THE
DIVINE
ARETINO

THE
DIVINE
ARETINO

A BIOGRAPHY BY

JAMES CLEUGH

𝖘𝖉

STEIN AND DAY/*Publishers*/New York

First published in the United States of America by
Stein and Day/Publishers, 1966

First published in Great Britain by Anthony Blond Ltd., 1965
Copyright © 1965 James Cleugh
Library of Congress Catalog Card No. 66-14949

Printed in the United States of America

Stein and Day/Publishers/7 East 48 Street, New York, N.Y. 10017

Contents

19171

Illustrations

Following Page 96

Portrait of Pietro Aretino by Titian (Galleria Pitti, Florence

Detail from portrait of Pope Leo X and Cardinals Giulio de' Medici and Luigi de' Rossi by Rafael (Galleria Palatina, Florence)

Portrait of Federigo II, Marquess of Mantua by Titian (Prado, Madrid)

Detail from portrait of Pope Clement VII by Sebastiano del Piombo (Gallerie Nazionali di Capodimonte, Naples)

Portrait of Giovanni delle Bande Nere by A. Bronzino (Palazzo Riccardi, Florence)

Detail from portrait of King Francis I by Titian (Louvre, Paris)

Detail from portrait of Emperor Charles V by Titian (Prado, Madrid)

Self-portrait by Titian, 1550 (Gemäldegalerie, Berlin)

Acknowledgments

Many of the translations quoted in this book are adapted from those which first appeared in *Aretino, Scourge of Princes* by T. C. Chubb (Reynal and Hitchcock, New York, 1940); author and publisher are here gratefully acknowledged. Also acknowledged are The Mansell Collection, London and Fratelli Alinari, Florence for their kind permission to include all the reproductions of photographs which appear in this book except that showing the self-portrait by Titian; the Gemäldegalerie and Walter Steinkopf, Berlin are gratefully acknowledged for their permission to include the latter.

Introduction

THE SUBJECT OF this biography was born towards the end of the fifteenth century. At that time Italians who spent most of their lives away from their native communities were sometimes called simply by the name of that community. The painter Pietro Vannucci, for instance, is known to history as Perugino, not Vannucci, Perugia being the chief city near the Umbrian village where he lived till he was nine. Thus the shoemaker's son Pietro del Tura of Arezzo, a cathedral town some fifty miles south-east of Florence, became merely Aretino, the fellow from Arezzo, to both friends and enemies as soon as he left home in his early teens.

He was born when the somewhat indefinite but resplendent period generally termed 'the Renaissance' was close to its climax. An attitude of mind characteristic of classical antiquity had been fashionable in Italy since about 1450. The great dim gulf that had once stretched between antiquity and Christian culture had been bridged for ever. The revived learning came to be called *humanismo,* for its practitioners were convinced that the present world of living men deserved at least as much attention as the future world of saved or lost souls. But the humanists were by no means all laughing heathen philosophers like Democritus. They were the schoolmasters of the day. A majority sank into ridiculous pedantry. It was not until a very few years before Aretino was born that Lorenzo de' Medici and his friend Politian, closely followed by Ariosto, invented humanism in the modern sense of the word. They stood primarily for erudition lightly carried, for love of both natural and man-made beauty and for deep sympathy with all the pains and pleasures that can be experienced by mankind. In art and science, in philosophy and education, this critical yet liberal spirit had already to a large extent substituted the idea of the gentleman for that of the saint in the more lucid and robust minds of the epoch.

Manners, accordingly, soon achieved far more social importance in Italy than in the rest of the continent. Refined diction, elegant attitudes on all occasions, an informed appreciation of luxury and agreeable objects in general, became the ideal, as in ancient Athens. But Italian high society at the turn of the fifteenth and sixteenth centuries fell short in practice of the Periclean theory. Mediterranean passions had been exacerbated by nearly fifteen hundred years of Christian austerity, and could not be restrained, always and everywhere, by a curb that lacked the terrors of supernatural sanction.

Under the brilliant surface of Renaissance Italy, therefore, a seething ferocity remained continuously apt to issue, generally when least expected, in cynical fraud and ruthless violence. In these circumstances the whole peninsula, a mosaic of mutually antagonistic yet relatively weak states, produced an inextricable network of ceaseless diplomatic intrigue without parallel in Europe at that time. The Italian intelligence, nurtured under such conditions, awed foreigners by its quickness. But Italian strength declined steadily. Other countries grew fascinated not only by the scholarship and the polish but also by the helplessness of the heirs of ancient Rome.

In 1494 the French king Charles VIII marched a cosmopolitan army, Spanish and German as well as French, overland to Naples, taking in every city of importance on the way. Italian social behaviour and Italian wealth excited the emulation and cupidity of the invaders. The prize could not be effectively defended. For there was no single major political power in Italy; there were five. Milan, Venice, Florence, Naples and Rome had a vigorous tradition of reciprocal hostility dating back to the central Middle Ages at least. For this reason Italy had to wait until the nineteenth century to become a unified nation. But in every field of civilisation, intellectual, moral and even political, as in the typical Italian unit of the city-state, the militarily vulnerable Italians were at full stretch, as the fifteenth century closed, in a task of critical significance. They were founding modern European culture upon an indestructible underground highway, more or less ignored elsewhere, that ran through time from Periclean Athens to the Paris that was to culminate under Louis XIV.

Renaissance men and women, the most interesting of them at least, were perhaps more various and versatile, within certain limits imposed by the general knowledge and conventions of their age, than any in history. Their saints and scoundrels, a Savonarola or a Cesare Borgia, their prosaic businessmen like Agostino Chigi, their solders of fortune like Giovanni de' Medici, could be matched in twentieth-century Europe; so could the courtesans and bluestockings, the dictatorial matrons, the cynical old bawds, the careful, industrious housewives and the romantic, headstrong boys and girls. But individuals frequently belonged to more than one of these categories.

There was a further notable respect in which Renaissance people differed from most of their modern descendants. The ambition, whether spiritual or material, to which outstanding minds are constantly drawn, was regularly tempered by the universal enthusiasm for all that has just been suggested as defining humanism.

But when the sixteenth century opened, the position which faced the princes of Italy, for the most part alternately vindictive and amiable, was a desperate one. Spain, France and Germany, the latter country disposing of the formidable Swiss mercenaries, were moving in on various pretexts to seize what spoil they could from the chaos of inter-state rivalry in the peninsula. The foreigners' own quarrels, however, for a while held up the approaching catastrophe. The balance of power swung backwards and forwards between France and Spain.

From about 1516, when Aretino, the shoemaker's son, acquired the good graces of Pope Leo X, the obstreperous young man began to exercise a certain pressure, growing stronger from year to year, upon Italian politics. Yet he took no personal interest in such matters, being neither a passionate patriot nor anxious to take charge of anyone or anything. He simply wanted to get hold of plenty of money and be admired for his literary talents. He saw that the quickest road to this goal in the existing state of political confusion was to use an exceptionally lurid and hard-hitting pen in contributions to a public excitement which left his own otherwise decidedly excitable nature perfectly cold. He didn't care in the least whether Charles or Francis, the pope or the Germans, would eventually rule Italy. He was only determined that the voice of one Pietro Aretino would resound as soon as possible from end to end of Europe. This position he knew would ensure him, with reasonable luck and good management, all the mistresses and the banquets, the splendid palaces and the gorgeous garments, the education in the highest and most intelligent society of his day, the incessant flow of wit and revelry, which in his view were the only things worth living for.

That he obtained all these appears a miracle to the twentieth-century mind. We are used to the rise of dictators and tycoons, comedians and pop singers, from the street-corner to affluence and power. But the loose constitution of modern society has rendered such ascents relatively easy for any talented boy or girl. In the more rigidly controlled communities of the sixteenth century, only just emergent from a millennium of feudalism and theocracy, the *parvenu* had a far harder task. It seems scarcely credible that the offspring, possibly illegitimate, of a poor cobbler and an artists' model, neither of whom could read or write, climbed to the top rungs of this steep and swaying ladder long before his thirtieth birthday.

The youth certainly had a glib tongue and an attractive personality. But so had thousands of his compatriots. Many Italian adolescents at this period were better looking, better schooled and endowed with better local and family connections than Aretino. Nevertheless most remained obscure, although as ambitious as Aretino. A few succeeded, but none to the extent of making such an impression as Aretino on popes and monarchs, statesmen and scholars like Guicciardini and Cardinal Bembo, soldiers like Giovanni de' Medici and artists like Titian and Ariosto.

These last two rare spirits, perhaps the noblest and most fastidious Italians of their time, unquestionably felt high esteem for Pietro Aretino, a man neither morally respectable nor intellectually distinguished. On the other hand a great many unscrupulous rogues feared him as they would have feared a warrior saint. Some unnecessarily tortuous dissemblers like Clement VII came to regret most bitterly their conduct towards one whom they discovered in due course to be anything but the heartless villain they had formerly considered him.

Big, blustering, amusing fellows with little formal education but of strong personality have at all times been popular at parties, taverns, clubs, in the theatre and wherever else men and women gather to be entertained. But mere blarney, even when coupled with great wit, rarely seduces serious professional people to the degree that Aretino's verbal fireworks imposed upon the mighty. Some other factor must have been operative in him to support the contemporary epithet of 'divine' accorded him by persons not in the habit of indiscriminate praise.

In hunting for clues to this mystery the investigator has to study as closely as possible the human environment in which it occurred. The depth and complexity of moves and countermoves at all levels of the higher reaches of power throughout the peninsula have already been mentioned. From the rulers of Milan, Venice, Florence, Rome and Naples down through layer after layer of petty potentates dependent on one or the other of these five separate states, each prince, duke or marquess lived in perpetual fear of ruin by a stronger neighbour and perpetual anxiety, therefore, to improve his own position.

All the threads in this labyrinth led sooner or later to the minotaur of Rome, the wealthiest and most dangerous of the competitors. The Vatican was determined to regain the omnipotence it had exercised in the comparatively recent past. One advantage could be relied upon. The secular if not the spiritual arm of the papacy still stood high in prestige. For not only could Rome afford to pay more mercenaries of better quality than the other states could command; she also disposed of a millennial experience of world-wide diplomacy.

Consequently every ambitious man wished to stand well with the pope, his favoured cardinals and his urbanely arrogant secretaries. A break with any of these authorities, for whatever reason, vital or trivial, tended to lead to disaster. The best way in which a non-Roman prince or other aspirant to glory could impress Rome would be to show himself both 'magnificent' like Lorenzo de' Medici of Florence and at the same time as outwardly devoted to Christian principles as any pope had to be, even the pernicious, if sometimes very able, Alexander VI.

Aretino's bold and subtle intelligence perceived at an early date that in order to enter effectively and permanently upon this equivocal scene more drastic measures than simple sycophancy towards the Holy See would be required, especially if one came from a provincial back-alley. He noticed that as the popes' characters varied the fortunes of despots big and little rose and fell with disturbing frequency. They were constantly being caught on the wrong foot, often too late to recover their balance. In this situation they understandably grew nervous, likely to clutch at any straw. It was even more interesting from the standpoint of a man bent on equalling or surpassing their status one day that in such a pitiable condition of uncertainty they might be knocked down with a feather. But what sort of a feather would do the trick best? What would turn them, at the appropriate moment, from haughty obstructionists to trembling suppliants?

There was one crucial way in which Aretino differed from his inconveniently numerous rivals. Many of them were as fundamentally unconcerned as himself with political or ethical conviction and as wholeheartedly devoted to purely personal and material ends. Yet, unscrupulous as he in thought, they lacked his instinct for going unscrupulously into action after due calculation of the odds. When they did act it seemed to be always too hastily or too timidly. Their prospective victims either saw through them because they had not surveyed and subsequently prepared the ground carefully enough, or else they perpended so long and elaborately beforehand that the opportunity was lost. Aretino's own rapid intuitions were of the kind which Machiavelli had praised in Cesare Borgia.

Aretino, though very far indeed from being a ruthless gangster like Cesare, resembled him in generally understanding just when, where and how to strike. The distinction between the two men lay primarily in Aretino's essential good nature. The treacherous and bloodthirsty Hispano-Roman always remained quite pitiless; the man from Arezzo genuinely disliked reducing people to utter misery and despair, though he enjoyed terrifying them. He never felt the hatred that seizes the chance to ruin and murder. Again and again, with contemptuous laughter, he allowed those who most persistently and dangerously attacked him to escape his vengeance. But he became in a very short time a past master at giving important or even unimportant persons such frights that they abjectly did whatever he asked them to do.

He was enabled to perpetrate such blackmail, in the special circumstances of Renaissance Italian society, as much through his unparalleled command of language as through a native shrewdness and resolution almost as rare. His eloquence owed little or nothing to the fashionable pompous rhetoric of the day; it was unique at the time in its alternately blunt and sharp realism, its cudgelling rather than thrusting wit. No one could doubt, either, that he meant what he said. If this or that prince or official or merchant or landlord did not immediately send him two hundred ducats, a pair of silver candlesticks, four gold-embroidered shirts or a present of anything from the duly witnessed cancellation of a debt to a brace of partridges, he was soon likely to find himself, somehow or other, in a disagreeable fix.

Aretino's reputation for such manoeuvres, which included the most barefaced lying, became so exaggerated by popular gossip that eventually, as he himself openly boasted, even a pope, an emperor or a king would pay him to hold that terrible tongue of his that, if irritated by neglect of its petitions, spared neither ladies of hitherto undoubted virtue nor saintly prelates nor internationally acclaimed scholars. All were accused of the vices opposite to the estimable qualities they possessed in reputation or in reality. The mud stuck. However, it would be removed at once, most efficiently, by the very man who had thrown it if Veronica Gambara, Bishop Domenico Bolani or that earnest literary critic Sperone Speroni did what had been demanded of them in the first place.

The eulogies would be just as uncompromising as the blame and expressed in equally pungent phrases; they would make their mark at once in an age when everyone who wore shoes expected to be addressed in conventionally flattering language. Spanish punctiliousness, derived ultimately from

15

the Moorish conquerors of Spain during the previous eight hundred years, had come to reinforce the new mode of conversation and correspondence introduced after the revival of learning. But Aretino's penned and spoken effusions, except for a few hackneyed forms of address when he felt they might be advisable, were not a bit like a Spaniard's or a mandarin's. His compliments resembled thumps on the back and digs in the ribs. They were normally as direct and heavy-handed as his insults.

Aretino's delight, however, in the fine arts was entirely sincere and had a basis of truly knowledgeable appreciation. His judgment in these matters won respect from both Titian and Sansovino, if not from that exceptionally obstinate intellectual Michelangelo. His good taste in this direction incidentally benefited him considerably in the main preoccupation of his life, the collection of largesse from the nobility and gentry, who also loved or pretended to love beautiful things. The spirit of the Renaissance all round them demanded at any rate lip-service to its life-enhancing revelations, though they were generally too busy to learn much about those qualities of a painting or a statue, a medallion or a jewelled dagger, that would make its possessor envied.

On the other hand the talkative connoisseur from Arezzo could tell a masterpiece from a fashionable fraud at a glance. Little lords anxious to impress bigger ones were always on the look-out for tangible proof of their own 'magnificence.' If Pietro Aretino recommended in language full of technical jargon the acquisition of a bust or a salt-cellar by some artist they had never heard of they could be fairly sure that important visitors would admire it, or better still, report the importance of the owner to people even more important than themselves.

Commissions had to be paid, of course. But the price would often be a low one, imposed by Aretino on the reluctant artist in the latter's own interests. For then the enraptured buyer might employ so modest a craftsman again and again, to the glowing enhancement of his reputation. This policy paid off in the case even of Titian and Charles V, both rather avaricious characters. The middleman, however, never dreamed of remaining satisfied with his commission.

He had bigger fish to fry. The potentate concerned soon found himself, as often as not, deep in correspondence with his originally deferential adviser; Aretino would gradually try to worm his way into the position of a trusted counsellor in the field of politics as well as of works of art.

If he succeeded all went well for a while. But once Aretino's new friend had found him useful demands for a salary began to be heard from the tipster. If the figure suggested seemed too high to the paymaster or if he showed signs of weariness of an association that might prove to be more trouble than it was worth, the situation altered. Threats, tactfully veiled at first, then plainly stated, appeared in the letters from Rome or Mantua, Reggio or Venice, wherever Pietro happened to be sojourning at the moment. For instance, rumours might be spread, he would write, that his 'good lord' was in the habit of committing incest or sodomy in his spare time, had not paid his mercenaries their wages or indulged in secret communion with some unpopular foreign ruler. Such gossip might be really dangerous in the precariously involved public circumstances of Renaissance Italy. Even today persistent adverse reports on the private life of a conspicuous person might damage his career. In the sixteenth century Italian chatterboxes were as ubiquitous and credulous as they were cynical and ill-natured, and stories of delinquency could be fatal to perfectly legitimate hopes.

Generally the victim of these tactics paid up or at least promised to do so. If he did not, off went the libels, sometimes in cold print. Even then, as already noted, the position could be retrieved by a timely capitulation. Despite the contempt usually felt for Aretino by 'well born' people he could always count on a wide audience for anything he had to say. Listeners or readers far above him socially did not necessarily believe his scandal; but it was more amusing and delivered in a more impudently confident style than anyone else's.

It was difficult to resist the jovial retailer of so many coarsely entertaining squibs and snap repartees. Other wits of his time and place tended to be aristocratically deliberate, condescending and sly, at best gaily ironic, in their comments. Aretino substituted for their cool sparkle a turbid torrent of picturesque verbiage which stunned hearers unaccustomed to such cinematographic effects. Conventional souls might shudder at a proletarian brutality then out of fashion even in the market-place, not to mention *palazzo* interiors. But Aretino's loud mouth and sledgehammer brain struck off such phrases as could be heard nowhere else. And it had to be conceded that his manners and in particular his dress were grandly ostentatious.

Personal adornments in fact exercised more momentum in carrying Aretino to the top than might now be assumed. Renaissance sensibility greatly increased both the wearing of chains, collars and rings and the subtlety of colour and cut in the clothing of those who could afford the best jewellers, fabrics, dyers and tailors. Such persons remained few while the crafts of industry, still unorganised, lagged behind the achievements of intellect. Gorgeous robes and ornaments accordingly acquired a prestige which would be laughable today. A man thus decorated, especially if tall, broad-shouldered and nobly bearded, could attract respectful attention even if not equipped with such a spellbinding personality as Aretino's. No one was likely to enquire how deeply so commanding an apparition might be in debt.

But of course Aretino made plenty of enemies once he had risen from the status of banker's lackey to that of papal favourite and pamphleteer. Hatchet-men employed by envious competitors or by men or women he had traduced often pursued him. Once at least he was nearly killed by a vicious dagger-thrust after midnight in a murky Roman street. One marquess, actually his host at the time, offered to arrange his assassination in the discreetest possible manner to please an exasperated pope. At an earlier date Adrian VI ordered Aretino's arrest for grossly impious attacks on the papal dignity after he had fled from Rome. If the emissaries sent from the Vatican had caught him the torture-chambers of the Castle of San Angelo might have engulfed him for ever. It was more by smiles of fortune than by dexterous expedients, though he was always careful to make powerful friends, that he escaped an early death.

Yet there were two other reasons why this incorrigible scandal-monger and blackmailer lived to be sixty-four, a ripe

old age in Renaissance Italy. In the first place, as already
mentioned, those who hated him most were often amazed to
find themselves positively benefited by his eloquent panegyrics as soon as he had reason to suppose they meant to
have his blood. They all had to acknowledge in the end
that he never bore any real malice against anyone, including
would-be assassins. He himself never considered having even
his most perfidious and merciless antagonists stabbed or
poisoned. Throughout his life he detested all kinds of violence, and preferred disconcerting moves on the chessboard
of intrigue to steel or arsenic. Sometimes he found it reward-
ing to ignore assailants altogether. Sometimes he used his
huge self-confidence to route or even convert a potential
murderer by his mere eloquent presence. This last proceed-
ing required moral rather than physical courage. Of the
latter he had no trace at all; of the former he possessed more
than any of his contemporaries except his crony Giovanni
de' Medici, who didn't need it since he had so much of
the other.

Secondly, by the time Aretino reached the age of thirty-
seven he concluded that he would be safer in Venice than
anywhere else. He decamped accordingly to that comparatively remote, orderly and independent city. He never left
it except for a brief visit to Rome in his sixties, when nearly
everyone who had objected to him was dead and admiration
of his literary and diplomatic talents had become so general
that he expected a cardinalate.

It must be repeated however, that luck cannot be left
out of account in considering this astonishingly successful
career. The exuberance and chaos of the Italian *cinquecento*,
its instant recognition of the *fait accompli*, its reverence for
printed and spoken scintillation, its immorality and mate-
rialism, its wealth and prodigality, offered every opportunity
to a 'brigand of letters'.

First Blood

HE WHO WAS TO BE called Pietro Aretino was born in a hospital in the little cathedral city of Arezzo during the night of April 19/20, 1492.

The buildings of Arezzo clung, as they still do, to the foothills of the rugged Apennines and spread down fanwise to the green valley of the confluence of the Arno and Chiana rivers. At the end of the fifteenth century the town did not differ much from a hundred other Italian settlements with its crooked lanes, gabled houses, a town-hall and Romanesque or Gothic churches, some of which, including the Arezzo cathedral begun in the twelfth century, remained unfinished. Wheat and olive fields, vineyards, lime-trees and palms could be seen from the highest windows.

A few days before the birth of Pietro, Lorenzo de' Medici, called the Magnificent, died. The Florentine Republic was at this time one of the five strongest states in Italy, the others being Venice, Milan, the papal dominions centred on Rome and the kingdom of Naples. Lorenzo had been the absolute master of Florence ever since 1478, a real tyrant in political and social affairs, but like certain other autocrats in both former and later times also a real intellectual. With his death the vast flowering of sensibility, erudition and adventurous thought known as the Italian Renaissance began to decay. The end of the fifteenth century involved the loss of a certain creative innocence and enthusiasm in Europe. The spiritual heirs of Lorenzo seem for the most part to have shifted the emphasis of their ideas from pure aesthetics to practical ambition. It was not only Pietro Aretino who was to discuss art and philosophy less for their own sakes than for personal aggrandisement.

No one supposed that the boy born in Arezzo on a Good Friday morning would make any more noise in the town, let alone throughout Europe, than any other Aretine citizen. But the fastidiously sophisticated Ariosto was to call him

'The Divine Aretino'. The slightly more censorious Titian was to call Aretino, at worst, the 'brigand chief of letters'. Many contemporaries were to accept unreservedly his own estimates of himself as the 'Fifth Evangelist' and 'Secretary of the World'. Modern biographers have declared him not only the first blackmailer but also the first democrat and publicity man in Christendom.

None of this seemed likely in 1492. Pietro's parents were poor shopkeepers, the presumed father being a tough shoe-maker named Andrea del Tura, though generally known, for some reason, as Luca. The mother, Luca's wife, had more claims to distinction, being a great beauty and a favourite model for the local painters. One Matteo Lappoli had copied her serene features for his fresco of the Annunciation in the church of San Agostino. Margherita Bonci, called Tita for short, may not have been a pattern of all the virtues. In fact there is some reason to suppose that some years after the birth of her son by Luca or possibly by someone else, the husband discovered an intrigue between her and a wealthy noble named Luigi Bacci and left home in consequence. Luca, with typical Aretine impulsiveness, seems to have joined a troop of mercenaries and never returned. Bacci on the other hand appears to have taken care that Tita and her children—she had two daughters younger than the boy Pietro —did not starve.

In later life Pietro repudiated gossip about his mother with furious indignation. In begging Vasari to copy the fresco in San Agostino he swore by 'the most tender love' he cherished for Tita's memory that her modesty and virtue were as well understood by her fellow-citizens as they had been nobly depicted by Lappoli. Vasari did the job for him. Titian, on examining the copy, told Pietro that in all his experience he had 'seen only one face less worldly.' The opinion was prob-ably sincere enough in a man not given to casual estimates of the art of painting.

At the same time Pietro managed to reconcile this filial reverence with the assertion, once he had grown famous, that Luigi Bacci was his real father and that gentleman's two legitimate sons, with whom Pietro voluminously corre-sponded, brothers to himself. Gualtiero and Francesco Bacci were delighted by the great man's condescension. In Pietro's old age however he had to withdraw this allegation of noble birth. For another Aretine, one Medoro Nucci, whom Pietro had befriended with his usual reckless hospitality in Venice, quarrelled with him—Nucci had a pretty young wife with whom his host probably flirted, if nothing more—and threatened him with proceedings before the Signory for fraudulently posing as an aristocrat.

With characteristic impudence, courage and agility the culprit coolly confessed his lie to the Duke of Florence. 'I glory in the title,' he wrote to the magnate in question, who happened to be the son of an old friend of his and owed his duchy largely to Aretino's own advocacy, 'which that villain' —Nucci—'has given me. May it teach the nobility to procreate sons like myself. begotten by a poor cobbler in Arezzo.' 'None of my line before me,' he told the sculptor Danese, 'were what I am. I give nobility to others, though I have received it from none.' He repeated again and again in later letters the phrase: 'I was born in a hospital'—i.e. a place where the great majority of patients were very poor—'but with the soul of a king.' He added pompously, when at last Arezzo made him an honorary magistrate: 'This unexpected dignity will call the attention of the young men of the town to the virtue of perseverance. It will show them to what heights base birth can rise through application.' He could have gone on to list some other less generally admired qualities conspicuous in himself which might be relied on to grease the wheels of hard work. But a letter of thanks for civic honours was not the proper place in which to talk of flattery, libel, pimping, perjury and unvarnished effrontery.

By the time Pietro was ten years old he could read, write and quote the Bible. He could also help his father to cobble. He had no other education but what he learned in the street. Such chatter included some doggerel by a notorious Florentine bard, a barber named Burchiello, 'whose Muse was a Venus of the crossroads bred among taverns.' Pietro enjoyed the rhymes of this early specimen of Fleet Street wit and tried to imitate them. It is improbable that Luca was amused, though Tita may have been.

In that same year, 1502, events occurred in Arezzo which made a lifelong impression on the restless, precociously intelligent and quick-tempered shoemaker's son, black-haired, square-chinned and already tall and robust for his age. They stamped his mind permanently with a hatred and fear of physical violence and an equal detestation of the arrogance, cruelty and sharp practice of those 'princes' of whom he was to call himself and be called by others—first by Ariosto—the 'scourge'.

A commissioner arrived from Florence to arrest the ring-leaders of a conspiracy to rebel against the authority of that city, then at war with Pisa. Someone who was in the plot at Arezzo declared that the Florentine had come to seize grain for the army, the troops of the hereditary oppressor of the Aretines. The church bells began to peal wildly. The enraged populace, Pietro no doubt among them, poured on to the *piazza*. A roar of menace went up: 'Down with the Florentines!'

The commissioner was seized and imprisoned. The houses of the rich, mainly supporters of Florentine policy, began to be plundered. Some were burnt to the ground. Vendettas started in the streets. A priest, the son of a family unsympathetic to the conspiracy, was dragged from his hiding-place in a drain-pipe at his monastery and butchered on the spot. One of his brothers was stabbed and flung out of a window. Other pro-Florentines were hanged from balconies or tortured as 'sodomites' by having a lighted torch thrust between their naked buttocks. Some committed suicide rather than fall into the hands of the maddened revolutionaries. Finally the castle, the outward symbol of Florentine rule, was destroyed.

Although the Medici had been expelled by the people of Florence for supporting the French invasion of 1494, the succeeding regime in that city was hated by an able general, Vitellozzo Vitelli, whose brother Paolo had been unjustly beheaded for treason by the Florentine Council of State. Vitellozzo arrived in Arezzo to lead the Aretines against their new tyrants, counting on the formidable Cesare Borgia, the Pope's son, for help. Cesare however changed his mind and backed Florence. Vitelli retired. French troops entered Arezzo, but in magnanimous mood; General Imbalt pardoned the conspirators, and after giving them some good advice about politics and economics departed on more important business.

The next day the vengeful Florentine army burst into the little town, sacked it and carried off thirty of the chief citizens as hostages for the future good behaviour of the Aretines. To the already shrewd young Pietro these turbulent scenes of merciless carnage, destruction and plunder, the gossip of treachery and deceit on all sides, the blind fury of almost everyone he met, threw a decidedly lurid light on the great world he had by this time firmly determined to enter and conquer as soon as he could stop people despising him as a child.

As the excitement gradually died down over the next two or three years, the boy made up his mind to 'soak' all these rich scoundrels who spent their lives mouthing pious rhetoric while they robbed and murdered their rivals and inflicted misery on their social inferiors. But apart from the moral aspect of this situation Pietro rather enjoyed reading or listening to their flamboyant speeches. To the end of his life he relished phrase-making and eventually outdid all his contemporaries in the dubious art.

It need not have been, as his enemies later alleged, the repercussions of a heretical sonnet or his father's discovery of Tita's affair with Luigi Bacci that caused the energetic boy, in 1505 or 1506, when he was thirteen or fourteen, to abandon the shoemaker's shop and tramp on alone over the fifty odd miles to Perugia. It is improbable that the local authorities would have taken much notice of the scribblings of an obscure artisan's brat still at the stage of physical correction by adults. Nor is it likely that a handsome and beloved mother's adultery, if any, even though followed by a less congenial father's desertion of the family, would have greatly perturbed a youngster whose thoroughly unconventional character must by then have been basically formed. Such events may have excited a son not long out of the nursery but already a bit of a scamp; they would hardly have induced him to forsake the domestic roof in disgust.

On the whole it seems reasonable to dismiss the speculations in question as the sort of malicious gossip to which any successful public figure, once he is duly established and envied as such, is exposed. If a person writes in defiance of authority at thirty and is at the same time known to be a sexual debauchee, there will be plenty of people to believe that he was just as bold at thirteen and had a whore for a mother.

However that may be, Pietro doubtless had other reasons for a departure perhaps not so hasty as it appears in the vague perspective of these years of childhood. Perugia was the first big town on the south-east road to Rome, the mightiest city in the world, its undisputed head, he had been told. He was to call it 'the world's backside' ('coda') before he was many years older. But to a penniless Tuscan teenager that vast and venerable constellation of both material and spiritual glory far away to the south shone like a guiding star to the only possible goal for inimitable minds such as he was already, as subsequently throughout his life, certain he possessed. There was in fact some degree of justification for such an opinion of himself.

He began his first experiments in cajolery along the white, dusty road under the blazing sun of early summer, less with his piercing black eyes and sturdy figure than with his long tongue and ready grin. They worked well both with sly, unscrupulous pedlars and suspicious peasants. If women were present the boy's boldly appreciative stares, amusing chatter and self-assurance turned the scale. At last, with hopes as high as ever, he reached the sprawling hillside city, already famous for its architecture, its university and its great contemporary painter Pietro Vanucci, called Il Perugino, then in his fifties.

At Perugia the 'foreign' lad was for the first time called 'the Aretine'. It was as Pietro Aretino that he plunged, with a precocity typical of Italian boys of fourteen then or now, into the wildest life he could find. But characteristically, he was looking as much for wit as for wantonness. He cultivated assiduously a boisterous youth of his own age but much better educated, one Agnolo Firenzuola, who later became a distinguished figure in Tuscan literature. Firenzuola, a Florentine, as his surname indicates, had already studied law at Siena and was now at Perugia for the same purpose. Subsequently he entered but soon left a monastery, practised as an advocate in Rome and eventually settled at Prato, close to his native city, in charge of the abbey of San Salvatore.

But in his early days at Perugia the future abbot was more

noted for shameless exuberance than for the subtle manipulation of a vernacular language he was later to polish into an exquisite literary instrument. He and Pietro, it is recorded, once indecently exposed themselves at a window in broad daylight. Agnolo wore only his shirt. But the bolder Pietro appeared stark naked. It seems that this tableau was staged in order to defy a certain old woman who had taken exception to this pair's previous antics. The whole quarter was roused to indignation and the boys had to make themselves scarce to escape a beating.

In 1512 Pietro somehow found means, at the age of eighteen, to get his first book of verse printed in Venice. It included folk-songs and epigrams of a burlesque sort, sonnets, facetious compositions in *terza rima,* letters in rhyme and a *Disperata*—probably a lugubrious elegy of some kind in fashionable terms and a mere literary exercise. The little book, though largely imitative of the work of others, showed clearly enough how Pietro's mature talent was going to develop. 'If the style does not please you,' he wrote to a correspondent, 'at least the boldness will . . . I dashed the stuff off almost in an instant.'

Pietro always remained incapable of and indeed uninterested in 'poetry' as distinct from 'verse'. He could use all sorts of verse forms with ease, but never with any striking point or depth. Prose was his true medium; here he could hit harder than anyone of his time. His prose was not read for intellectual or aesthetic profit, but for sheer, usually malicious enjoyment of its imagery and earthiness. As a twentieth-century journalist he would have quickly become a star reporter and the editor of a popular daily newspaper.

Like many other bright young men in the city of Pietro Vanucci, he also tried his hand at painting. He soon mastered the rudiments of the art of representing three-dimensional objects on a flat surface and became fascinated by the process. But his shrewd mind could not be content with mere enthusiasm. In discussions with his coevals he criticised as much as he raved. Such were the foundations of a concern with pictorial technique which eventually rendered him an authority to whom even Titian listened with respect. But Pietro never achieved distinction as a painter himself. With his usual realism he recognized early that the self-discipline necessary for success as an artist, however passionately involved in self-expression, would be impossible for his essentially restless, prosaic and peremptory temper.

He turned back to literature. Firenzuola's example and the high cultural level of a cathedral and university city had long caused him to lament his lack of formal education. But he was still too poor to buy books. In order to get at them he obtained a job first as valet to a lawyer and then in a bindery, where he spent more time poring over the printed sheets in the workshop than in glueing and sewing them to their covers. He learned fast in this way. Yet he still found leisure for escapades. According to the Perugian poet Caporali he had been offended by the sight of a mediocre fresco in the Piazza Grande depicting Mary Magdalene at the feet of Christ. Her arms outspread in an absurdly awkward attitude of adoration and the too conspicuous tears rolling down her cheeks lent in Pietro's view an utterly incongruous aspect to the buxom citizeness who had been used as a model. He decided to correct this artistic impropriety and call the perpetrator to order in the only way he could be expected to understand—pictorially.

One morning, early risers were horrified to find that the pious Magdalene had been transformed overnight into the courtesan she was said to have been before her conversion. A lute had appeared in her hands and she was gazing at Jesus with a far from sorrowing expression. Pietro had spent a couple of hours the night before with his brushes and palette, and a discreet torch, on a ladder propped against the wall. Always a good Catholic in theory, though a bad one in practice, he was certainly a better critic of painting than of religion.

The joke, however, did not amuse the clergy or the ruling Baglioni family or the municipality of Perugia. Pietro could usually talk himself out of trouble, but this time his laughing apology did not help him. While the picture was being restored he was sternly given to understand that if he did not remove himself forthwith from the precincts of the city he could expect an examination by the Holy Inquisition. He was no more amused by such a prospect than the Perugian authorities had been by his exploit.

However much truth there may be in this story of

Caporali's, it is certain that Pietro left Perugia almost as poor as he had entered it half a dozen years previously, although infinitely richer in his knowledge of society. His self-confidence, moreover, was now based upon practical achievements in literature, art and book-binding as well as upon mere temperament. He was richer, too, in courage— moral rather than physical—tested in plenty of dealings with petty tyrants whom others could only fear. It was from this source that he drew his characteristically reckless optimism, that of a born gambler. But Pietro never gambled with cards or dice; he gambled with men's minds. Now he looked beyond Perugia.

He was bent upon Rome, where all roads led, where he had been aiming all along. It was there that all the big fortunes were made and the great posts obtained. There were people in Rome who swayed the destinies of mankind. Why shouldn't he, one day, be one of them?

It was not difficult for a personable young man who could paint, write and make tired business men roar with laughter to earn a tolerable living in the huge, gay, cultivated and unscrupulous metropolis ruled in those years by Pople Leo X. The pontiff was himself a man after Pietro's own heart, generous, learned and outwardly pious. Bull-necked, pop- eyed, red-faced and in his late thirties, born Giovanni de' Medici, the second son of Lorenzo the Magnificent, he had at once achieved general popularity through the affable ease of manner which his father had known so well how to employ on occasion. Pope Leo sedulously cultivated the political principles of Niccolo Machiavelli.

The Roman artistic world, to which Pietro, as a painter and critic of paintings himself, naturally gravitated, was dominated at this time by the thirty-year-old Raphael, fated to die prematurely only six years later. Michelangelo, aged thirty-seven, was already in Rome, as well as Raphael's former master, Pietro Vanucci the Perugian, Signorelli, Pin- turicchio and many other brilliant figures. But Pietro could not see himself rising to glory in any of their studios; he knew himself to be no more than an average hand with the brush. Realistic as ever, he made for the secular magnates who financed the painters.

The enormously rich banker Agostino Chigi, Sienese by

birth, a patron of Raphael and treasurer to the papal court, was eventually persuaded to engage Pietro as a lackey. (According to Pietro's sworn enemy Nicolo Franco two years of vagabondage preceded his appointment to Chigi's household.) In that capacity he could at least see at a distance the most important people in Rome and pick up perquisites here and there.

Any biographer of Pietro Aretino must always bear in mind that he was a great liar all his life, with an extravagant imagination intent upon representing himself as a reckless, picturesque swashbuckler who had drunk life to the dregs before he was twenty-five. His letters were all written with an eye to subsequent publication, in order to maintain this legend among a great many others dealing with his recent as well as his distant past. Carefully composed to amuse or impress the various persons to whom they were addressed, they were often inconsistent. He did not care in the least if he were found out in one of these fabrications.

So the highly entertaining letters of this master of the epistolary style—he revolutionised the conventionally pompous communications usually penned by correspondents in his day—have to be taken with several grains of salt. They cannot be regarded as reliable evidence of actual experience. But their details, whether fictitious or not, are significant for a close reading of the writer's remarkably complex mentality.

Nor can the letters of such hostile witnesses as Franco be swallowed whole. Franco alleges, for instance, that Aretino lost one job he held in Rome for stealing a silver cup from his master (unnamed by Franco but whom others among Pietro's enemies named as Chigi), but that a subsequent employer, Cardinal San Giovanni, liked him well enough to bequeath to him a piece of valuable old brocade, a chain worth ten ducats and a velvet cap. He is stated to have sung for his supper in the streets of Vicenza, masqueraded as a wandering friar, worked in the stables of the Sheep Inn at Bologna and run errands for money-lenders and tax collectors. He had also, wrote Franco, driven mules for a living, held ladders for hangmen, been sentenced to a term in the galleys, and thereafter served an apprenticeship to a miller. He had been a courier, a pimp, a mountebank, a confidence trickster, a scholar's groom 'and worse'. The catalogue, which perhaps owes something to the author's reading of medieval romances, is clearly malevolent and distorted, but it may have had some foundation in fact. There is no indisputable evidence as to its truth.

Pietro may or may not have been, as he himself asserted, a servant in a Franciscan monastery near Ravenna, where he bound books and noted the improper sexual antics of both monks and nuns. The Father Superior, he claimed, kicked him out for joining in these orgies, pardonable in the clergy but disgraceful in an attendant layman. As an example of Pietro's mature manner in prose, a speech from his comedy 'Court Life' (*La Cortigiana*), published in 1524, may be cited. The points are so vividly and precisely made that it would seem based on personal experience as well as hearsay, though, like any good journalist, Pietro was quite capable of taking exact notes of anybody's conversation. It is perfectly certain, however, that he had himself been a domestic drudge in Rome.

'If your bad luck forces you to enter a servant's hall, as soon as you come in you will see before your eyes a tomb so damp, dark and horrible that even a sepulchre would have a hundred times more gaiety. If you have ever seen the prison of the Corte Savello when it is full of captives you have seen a servants' hall full of servants at meal times. For those who eat in a servants' hall seem like prisoners just as the servants' hall seems like a prison. But prisons are much more comfortable than servants' halls, for prisoners are as warm in winter as in summer, while servants' halls boil in summer and in winter are so cold that the words freeze in your mouth. And the stench of a prison is less disagreeable than the stink of a servants' hall, for the former comes from prisoners and the latter from the dying.

'And listen! You eat off a table-cloth of more colours than those of a painter's apron. It makes you vomit to think of it. Do you know what they wash the table-cloth with at the end of a meal? With the pigs' grease left over from the candles of the night before! Yet often enough we eat without any light at all. Then we are in luck. For in the dark our stomachs are not turned by the sight of the foul repasts they bring us. Since we are starving they satisfy us, but in the process drive us to despair.

'For meat we have some ancient scrap of beef. Then comes the fruit. When melons, artichokes, figs, grapes, cucumbers and plums are no longer worth keeping they pass them on to us as if they were a State's ransom. Sometimes, instead of fruit, they hand us out four slices of ox milk cheese so hard and dry that it brings on a colic which would kill a statue. Prolonged and pitiful supplications to the cook for a little thin soup produce only a saucer of dish-water.

'If you do get soup it's like the muck friars are given. Do you know why so many friars quit their Orders every day? It's because of the soup. The cooks ruin it just as courts destroy the faith of those who serve them. And who could enumerate all the false tricks they play in Lent when they make everyone fast? They go on like that not for the good of our souls but simply to save money on our keep. For when Lent comes round, lo and behold, the first course consists of a couple of anchovies followed by a few Sardinian weeds, burnt rather than cooked. With them comes a bean soup, innocent of salt or oil. It's enough to make you curse heaven. Then in the evening for supper we enjoy ten nettle leaves and a musty roll at their bidding.

'All this wouldn't matter so much if only they showed us a little consideration in hot weather. At that season we not only have to endure the vile stench of the heaps of offal which are never swept up and attract all the flies in the city, but we also have to drink wine diluted with tepid water. It has stood for four hours in a copper vessel before you touch it. We all drink out of one pewter mug which all the waters of the Tiber could not clean. As we eat we have to watch one poor wretch wiping his hands on his breeches, while another uses his cloak for the same purpose, another his jerkin and another the wall.

'For our greater torment we have to gobble our food at a terrific rate, like so many buzzards. For, as soon as that venerable and respectable man, the steward, has twice intoned the benediction, we have to rise. Is it not shameful? For we are not only forbidden our fill of food but also our fill of talk.

'Once in a lifetime we get a banquet. Then you should just see the procession of heads, feet, necks, carcases, bones and skeletons. It looks like the one which goes to San Marco on the day of Messer Pasquino.[1] For just as on that day the vicars, arch-priests, canons and similar gentry carry the holy relics of martyrs and confessors, so the lousy fellows from the kitchen bring us the remains of a capon or a partridge, after keeping portions for themselves and their trollops. The rest they toss to us.

'Yesterday I saw one of our gang begin to weep when he heard the dinner-bell, that ambassador of starvation, just as if it were knelling the death of his father. When I asked him the cause of his tears, he replied: "I weep to hear that bell call us to eat the bread of sorrow, to drink our own blood and feed upon our own flesh, cooked in our own sweat." This man was a priest. That evening he broke his fast with four nuts. The chamberlain had three, a squire two and I but one.'

The exaggeration, the phrase-making and the invective, the specious underdog's propaganda, are cunningly contrived to elicit the laughter which is always loudest at other people's misfortunes. Pietro had little to learn about writing farce.

Pietro probably entered the gorgeous household of Agostino Chigi about 1514. This self-made millionaire once told Leo X that he had no idea how much money he really had. He shared that pope's delight in hunting and lavish banquets. After one of the latter he grandly threw a dinner service of solid gold, from which Leo and a group of cardinals had eaten and drunk, into the Tiber. But nets, though no one present except the host knew it at the time, had been stretched under the water to catch the treasure, which was duly recovered.

This typical business man's prudence was the least conspicuous, though the most important trait in Chigi's char-

[1] See page 46 for an explanation of this reference.

acter. Most people were merely astounded at his magnificence. His mistress, the cultivated courtesan Imperia, who
spoke Latin and Greek, knew Petrarch and Boccaccio by
heart, wrote her own songs and accompanied them on the
zither or lute, was lodged in unexampled splendour. The
Spanish ambassador, on a formal visit to this powerful and
accomplished lady, told the novelist Bandello that everything he saw in her apartments was so precious that when
he felt the need to spit he was obliged to let fly in the face
of his own servant, the only object anywhere near him
that he considered of no value.

'A young man'—Pietro wrote long afterwards—'when he
goes into some great man's service, is like a pearl on
bombazine. He is adorned with grace, filled with polite-
ness and simplicity, is all modesty and purity. He has two
sets of clothes and they are in as good a style as his father's
purse and generosity permit. He goes up the long stairway. And as those in front of him and those behind him
look him over from head to foot he seems like the Lamb
of God in innocence. Blushing rosily in his shyness and
timidity, he kisses the hand of his new master, who gives
him a sly leer and then greets him with bawdy laughter.
In about three days he has found his place and is set
to work cleaning privies, polishing chamber pots, lighting
candles, sweeping out bedrooms and performing lewd
offices for cooks and stewards, who soon see to it that
he is all pricked out and embroidered with the French
disease. Meanwhile his shirt, though stained with sweat,
is not laundered. His breeches are reduced to rags but
are not patched. His shoes wear out and are not resoled.
His hair grows lousy but is not washed. A smell of stale-
ness which is musty enough to make ten iron stoves sick
takes possession of him. The good youth has come to
resemble an apple out of which two bites have been taken
and which now lies in the gutter for flies to feast on.'

All the same, Chigi's new lackey found an opportunity to
show his burlesque verses, both published and unpublished,
to those of his master's guests who took an interest in litera-

ture. There were a good many who would not have looked at love elegies. But nearly all of them enjoyed having witty and discreetly obscene sallies in rhyme read out to them.

Nothing very much came of this situation for a year or two. Pietro was a popular servant and had a good deal of patronising freedom allowed him, like an official jester, among the great men, cardinals and secular lords, popular writers and artists who came to see Chigi. With many of them Pietro was afterwards to maintain quite intimate relations. But at this date he remained dissatisfied. He could now wear decent garments, eat well, and appreciate the caresses of minor courtesans, 'candle girls', as they were called, because they set candles at their windows to attract clients.

But none of this was enough for a man determined to give rather than receive orders. He intended, and soon, to have all Rome at his feet. He knew he could do it in only one way. Most people, he could see, succeeded by force or fraud: he had no objection to the latter but was not interested in the former. Fraud, however, must be on a great scale to provide the position he was sure he could fill; petty swindles, he had quickly realised, would get him nowhere. Yet big business required capital. Moreover, its details bored him stiff. On the other hand, a talent for clowning could be seen enriching all kinds of men and women vastly inferior to himself, buffoons and the more lively sort of whore, with apparently the greatest of ease. They must have begun somewhere, somehow.

Pietro's chance came in 1516, when the Pope's pet elephant died. The beast came from India, but had a Carthaginian name, Hanno. It had been presented to Leo by the Portuguese ambassador, Tristan da Cunha (after whom the island is called), two years before. But in 1516 the German humanist Ulrich von Hutten, who was in Italy at the time, wrote to a friend:

'You have all heard how the Pope had a great animal, an elephant, which he held in high honour and loved much. You must know that this animal is now dead. When he was sick the Pope was filled with woe. He summoned many doctors, saying: "If it is possible, cure my elephant." They all did the best they could. They examined the ele-

phant's urine and gave him a great purgative which
weighed five hundred ounces. But it did not take effect
and so he is dead and the Pope greatly grieves. They say
that he would have paid five thousand ducats to anyone
who cured the elephant, for he was a remarkable animal
and had an enormous nose. He always knelt down when
he came into the Pope's presence and trumpeted resound-
ingly the syllable, "Bar, bar, bar!" '

Leo ordered Raphael to paint a life-size picture of the
dead monster on the wall below which it had been buried.
The pontiff himself composed a pompous epigraph in Latin.
All Rome was still talking, with discreet laughter, of these
events when innumerable copies of a printed pamphlet began
to be offered for sale at every street-corner. It was entitled
'The Last Will And Testament Of The Elephant'. The text
related that Hanno, having realised that his end was near
owing to the unhealthy air of Rome and the short rations
on which he was kept by his miser of a keeper, Zuan Battista
of Aquila, had commissioned the anonymous author to make
copies of a Will drawn up by the Consistorial Court lawyer
Mario de' Previchi. The document continued:

'Item, to my heir, the workshop of St Peter, I give the
golden covering which I wear on festal occasions, on condition that they do not put the alms of the said workshop
to unholy uses . . . Item, to my heir Cardinal San Giorgio
I give my ivory tusks, so that his thirst for the papacy, as
intense as that of Tantalus, may be moderated . . . Item,
to my heir the Cardinal Santa Croce, I give my knees, so
that he can imitate my genuflections, but only on condition that he tells no more lies in Council . . . Item, to my
heir Cardinal Volterra I give my wisdom, if he will promise to be generous, for a change . . . Item, to my heir
Cardinal Santi Quattro I give my jaws, so that he can
devour the revenues of Christ the more readily . . . Item,
to my heir Cardinal Medici I give my ears, so that he
can hear the doings of everyone . . .'

Cardinal Grassi, said to be the most incorrigible fornicator in the Sacred College, was left the elephant's generative organs.

Between guffaws every reader speculated about the authorship of this scathing document. Before long Chigi's lackey, Pietro Aretino, coolly let it be known that he was the author. He circulated a dramatic sketch in verse which included the lines:

'Take care that Aretino be your friend,
for he's a bad enemy to wrong.
His words alone the Pope's high fame could rend,
so may God guard us all from such a tongue.'

Pietro had decided to wait no longer before taking a dangerous risk in order to bring himself before the public. As usual he had calculated the odds carefully beforehand. If a different sort of pope had been in charge the dice would have been too heavily loaded against a scurrilous traducer of the highest princes of the Church. Immediate arrest, torture and imprisonment, perhaps even assassination by a band of hired killers in the small hours, would have followed. But everyone knew that soft-bellied Leo loved a joke at the expense of the ambitious fops, ecclesiastical or lay, who surrounded him. He had permitted the greatest freedom of speech often enough in his fairly frequent moments of relaxation. As a Florentine, too, he had no objection to seeing Romans having their legs pulled. Pietro, whose moral courage and mental dexterity in self-defence exceeded those of any of his contemporaries, rightly guessed that the elephant's death had been a heaven-sent opportunity for personal advancement. He confidently awaited favourable reactions to Hanno's 'Last Will and Testament'.

They soon came. It was not only Chigi and his guests who heartily congratulated their bold footman on his literary talent. The Pope himself sent a request to the banker to release this jester to join the papal household. Such a demand could not be refused. Pietro hastened to present himself before the jovial Vicar of Christ, who asked him facetiously:

'Well, *Messere,* which would you rather be, Virgil or Camillo Querno, my poet laureate?'

'Your Holiness's laureate, of course,' retorted Pietro instantly, 'For he can drink more good mulled wine in the Castello in July than old Virgil could have got from the Emperor Augustus for two thousand fawning Aeneids and a million Georgics.'

The answer was characteristically cunning in its implied sharing of the Pope's taste for strong liquor, to which in fact his new servant always remained quite indifferent. He was never drunk in his life, though he often pretended to be if occasion warranted it.

Leo was delighted with him. The die had been well worth casting, Pietro reflected. It had turned up a six. He had drawn the first blood from the world he meant to subjugate. While still four years short of thirty he could look forward, he now believed, to a career that would take him far beyond the stuffy precincts of the Vatican.

The World's Backside

IN 1519, WHILE the ex-lackey and poet Pietro Aretino was still making hosts of friends and enemies as a popular clown highly skilled in backchat, verse-making and art criticism at the papal court in Rome, two important events occurred which were destined to have great influence on his future. In the first place Charles of Habsburg, aged nineteen, was elected Holy Roman Emperor, to the great wrath of King Francis I of France, aged twenty-five, who had tried in vain to bribe his own way to the imperial throne. But Charles, as the grandson of the emperor Maximilian I, had the better claim both in law and territorially. Leo X soon deserted his former ally Francis.

Secondly, either in that year or a little earlier – the evidence is contradictory – Pietro met a holy terror of a young soldier named Giovanni de' Medici, still only twenty-one but already a seasoned campaigner. Giovanni was a nephew of Lorenzo the Magnificent and thus a cousin of the Pope, who let him do pretty much as he liked in Rome, which he visited only during one or other of his frequent rows with more senior commanders. This Giovanni, exactly six years younger than Pietro, was the son of another Giovanni de' Medici, a handsome and tolerant but otherwise undistinguished gentleman who died of a fever in the year of his son's birth, 1498. The mother of the second Giovanni, however, Caterina Sforza, differed entirely in temperament from her easy-going third husband. With the fierce military masculinity of certain medieval queens and even abbesses, the prototypes of those invincible female knights who figure in fifteenth-century epics and whom Pietro, following earlier models, was to attempt to describe in his own experiment in this kind of poetry, Caterina combined an alarming intelligence. At the end of 1499, when she was about forty, she held her castle at Forli in the Romagna against Cesare Borgia till all the defenders except herself had perished. Cesare kept her a captive in Rome until 1501. She died in 1509, when her son Giovanni, at eleven, showed every sign of following in her footsteps.

He already looked like a miniature but lean and athletic Napoleon. Hardly ever out of the saddle, when in it he usually rode at full gallop. He swam rivers in the depth of winter, hunted his hounds, raided neighbouring villages and robbed passing travellers in the spirit of a baron of the Dark Ages. At twelve, he visited a brothel for the first time and killed his first man. At fourteen, after his cousin Leo X had assumed the tiara in 1513, he was sampling Sienese, Roman and Neapolitan courtesans. At sixteen he unhorsed eight antagonists, one after the other, in a tournament in Florence.

Next year Leo sent his nephew Lorenzo de' Medici to attack the city of Urbino in the Marches. Giovanni accompanied his cousin on this campaign and after Urbino had been stormed returned with him in triumph to Florence. Lorenzo, now Duke of Urbino, had put him in command of a hundred light horsemen, Corsicans whose 'sombre courage' he was ever afterwards to swear made them the finest soldiers in the world. It is curious that Giovanni, who was to prove unquestionably the greatest commander of his lifetime, should have borne a distinct physical resemblance to the Corsican Napoleon and also shared in some degree the latter's special aptitude for tactics in the field, so far as the cruder armaments of the early sixteenth century permitted.

That year Giovanni married Maria Salviati, the daughter of his former tutor, a thoroughly domesticated, somewhat pathetic young woman, about the same age as himself. He had known her since they were both children. She never meant much to her husband, though he always treated her with courtesy.

It may have been at this period, 1516–17, that Giovanni first met Pietro, now in a position, as Leo's favourite buffoon, to introduce the dashing young cavalry officer to celebrated courtesans, such as the wealthy, pseudo-pious Spanish Jewess Niccolosa and the 'angel-faced, devil-hearted' Lucrezia, a great favourite of Pietro's, whom he had nicknamed, for her absurd pretences at modesty, 'Mother-won't-let-me'. But Giovanni never stayed long in Rome. By March 1517 he was fighting the Spaniards in the Tuscan Apennines. The foreigners had been called in by Francesco Maria della Rovere, the expelled Duke of Urbino, to help him regain his property. But Giovanni's wild Corsican riders proved more than a match, even in the hills, for the world-famous Spanish infantry; Francesco Maria sued for peace at the end of the year.

This useful experience on active service in difficult conditions began the young commander's disillusion with the average Italian general officers of his day, whom he accused to their faces of negligence, treachery and cowardice. History seems to prove that he was largely right in considering that most of them thought only of their personal profit and, if that were assured, could not have cared less which side won a victory. But he himself lived pretty ostentatiously at this time. He seldom sat down to a dinner for less than fifty and kept thirty horses in his stables. Moreover, the stubborn violence of his unending personal quarrels, some of them with relatively decent people, was becoming beyond a joke.

On November 25, 1517 he wrote to a rival *condottiere*, a more or less respectable officer of good family, one Camillo degli Appiani, then in residence at the Tuscan port of Piombino opposite the island of Elba:

'Lord Camillo. Recently a man in my service called Il Corsetto' – the 'Little Corsican' – 'arrived at Piombino and asked if you had any message for me. After making him wait a while in your house you inflicted five or six wounds upon him. You call yourself a gentleman. The greatest rascal in the world would not have done such a shameful thing. I call upon you to meet me in arms, when I will punish you for your ignoble behaviour. If you have any honour left you will not fail to meet me, though I doubt if you will dare to fight me. I will send you word of a safe meeting-place, suitable for persons of our rank. If you do not accept battle I will treat you as such cowardice deserves. I will give you fifteen days from that on which you receive this letter to reply to it.'

Friends and relatives on both sides intervened to prevent a duel. Camillo degli Appiani eventually retorted to a second equally offensive challenge by pointing out to his excited young correspondent that the alleged 'Corsican' was a Calabrian vassal of the Appiani family named Antonino da Cola and that he, Camillo, had been obliged to chastise the fellow, by the sword, for insufferable impudence. Giovanni, infuriated by being given the lie in this fashion, rushed with his 'Corsetto' to the Glove Inn at Florence, where he had been told that Camillo's chancellor and clerk were staying. Bursting into their apartment, he wounded both men so seriously that they subsequently died.

The two assailants galloped off to Ferrara, beyond Florentine jurisdiction. From that city Giovanni issued another frantically abusive challenge to Camillo. But even in sixteenth-century Italy this super-aristocratic behaviour could not be ignored. The young Medici found that everyone was against him, including his cousin the Pope, who summoned him to Rome to explain his conduct. At last, early in March 1518, he sullenly condescended to apologise. But he was sentenced to five years' banishment from Florence. The 'Corsetto' confessed under torture that he had in fact baited Camillo and was duly beheaded for his part as prime mover in this somewhat mysterious affair. Apparently he had merely posed as a Corsican in order to enlist Giovanni's help in revenging himself upon Camillo for some real or fancied injustice.

Yet in December 1518 the most successful young soldier in the country again appeared in Florence, overawing the magistracy, using his incorrigible sword in street brawls, contemptuously apologising, piling up debts, writing letters to everyone except his appalled wife, sending the worried Leo a present of falcons and being generally such a nuisance, in the absence of any war in which he could be usefully employed, that the Pope in March 1519 again called him to Rome, paid his debts and gave him a hundred men-at-arms to drill. It is said that once he had occasion to rebuke one of these tough mercenaries and strode up to him in his usual menacing fashion. The fellow laid a hand on his sword. 'One step nearer, Captain, and you die!' Giovanni, enraptured with this prompt exhibition of ferocity, promoted the soldier on the spot to command a company. The man, needless to say, was a Corsican!

Clear evidence exists that Giovanni de' Medici and Pietro Aretino revelled together in Rome at this date, whenever the former could spare the time from his military duties. The story that he and Pietro met at Ravenna about 1517–18, while the latter was employed at a monastery in the district, and thereafter became 'inseparable' until in the summer of 1519 Giovanni sent Pietro to Rome with a despatch for the Pope, is conceivable, but rather unlikely in view of Pietro's unquestionable aversion from every aspect of warfare and his well documented presence at the papal court in those years.

In any case, whether old or new friends in 1519, the two young men certainly spent a lot of time together in Rome towards the end of that year. Their intimacy was uninterruptedly loyal and affectionate on both sides. Its basis was the respect each felt for the daring and irrepressible independence of mind shown by the other, a quality rare in an age when success in life normally followed only upon sycophancy and obsequiousness to one's social superiors. Each also admired in the other achievements he could not imitate. Giovanni took no interest in art, literature or political intrigue. He hated complication of any sort except in the field, where his inborn gift for tactics repeatedly baffled the enemy. But he was profoundly impressed by Pietro's ability to make the most dangerous people either laugh or squirm by simply scribbling and talking. Pietro, for his part, found in his friend a fiery honesty and courage which not only formed an agreeable contrast with most of the persons in their circle, but also might well make Giovanni the 'saviour of Italy', that is to say the physical bulwark behind which he, Pietro, could rise to command the destinies of his country. Detesting hard knocks and slaughter himself, Pietro realised that they were essential for the acquisition of power in any practical sense, and such power he was now intent upon.

For the rest, both these youthful playboys loved women, parties and mockery of pretentious priests and courtiers. In such amusements the younger man was notable mainly for riotous pride, while his companion excelled in ostentation and sheer publicity-mongering, as well as the exploitation of feminine wiles and masculine debauchery to further his own ambition.

A light horseman by preference, Giovanni behaved like a Prince Rupert in battle, though he kept his men under far better control. They knew he would not hesitate to run them through with his own sword if they defied him in the field, as was common enough in the ill-disciplined armies of the period under less resolute commanders. On the other hand, he was always just as ready to cut down their enemies, whether official or unofficial, as the scene in the Glove Inn at Florence early in 1518 proves.

This bloodthirsty brawler, soldier of genius and indefatigable overwhelmer of courtesans was already short of the ring-finger of his right hand – lost in one of his innumerable skirmishes in the Marches – when he and Pietro began their Roman revels. In appearance a low-browed athlete of average height, with a rather large head, a full but pale face, a short aquiline nose, and terrifying, sparkling eyes, the formidable captain had a voice that on occasion frightened civilians out of their wits. His hands and feet were noticeably small, but his arms and legs extremely muscular. The art critic in Pietro was fascinated by these physical peculiarities.

Pietro also saw that the *condottiere*, though he didn't know a sonnet from an elegy or a Raphael from a Fra Bartolomeo, had more in him than any of the swaggering courtiers, learned or otherwise, around Leo. Giovanni, on his side, duly fell under Pietro's spell, irresistible when the satirist chose to deploy it for the few males he favoured. Keen lechers, keen haters of people with more money than they deserved, the two friends were equally generous to a fault, quick-witted and at bottom anarchists impatient of any authority but their own. Giovanni, unlike his companion, hardly troubled to disguise this tendency in himself.

Pietro particularly adored his friend for fighting because he loved it, quite regardless, unlike all other mercenary commanders, of the wealth to be gained. Pietro, too, was always indifferent to money for its own sake, and wrote because writing was what he loved best. The dark, fierce Medici, an aristocrat to his finger-tips, appreciated, for his part, the flamboyant small-town shoe-maker's son's calculated insolence and adroit changes of ground when cornered.

Pietro and Giovanni roamed the steep, teeming streets of the 'world's head' together and found that even by daylight it bore a distinct resemblance, here and there, to the world's backside. They indulged in friendly competitions for the favours of prominent courtesans, the more notorious for fraud and malice the better. Pietro was always ready to withdraw in favour of his boisterous companion if the latter showed signs of losing his temper. For Giovanni, a member of one of the most powerful families in Italy and also the Pope's nephew, again and again frightened off, with his prompt sword or his mere name, the bravos hired by the sharp-tongued satirist's foes to teach him a lesson. The public progress of the two friends often resembled that of a late eighteenth-century English 'milord' with his attendant pugilist. For Pietro always dressed splendidly (often on credit) and strutted, while the other, more soberly garbed, marched with a wary, professional soldier's tread at his elbow.

But war soon flared up again in Lombardy. Giovanni rushed off to defend the papal and imperial forces against the invasion of Francis I, directed on Milan. The young *condottiere* greatly increased his reputation for dashing heroism – and bursts of ill-temper against elderly allied generals – during the campaign. Like Horatius he swam a river in full armour, though on horse-back. On the road to Milan, while hurrying to meet the imperial troops marching to relieve the city from the close pressure of the French, he put to flight, single-handed, a mob of Italian refugees who had brought his horse down. His sword whirled, they said afterwards, in all directions at once, like that of a true Orlando Furioso. In the end Milan was saved from the French and the restored Duke of that city, Francesco Maria Sforza, personally thanked Giovanni de' Medici for his conspicuous part in the victory.

Meanwhile, Pietro in Rome sorely missed his bold play-fellow and protector, and began to look for a second useful patron, one who might be expected to live longer than the gluttonous, wine-bibbing Pope, who took so little care of a weak constitution. The poet found such a champion in another Medici, the Cardinal Giulio, a robust cleric in his early forties, son of the only brother of the Magnificent Lorenzo and there-fore Leo's cousin. Giulio had been advising the pontiff for some years and was obviously in the running to succeed him when the prematurely aged pontiff died. The Cardinal, of whom Pietro had probably seen something while serving as a lackey in Chigi's household, seemed a cultured and accessible magnate, not at all a bigot and full of generosity. In truth he was courting popularity right and left for the papal election that was expected soon, Leo being considered too fond of hunting, among other diversions, for so corpulent a man to last much longer.

Pietro's shrewd judgment of human character did not allow him to trust Giulio de' Medici. One never quite knew what so subtle a mind might be up to. Were those dark, strongly marked, somewhat stern features in fact a sign of honest industry, courage and true piety, or of something more like Pietro's own outlook on the world? Was the Cardinal really unscrupulous and unprincipled? Was he what Giovanni de' Medici would call in his blunt fashion, with a rattling warrior's oath, 'shifty'? Time would show. Meanwhile, one thing seemed clear to Pietro. No other cardinal but the Medici had a chance of the tiara.

As many people who knew the Pope well had in private prophesied, Leo X died suddenly, a few days after a chill caught on a November hunting trip down the Tiber. He was only forty-six, but had been in poor health for a long time and looked much older. The day of his death was December 1, 1521.

As usual on these occasions in Renaissance Italy some rejoiced while others mourned. When the news broke, the enemies of the Medici in Ferrara and Venice, even in Florence, where that family now ruled again, hoped for better times, since Medicean 'faithlessness and cruelty' could no longer look for support from the highest seat in Christendom. But bankers who had lent the late pontiff enormous sums, cardinals and bishops who had staked their careers on his continued existence, writers and artists whom he had patronised so lavishly, were all inconsolable.

So was Giovanni de' Medici, still facing the French in the Lombardy field. He replaced all the flags, pennons and other draperies of his squadrons, which had been white, with black cloth. He thus acquired the name by which he is known to historians, Giovanni delle Bande Nere ('John of the Black Bands'). It was a name which struck terror into Frenchmen, Spaniards and Italians alike, whether friends or foes, wherever his dreaded light cavalry's trumpet sounded.

The comments of smaller men on Leo's death were simply malicious. 'He took office like a fox', growled one street-corner orator. 'He ruled like a lion – well named Leo, forsooth – and he died like a dog'. Pietro could have bettered this rude epigraph. But he had more important work to do just then than speaking ill of the dead.

In the Piazza Navone at Rome stood an ancient statue, armless, legless, and with a broken nose. It was supposed to have once represented Hercules. But the Roman populace called it Pasquino, probably after some well known wit of earlier times, perhaps a schoolmaster. A 'feast of Pasquino' was initiated about the year 1500. On that occasion the pedestal of the image

would be plastered with scurrilous Latin epigrams – 'pasquinades' – of varying merit, attacking important public figures.
After a while this habit came to be indulged in at any time, not
necessarily during the April 'Feast of Messer Pasquino'. Pietro
rose voluminously to this chance of promoting both Cardinal
Giulio's candidature for the papacy and the writer's own rising
reputation as a reckless and popular castigator of the great. He
pasted on the statue, night after night, sonnet after biting sonnet,
to the number of over fifty in the end, trouncing all and sundry,
but mostly Giulio's rivals.

Rough English translations can reproduce little of the sizzling
effect of these verses in the original, packed as they are with
local slang and now indecipherable local allusions. But their
general nature can be suggested in a couple of examples.

'If Flisco's pope he'll go for a whole year
without a lawsuit and for that same time
Farnese will not talk and of all crime
Colonna Armellino sure will clear.
Mantua to small boys will not go near,
Ponzetta money lavishly will throw,
Campeggio'll be less civil and more slow,
and Grassi will desert his wife, poor dear.

Ancona's rages shall obey his needs
and Pucci will draw up no further deeds
and Valle will not care if his heart bleeds,
but he'll give up his brats, Cesarini his whore,
and Trani his poor ma, who loves him sore.
Cortona, too, will drop his plots and more.'

'We have a Pope! And each low hostelry,
each custom-house, each corner butcher's store,
blazes with light and sound and trumpet's roar
to see fulfilled Pasquino's prophecy
about the bleating, braying hierarchy
of geldings, sheep, slow oxen, bullocks, cows.
Lord of high-bellowed but of broken vows,
Armellino's Pope on fools' epiphany.

And though he can't put on his triple crown
until, like dulling lead instead of rain,

47

The Holy Ghost descends from the still air,
yet since his name is vaunted through the town
it sudden comes to make his boast more plain,
more like a donkey than a dove so fair.'

It was doggerel, but better doggerel than anyone else could write in Rome at the time. Pietro knew that well enough. He boldly confessed his authorship in such lines as

'It's really surprising that the Cardinals' College
can find no way of stopping Aretino's verbiage.'

or

'Master Pasquino's inn
is the school of Peter Aretin.'

The verses became so popular that they travelled all over Italy and a good part of Europe. Everyone was interested in what was happening in Rome and who was going to be the next pope. Crowned heads and other dictatorial persons heard for the first time the name of Pietro Aretino, the 'Chancellor of Master Pasquino', which some of them would later come to fear more than that of the Sultan or the devil himself.

Meanwhile a peculiar situation had developed in the locked chapel where the cardinals debated. Their deliberations lasted so long that the very man whose chance of election, on the whole, stood highest, began to grow uneasy. The enemies of the Medici in the north, Cardinal Giulio heard with anxiety as the new year of 1522 began, were taking advantage of the confusion in Rome to bid for a restoration of truly republican conditions, involving a second expulsion of his kinsmen, in Florence. Troops from Perugia and exiles from Urbino were on the march for Siena, although their objective was clearly the city which the Medici family now regarded as their own. Giulio resolved to meet this situation by getting himself elected Pope forthwith.

All Italy was seething with impatience. Baldassare Castiglione, the most elegant stylist of the day, who had already written but not yet published his famous treatise on the ideal qualities of a gentleman, *Il Cortigiano*, was then in command of the papal troops in Lombardy. He expressed the mood of sarcastic irritation throughout the peninsula when he remarked in a letter: 'Every morning we await the descent of the Holy Ghost. But it seems that he is out of town.'

In these circumstances Cardinal Giulio de' Medici resolved on a bold move. He already controlled about a third of the votes in the Sacred College, mostly those of the younger cardinals. But a two-thirds majority was necessary for a candidate to secure the Chair of St Peter. The older cardinals objected to Giulio on account of his age, still well under fifty. However, they could not agree on an over-fifty substitute for the Florentine. He proposed several plausible names, but they were all vetoed, generally by the French cardinals, who were dead against anyone friendly to a Medici. They had not forgiven the late Pope Leo's betrayal of their king.

Faced with this dilemma between the Medicean and anti-Medicean factions in the Sacred College, Giulio astutely determined to propose a candidate so obscure that the reluctance to vote for such a nonentity would force the cardinals to call for the best known man in an assembly where no one could be implicitly trusted. He proposed Adrian of Utrecht, a Fleming of sixty-three who had started life either, like Christ, in a carpenter's shop or, as some said, in a shipyard or a drapery store, and had risen to become a tutor of the Emperor Charles, thereafter being appointed Cardinal of Tortosa in Spain. Adrian had not even troubled to attend the Sacred College on this momentous occasion. He was a worthy and learned prelate but otherwise quite unremarkable. In the circumstances, Giulio expected ironical smiles from his colleagues, followed by an overwhelming vote for himself.

However, after some equivocal debate the requisite decisive number of twenty-six cardinals voted for Adrian. When the new Pope's name was announced from the balcony of the still unfinished church of St Peter, the crowd in the muddy square below greeted the news in shocked silence. Then catcalls, whistles and finally a raging roar of jeers broke out. For a while the Roman populace was in a dangerous mood. They would have cheered for a Medici or a Colonna. They might have grudgingly accepted a Spaniard or a Frenchman. But a Dutchman! The Venetian ambassador wrote home that he was 'stunned' at the news and could hardly believe his ears. The cardinals themselves seemed to regret their decision as soon as they had taken it. When they emerged from St Peter's after the announcement they looked, according to the Roman poet Tebaldeo, 'like ghosts from limbo, so white and distraught were their faces'. Tebaldeo continues, 'Almost all are dissatisfied and repent already of having chosen a stranger, a barbarian and a tutor of the emperor – a monarch most dangerous to the temporal power of the papacy.'

The nervous ecclesiastical princes were almost mobbed. One enraged citizen seized Cardinal Minerva and bawled into his ear that the members of the conclave ought to be 'roasted or boiled or pounded into a jelly.' The Cardinal of Mantua told another rioter: 'We deserve the most rigorous punishment. I am glad that you do not avenge your wrongs with stones.' He was probably one of the minority who had not voted for Adrian.

Next day lampoons and caricatures were printed. One drawing showed St Peter making off from Rome with a bag of plunder, like a burglar, while a prostitute, somewhat rudely typifying the Eternal City, vainly tried to stop him, yelling: 'I got away from the money-lenders, but now the Jews have me!' Everyone understood what she meant. The 'money-lenders' were the Florentine bankers of Leo X. The 'Jews' were the men of Spain, where Adrian had lived. To the Roman rabble the hated Spaniards were all 'Jews' or 'Moors', since both these races had exercised great influence in Spain. Another cartoon showed the old Dutchman dressed as a schoolmaster and flourishing a ruler or cane, with which he was beating the bare backsides of a fugitive group of cardinals on horseback. A Latin inscription sneered: 'See what a wretched pass their wrangling has brought them to!'

But by far the hardest hitting of the flood of lampoons and 'pasquinades' were those of the fastest pen in Rome, that of Pietro Aretino. For once he dropped his laughing irony and burst into a furious sonnet, rhyming throughout on the Italian words *noi* and *voi*, 'we' and 'you'. So startling an innovation in the traditional scheme of this form of composition conveyed by its monotonous violence, like the blows of an axe, a kind of savage indignation that could have been registered in no other way.

'O cardinals, if you were changed to us –
and not for anything would we be you –

and we had done the same bad things as you,
tell us quite frankly, what would you do to us?
We are most certain that you would hang us,
as we should like to hack to pieces you.
Indeed, had we the same power as you,
you would be crucified at once by us.
But since all honours are but shames to you
and not yet infamous can you call us,
we will no longer deign to speak of you.
O filthy rabble, foe to Christ and us,
to burial alive we'd like to sentence you
now that you've brought to ruin you and us.'

The author had a personal reason, of course, for his outburst.
He had been banking on the generous Medici. He knew nothing
of this old Dutch bigot, who did not even live in Italy, except
that he was reputed to scorn the vanities of this world, including
everything Pietro himself so hugely enjoyed – witty literature,
grand painting, gorgeous young women, brilliant banquets and
dazzling garments. It would be useless, Pietro concluded, to try
his usual sparkling style of conciliation. Adrian of Utrecht had
probably never laughed in his life. But, like so many puritans,
he might be effectively vengeful. There was no point in exposing
oneself, as the most talkative rebel against the cardinals'
decision, to his possibly homicidal wrath. As soon as Messer
Pietro heard that the new Pope had set sail from Tortosa for
Rome, he himself made off at a good round pace for Bologna,
the famous university town two hundred miles to the north,
where, according to Niccolo Franco, he had once acted as
stable-boy at an inn.

A letter he received at Bologna from a certain Andrea, a
Roman painter – not the contemporary Florentine Andrea del
Sarto – and one of Pietro's most assiduous admirers and imita-
tors, as well as a good Medici man, shows the sort of impression
Pietro had made on the average lively Roman citizen. Andrea
pretends to have been much exercised as to how he should
address his friend. He gives a long list of possible honorific titles
of a burlesque character, all eventually rejected as more suitable to other prominent Italians.

'Respected Sir' would be appropriate only to merchant-
bankers like Chigi. 'Your Excellency' made one think of military

men like Giovanni the *condottiere* or noblemen like Malatesta
of Rimini. 'Most Christian and Catholic' should be reserved for
people who, unlike his correspondent, went regularly to mass.
'Distinguished' was for lawyers, 'Illustrious' for princes,
'Reverend' for priests, 'Prudent' for business men who would
not stir without written contracts, not at all Messer Pietro's
way. 'Magnificent' is for 'Venetian louts' and 'Ser Pietro' only
for Spaniards or Neapolitans, equally unpopular with the
Roman masses. So the catalogue goes on for a page or two,
citing well known Romans who would object to their favourite
complimentary phrases being applied to the 'One and only'
Pietro Aretino. Andrea continues:

'Even the illustrious Cardinal Medici, our common patron,
would call me a liar if I addressed you as 'Speaker of Evil',
while 'Speaker of Good' would only bring down on my head
the anathemas of Cardinals Soderino, Colonna and Cornaro.
So I will simply call you "Dear Aretino" and say how much
your departure has increased the sorrows of Rome. Master
Pasquino has not spoken a word since you left. He is wearing
deep mourning.'

Andrea dated his letter 'from filthy Rome in the last days of
this executioner of a July 1522, a thieving traitor of a year.' The
style somewhat resembles that of its addressee, and it is quite
possible, though improbable, that Pietro forged the letter, as he
often in later times forged flattering missives purporting to have
been written to himself, or re-wrote genuine communications
which he did not consider flattering enough. Andrea, however,
scarcely seems to have been sufficiently important to merit this
treatment. But the letter, if genuine is evidenec for the exile's
personal popularity at this date among ordinary people, his continued good standing with Giulio de' Medici in spite of the
latter's vexation at not being elected to the Chair of St Peter,
and the identification of Pietro in most Roman minds with the
author of Messer Pasquino's more embittered comments on
public events.

One of Adrian's first acts as Pope was to command this
statue to be thrown into the Tiber. But he was persuaded to
countermand the order, being logical enough to see that the
image's destruction would only perpetuate a legend of martyr-

dom among the populace and the jollier of the courtiers, who had already reason enough to hate the Pope as a killjoy. The austere pontiff had no more use for literary men than he had for high living in general or the splendours of the Vatican in particular. He had called the magnificent 'Laocoon' in the Belvedere sculpture gallery a 'heathen idol'. Adrian eventually directed that all those who could be proved to have acted as mouthpieces for Messer Pasquino's shocking gibes should be 'hunted down and severely punished'.

There were plenty of unscrupulous priests and laymen ready to carry out this order and so curry favour with Adrian VI. Pietro, really losing his temper seriously for the first and not the last time in his life, was not prepared to remain silent under this 'barbarian' of a pope. He continued his attacks on Adrian from Bologna. But he was beginning to wonder whether that agreeable city stood far enough away from the papal court and would be strong enough to protect him from the Holy Father's minions. Messer Pietro hated bodily pain, confinement and discomfort as only a born sensualist can. But physical coward as he always was, Pietro remained, through sheer vanity, shamelessness and high spirits, eternally irrepressible. He invariably found a way of outwitting the torturers.

Giulio de' Medici, he decided, must be trapped, if he could not be tactfully induced, into opening the door to freedom from Adrian's vengeance. The Cardinal was in Florence, where he had taken charge of the government on the death of his nephew Lorenzo de' Medici the Younger in 1519. Pietro set out for that restless city and let his old patron know of his presence there. Giulio, in a delicate position between an uncongenial pope and the turbulent Florentine citizenry, was not quite sure how useful or how much of a nuisance Pietro might now prove to be. After prolonged hesitation he consented to see his fluent, ostentatiously devoted yet not altogether trustworthy retainer.

The interview had a confidential character. The titular ruler of Florence explained to his client that there could be no question of a possible successor to Adrian offending the pontiff by protecting a man who had never ceased to be a thorn in the flesh of the Vicar of Christ. There were, however, the Cardinal continued suavely, other notable gentlemen among the many admirers of the visitor who might be prepared to take his part.

The Marquess of Mantua, for instance, had spoken well of him. And Mantua, a very strong city on the river Mincio in the far north of the peninsula near the Lago di Garda, was surrounded by a maze of lakes and marshes and considered impregnable by military men.

The Marquess, still in his early twenties, may or may not have already met Pietro personally at this date. A recent authority mentions casually that Pietro had made his way to the Mantuan court, where 'he did not stay long', before the death of Leo X. But other biographers are silent on this visit and the Cardinal's reported language, when Pietro called on him in Florence, seems to imply that the two young men were not personally acquainted.

'I will give you a letter to take to his lordship if you like', Giulio told Messer Pietro, who had been unusually silent after the first florid exchange of mutual compliments and apologies. Two of the subtlest minds of their day exchanged wary smiles. Pietro, very much on his guard, could not help suspecting the Cardinal of a manoeuvre to get rid of him at all costs, even at the cost of a life so exceptionally valuable to its owner. The Medici, for his part, did not wish Pietro to think so, and perhaps did not at all desire a potential future champion finally put out of the way. But the fellow was definitely a liability to Giulio's plans so long as that exasperating old fanatic at the Vatican held on to the tiara.

'The Marquess is a man after your own heart, Messer Pietro', the sly prelate went on in a lighter tone, with a great display of unbending. 'I'm sure you will become great friends. He's very fond of painting and sculpture. He has an ear, I'm told, for a good laugh, or he wouldn't have asked Baldassare Castiglione, as I happen to know, to get him all your writings. He also – they tell me, though I oughtn't, as a priest, to say so – has two eyes in his head for a pretty face'. This last piece of information was an understatement. Federigo Gonzaga, Marquess of Mantua, had achieved notoriety, even in Renaissance Italy, for his tireless pursuit of every personable young woman within sight.

'I am very deeply indebted, as so often before, to your Eminence's kind heart,' said Pietro Aretino. 'I should certainly like to pay my respects to the Marquess under such auspicious circumstances.'

He had decided to risk it. Early in February 1523 he reached the outskirts of Mantua and liked the look of the place, both for its marshy environment (the best defence against military assault in those days) and its picturesque architecture. After all, he reflected, Virgil had been born there. Why shouldn't Pietro Aretino confer a further celebrity on the city by residing in it for a few carefree weeks or months under a new, rich and affable patron?

Federigo, a handsome, dark-haired and full-bearded young nobleman, whose sensual, sensitive, good-natured but weak features are perfectly caught in Titian's portrait of him, made an excellent first impression on everyone he met, not excluding crafty Pietro. The Marquess was not the son of that brainy beauty Isabella d'Este for nothing. Castiglione puts a flattering account of him into the mouth of one of the participants in the discussion at the palace of the Duke of Urbino recorded in *Il Cortigiano*:

'Today in Italy you may find certain sons of illustrious lords who may not have the power of their ancestors but make up for it in talent. The most promising of these young men is Federigo Gonzaga, eldest son of the Marquess of Mantua. In addition to his excellent manners and the discretion he shows at so tender an age he is said by those in charge of him to be wonderful in wit, desire for honour, courtesy and love of justice. From such a beginning one can only expect the most admirable of ends.'

But under this amiable surface Federigo had now, as a marquess in his twenties, certain shortcomings which Pietro soon noted. The Mantuan ruler's lack of moral principle and excessive sensuality both amused and interested his new guest. These weaknesses could easily be exploited by an ambitious and unscrupulous companion who, while sharing them, indulged them in a considerably more level-headed fashion than his host. On the other hand, Federigo's avarice might prove troublesome, though Pietro was fairly sure of the protection to be afforded by a certain weapon he had already tried out on a small scale with notable success, namely the application of shock treatment to shame the subject into behaving like a gentleman by threatening to reveal occasions when he had not

behaved like one. But for the moment the dangerous newcomer
to the Mantuan court bided his time. He wrote exultantly to
his 'brother' Gualtiero Bacci:

'I am now in Mantua in the house of the Lord Marquess,
and so much in that lord's graces that he gives up eating and
sleeping to talk to me. He says that he has no other real
pleasure. He has written things about me to the Cardinal de'
Medici which truly and honourably give me great joy. He
promises that if I stay with him I will have an income of
three hundred *scudi* a year. He has given me the very apartment occupied by Francesco Maria, Duke of Urbino, when
he was driven from his dominions, and has assigned me a
personal steward to take charge of my meals. At my table
there are always great gentlemen, and in short he could not
have done more for me if I had been some mighty noble. As
a result all his court bows down before me and any member
of it who can get even one of my verses calls himself lucky.
And as fast as I make them, the Marquess has them copied.
I have already composed several singing his praises. In this
manner I live here and each day he gives me presents, fine
things I will show to you in Arezzo.'

Federigo, on his side, writing from his country villa at
Marmirolo, informed Cardinal Giulio de' Medici:

'Our Pietro Aretino is like a festival of joy and pleasure to
me. The fact that I am away from Mantua hardly bothers
me at all, for being with him is like being in a whole crowd
and his conversation takes the place of many talented men.
Indeed, if it were not for the reverence and obligations which
I feel towards Your Eminence and the loyalty, second to no
one's, which Messer Pietro cherishes for you, I would attempt
to decorate my court permanently with this precious jewel. I
cannot do so for the two above-mentioned reasons. But I shall
be allowed, I hope, to enjoy his presence for a certain time,
subject to your contentment. I know that to a person so busy
as Your Eminence such a man must be the greatest recreation
and pleasure. Therefore I will restore him to you soon. And
if my 'soon' seems late to you, to me it seems very early
indeed. Would I could keep him much longer!'

The Cardinal replied complacently. Obviously feeling great relief at getting Pietro off his hands for the time being, he wrote to Federigo:

'I wish Your Excellency to keep and enjoy his services as long as you see fit and wish to do so. I assure you that I could have no greater pleasure than hearing of Your Excellency's satisfaction with anything I can do for you. Nor do I think it will displease Messer Pietro to stay with you. I have always known him to be desirous and eager to serve you. If he does so, it will please me more than if he were serving my own person, for I regard his service to you as service to myself. If there is any other way in which I can serve Your Excellency, I pray you to advise me of it. For I will always be most ready to carry out every wish of yours.'

But Pietro was already beginning to see through the Marquess, whom he could not forgive, though he did not show it at present, for his stupidity. At a much later date he was to let fly in highly characteristic fashion.

'Sardanapalus, I mean Federigo' – he wrote – 'is capable of making a hundred herds of swine citizens and after offering up his sword in the temple of Venus, the pleasure-giver, he will announce that the greatest good is Petrarch's "sloth, gluttony and lazy lassitude". Master Abraham, his doctor, finds in the ducal constellations' – the Marquess had by then been made a Duke – 'that he is in danger of going to the Antipodes because of some gravel in his kidneys which has been aggravated by his drunkenness and his continual erotic relations with both men and women.'

Long before the time of this letter, however, Pietro, while still enjoying the early spring weather of 1523 at Mantua, hunting during the day and holding a gay company spellbound in the evenings with his brilliant gossip of Roman life, had decided that this northern city could be nothing but a temporary refuge. Rome, or at least Florence, would certainly pay better dividends.

He discussed these feelings, tactfully enough, with the equally tactful Marquess. They agreed that the first step must be to sound the Cardinal who had meanwhile much improved his prospects in both Florence and Rome by being more tactful than either. The Mantuan ambassador in Florence was directed by his master to discover the views of Giulio de' Medici regarding a possible return of Messer Pietro Aretino. The envoy's reply was prompt and disappointing.

'I have spoken to his Eminence regarding Messer Pietro and Your Excellency's reluctance to keep him in Mantua because he wished to return to Florence at all costs. I added that he had already repeatedly asked your permission to do so. The Cardinal answered that the Aretine was a loud-mouthed and unreliable trouble-maker. He said nothing more. It seems to me, therefore, that he is well aware that you cannot manage the Aretine and that so far as His Eminence is concerned you may dismiss Messer Pietro any time you like. But before doing so you should warn the Aretine that I have heard from Messer Paul of Arezzo that certain new writings against the Pope and some of the Cardinals are going the rounds in Rome and on this account the Pope has sent Cardinal Medici a brief ordering him to arrest Pietro Aretino and send him under guard to the papal authorities in Rome. I therefore doubt whether His Eminence would be in a position to protect Messer Pietro in Florence, were he to arrive there.'

Pietro's counterstroke to this devastating rebuff was worthy of Giovanni de' Medici himself on a stricken field. He haughtily dictated to the compliant Marquess a fulsome letter of commendation of the latter's parting guest, Pietro himself, to the Cardinal, just as if the ambassador's letter had never been received.

'I desired the excellent Messer Pietro Aretino even before Your Eminence allowed me to have him and I shall do so still more after his departure, which will take place soon. For during these days, which to me, however, have been but a moment, I have enjoyed so thoroughly his engaging virtues and agreeable wit that I would never have been able to dismiss him, though he asked me to do so again and again, were it not that he goes to Your Eminence. I am well aware, indeed, how much I am in your debt, since your affection for me has deprived you so long of the company of a man who should always be desired. I thank you infinitely for the gift you have made me. It is a favour among the greatest that I have ever been granted. Furthermore, though it may seem impertinent to recommend to any man what is already his own property, yet, since Pietro has become mine also, I beg to recommend him to you. Had I anything of equal worth I would offer it to Your Eminence in exchange for him. But in this affair there can be no just exchange and I am to that extent the more indebted to you.'

Then the subject of this encomium coolly set out for Florence in his best clothes, with the dictated letter in his pocket, to interview the man who had a warrant for his arrest in *his* pocket. He charged straight into the palace of the Medici, brushing everyone aside with the thunderous announcement: 'I AM PIETRO ARETINO!'

The Cardinal, too, must be admired for the courtesy of the reception he accorded to his formidable client. He merely raised his beetling black eyebrows.

'Didn't you like Mantua, *messere?*'

'On the contrary, I enjoyed every moment of my stay there. But my heart was always with Your Eminence and I couldn't keep away from you any longer.'

Giulio de' Medici bowed in dignified acknowledgement of these sentiments. No doubt he was thinking, as so often before, that he really could not afford to make an enemy of so daring and able an ally.

'You will realise,' he said quietly, 'that I can't openly defy His Holiness's orders, of which you must be aware. But I am ready to recommend you to the protection of a member of my family whom I believe you already know, the great captain Giovanni delle Bande Nere. I dare say you would like to see him again?'

Pietro's heart leapt. But he did not choose to smile. The Cardinal must not be allowed too easy a triumph.

'If your Eminence advises such a step I can only agree to take it,' he retorted gravely.

Giovanni was in camp at Reggio in Emilia, not at present fighting but sampling the courtesans and officers' wives of the merry garrison town. The most interesting of the professional ladies was one Paola. According to Pietro she was a decent sort,

for a change, and relatively honest. She compared most favour-
ably with the half-bred Greeks, Venetians and Jewesses the two
young men had cultivated in Rome, glamour girls 'with the
faces of angels and the hearts of devils'. Giovanni seems to have
behaved in bed much as he did on the battlefield, lying incomprehensibly low for a while and then bursting out with
shocking suddenness upon his startled companion, as if he were
confronting her sword in hand. Pietro wrote on arrival at
Reggio:

'Joy filled the hearts of all. For the young leader had just
given his soldiers a night of liberty. Torches were blazing
everywhere. The whores of the city had come to the camp in
great numbers. Some of the troopers were leaping from their
horses, having just returned from a foraging expedition.
Bottles of wine, well cured hams, baskets of fruit and even
bleating lambs were slung across their saddle-bows. Such
provisions had cost them nothing, for they had robbed everyone for ten miles around. A few of the women in the plundered
families wept and tore their hair, while their husbands and
fathers clamoured and argued, pleading for restoration of
their wives, daughters and livestock. But these male peasants
were beaten back with the flats of daggers and halberds.
Enormous campfires gleamed under groves of oaks. The
shadows of the soldiers drinking, gambling or making love
were flung hither and thither in the ruddy light of the
cressets.'

Long afterwards, Pietro described these days in a letter to a
respectable feminine correspondent who had been the wife of
one of Giovanni's best lieutenants.

'I used to dart all over Reggio on the back of my palfrey,
which in whiteness surpassed the snow. I was head over heels
in love with Laura, so as to keep company with the amorous
pre-occupations of that often easy-going, often temperamental
Giovanni de' Medici. In those days my beard was ebony,
not ivory. In those days I had wings, not feet of lead. Did you
ever see a more continent or timid lover than Giovanni?
Don't you remember how for three days he ate nothing and
thereafter was like some engine in his new ferocity? Often
enough Orlando' – the contemporary epic poet Ariosto's

hero – 'wished to carry away Angelica. But our youthful great one never even thought of eloping with his lady-love. Owing to the grandeur of his soul he was able to quench the fire that was truly burning up his heart in festivals, banquets and jousts, when he shattered with lustful thrusts of his lance the very columns which supported her portico. I used to think that heaven and earth would be riven asunder when he harnessed his furious chargers to their chariot and drove madly about the streets with an outcry more diabolical than loving. Where in your ladyship's house has he not been brought in, utterly exhausted, beside himself, like a man possessed?

'Yet the good Paola, who inflamed him with her divine graces, could take glory from his respecting her chastity.

'Alas, all these things are resolved into the air that carries away the sound of voices. They pass like a dream. It seems to me only a short while ago that I saw the leader of those incomparable troops embraced by your late husband, who was more to him than a brother or a friend. It seems to me that I still hear them, still see them talking and jesting together.

'As for myself, my eyes fill with tears when I remember how affectionately, in church and in the streets, the dear, sweet, lovely little Countess Madrina used to kiss me. The mischance through which I fell asleep beside her when I found her ill is now a stock scene of comedy. Having talked a while by her bed and being overcome, almost senseless with heat and fatigue, I laid my head on her pillow and snored till her idiot of a husband, the Count, woke me with a furious shaking. "Why not undress," he shouted, "and get into bed?" I heard that the learned Messer Aurelio de la Fossa nearly split his jaws with laughing when some great ladies told him that story. So did I when that same Countess, after reading a letter I had brought her from Milan, turned to me and said: "My husband writes that I am to treat you just as I would him. So will you sleep with me tonight?"

'And I wonder what has become of that other wife, one Martha, who confessed to her husband that while she was still a girl she had been madly loved and added: "Pardon me, husband. I had to do the poor fellow some kindness, since he lived in the house with me."

'But now let us make an end of chatter. For although jests will not keep us from growing old and dying it is true that thinking continually about the wild recklessness of youth makes time walk with a slow pace. Thus memory drives ruthlessly away the thought of the death sentence which every man living carries in his head. In spite of that my motto shall still be "I will", not "If I am able". For no living man has been able to escape love entirely and so long as there is beauty and there are eyes to see it no man ever will.

'O Reggio, I salute thy grace! O good Reggio, courteous Reggio! I have the same desire to see you as I have memory to exalt you. Nor do I know which holds more of my good will, Reggio or Arezzo, where I was born. Reggio is so hospitable! Her advantages are free to all. She almost persuades me to break my oath that I will never leave these mighty and renowned waters!'

Pietro was writing from Venice, the city of lagoons and canals.

That autumn, on September 14, 1523, the stern and parsimonius Pope Adrian VI died. He had lasted only two years; it was probably conscientious overwork that had killed him. But there were rumours of poison. Some exuberantly grateful citizens gave the papal doctor, a Perugian, a rattling good dinner, much to that functionary's embarrassment, especially when in uproarious speeches at the banquet he was named in Latin as, like Cicero, the 'saviour of his country'.

Two months later, Cardinal Giulio de' Medici was duly elected as Clement VII to the Chair of St Peter. He had heavily bribed his principal rival, Colonna, and had promised the delegates of Francis I, who had also resolutely opposed him, a thoroughly francophile, anti-imperialist policy once he was elected Pope.

Pietro heard the good tidings at Giovanni's camp, on guard before Milan. Before setting out to join his patron, who had now attained the highest possible ambition of a prince of the Church, he dashed off a jubilant screed to the Marquess of Mantua:

'I, my lord, set out very shortly for Rome and great is my delight to realise that in spite of all Ponzetta could do I shall find that my patron has become Pope, though he was only a cardinal when I departed. But, God forgive me, I no longer wish to speak the truth about cardinals, since they have conducted themselves so well. What a good man Colonna is! I would like to murder Pasquino, who called him a base rogue and accused old Del Monte of practising the Black Art, while he charged the other sage and sainted *monsignori* of even worse offences. But to go on to other matters, I enclose an epitaph for poor Master Adrian, who was, by the grace of God, such a dear friend of ours. I know how much you loved him while he was alive!'

The irony here could hardly have escaped even the Marquess of Mantua. The epitaph was also in Pietro's best vein.

> 'Here lies poor Adrian, made by wine divine.
> He was a Dutchman, a shipbuilder's son.
> To be a cardinal he surely won
> by teaching Charles the alphabet to whine.
> He was a pedant and he used to hold
> a school for janitors. This makes me weep.
> He was named shepherd, though himself a sheep,
> and he chased Soderini from his fold . . .'

There was much more in the same style, neatly forged couplets packed with stinging insults. The Marquess was delighted. He sent copies of the verses to all his friends. Few failed to applaud them. Pietro had been rising to the top of his epistolary form ever since he joined Giovanni at Milan. The company of the superb *condottiere*, who knew less about literature than any of his girl friends, always stimulated Pietro to his best efforts, which mostly went to the fortunate Marquess.

'What a fine comedy I saw in this siege!' – he wrote to his secular patron a short time before the news of the election of Clement VII. – 'By God, my lord, every vexation would desert you if I could only spend an hour telling you of the things done in this war! I would make you laugh most of all in relating the deeds of the Sforza whelp.' – This was Francesco Maria Sforza, Duke of Milan while the city was under siege by the French as a Spanish dependency in that year – 'As the devil would have it, one day, in his absence, a company of his took one single miserable Frenchman prisoner. The Duke sounded his trumpets and went round and round the city as if he had routed the whole French army. All the women rushed to the windows with lights in their hands and screamed "Victory, victory!" Next morning, in the cathedral, a sermon was delivered celebrating the ducal prowess. A solemn and villainous procession, robed in white, was then organised and little Sforza paraded the streets in a triumphal chariot drawn by four German lancers. He had the prisoner in front of him with a sign reading VENI, VIDI, VICI and a thousand other follies of which I couldn't say which was best.'

It was perhaps by deliberate policy that in November 1523 the author seemed in no hurry to pay his respects to Clement. He returned first to his delightful Reggio, where he had spent much of the summer dancing attendance on a cookmaid named Laura. Unlike most of the girls approached by this tall, black-bearded and loquacious amorist, the cook declined for months to accept him as a lover.

But Pietro probably had another reason for keeping away from the new Pope that autumn. He did not want to seem too eager for Giulio's favour, on the principle that absence makes the heart grow fonder. In any case too precipitate a rush to Rome would have been fatal to his interests with so incalculable a patron. Moreover, it was already clear that people of Pietro's stamp would not be particularly welcome at the papal court just yet.

'His Holiness' – wrote the Venetian ambassador – 'is temperate in every human action, particularly in eating and drinking. And he gives such an example of sexual continence that nowadays – I can't speak of the past – no one can censure his conduct in that respect. He indulges in no sort of vice, and does not spend anybody else's money, sell any benefices or practise simony. He gives much to charity. Since his election he has not been to Leo's hunting-lodge more than twice. Nor does he care for music or buffoons.'

Pietro must also have reflected on the situation's political angle. Despite Clement's promises to the French cardinals he was taking no special steps, at any rate no obvious ones, to favour the ambitions of Francis as against those of Charles V. In northern Italy, in Naples, in the Netherlands and along the Pyrennees the opposing generals were still vainly guessing which way the new Pope would jump. Pietro wanted to jump one way or the other. He didn't care which. But it might be dangerous to jump before Clement did. The poet waited anxiously in Laura's kitchen, or her bedroom, for definite information from Rome.

It did not come. As usual Pietro grew impatient. Soon he took the risk he calculated to be the best, counting on the Pope's known promises to the French. By the end of November 1523 he could wait no longer. He moved south, down through Tuscany to Rome, intending to present himself, if not to the still enigmatic Pope, at any rate to Clement's right-hand man, Giovanmatteo Giberti, head of the French faction at the papal court, holding the office of 'Datary' or registrar of appointments, a position which controlled all the other posts in the Vatican.

Giberti was known only by reputation to Pietro. He was said to be both cultured and morally austere, an unusual combination since Savonarola's time in Renaissance Italy. It appeared too that the Datary was not personally ambitious, though a most resolute, resourceful and knowledgeable diplomat and politician. On the whole Pietro, always attracted by anyone of superior intelligence, felt he could handle Giberti, not by his normal riproaring methods, but by discreet flattery, subtlety and tact. Confident as ever, he rode at his leisure through the damp December weather, making up sonnets in praise of Giberti. But once in Rome he took a decision which very nearly cost him his life.

Court and Camp

PIETRO BEGAN BY sending certain odes and sonnets to the pious and accomplished poetess Vittoria Colonna, wife of the Marquess of Pescara, an able soldier soon to win the battle of Pavia against Francis I and take that king prisoner. Vittoria, in so far as she took any interest in politics, naturally favoured the Emperor, not the French. But her character was unimpeachable and she moved in the highest Roman intellectual circles. Pietro, with consummate audacity, was planting a foot in both camps. For all the poems he submitted to Vittoria, the literary queen of Rome, eulogised the francophile Datary, Giovanmatteo Giberti. The lady, as Pietro had anticipated, informed that official accordingly, perhaps with a certain irony. In any case, the author of these insurance premiums in verse was already shifting his ground again.

The Spanish faction, he had quite suddenly realised, might be stronger in the society close to the Vatican than he had supposed. He promptly wrote a series of scurrilous epigrams against the Datary and simultaneously addressed compliments to Nicholas Schomberg, Archbishop of Capua, the German leader of the imperial cause at Rome.

But he had acted, as so often, over-hastily. The papal court had by no means decided to drop France. Giberti was infuriated by the provincial newcomer's insolence. 'Let that lewd speaker,' he is related to have hissed, 'praise the German' – Schomberg – 'as he will. But since he has dared to snarl at me I shall find a way to cut his tongue from his loud mouth.'

The opportunity for this operation soon arose. Raphael, dead four years previously, had been succeeded as the head of the Roman school of painting by his favourite pupil Giulio de' Gianuzzi, known to art historians as Giulio Romano. Giulio, however, worked chiefly for Pietro's old friend the Marquess of Mantua in that city. Neverthless, in the summer of 1524 the distinguished painter and architect was in Rome, finishing some murals begun by Raphael in the Vatican.

Giulio, then aged twenty-five, was persuaded by friends or decided on his own account, for he was a great lover of fun and games as well as of his art, to dash off no less than sixteen sketches of distinctly obscene character. Vasari writes that these dealt with 'the various attitudes and postures in which lewd men have intercourse with lewd women.' These pictures were circulated in private. Some authorities state that they were produced at least three years earlier, to amuse Leo X. There is nothing in that pontiff's character to render such a supposition untenable. It is clear enough that he enjoyed scatological anecdotes on occasion. But they did not play so large a part in his life as they did, for instance, in that of his predecessor, Alexander VI. Leo was not the sort of pope to commission erotic cartoons, though he might have laughed at them, in his gross way, amongst friends.

The question, however, of exactly when these drawings were done is unimportant, as we shall presently see. It is certain only that they were well known to the more exuberant artists of Rome in the summer of 1524. At that date it so happened that the new technique of engraving, by which many copies of a single original could be rapidly manufactured, had just become generally known in the metropolis. The good-natured Giulio, inquisitive about the claims made for this relatively recent process, allowed the most skilled engraver in the city, one Marcantonio Raimondi from Bologna, to reproduce for a wider market the sixteen pornographic sketches. No doubt arrangements were made to share the enormous profits expected.

Raimondi had long been an important figure to Romans concerned with pictures. His abilities had by 1524 sunk below their highest level. But such reputations die hard – no doubt he continued to be regarded as the chief Italian master of his art. He had reached Rome about the year 1510, while Raphael was still alive. Soon a series of prints after the latter's designs began to be issued by the Bolognese engraver. These fairly free reproductions remain Marcantonio's best work, a great improvement on the copper counterfeits of Albrecht Dürer's woodcuts he had been making in Bologna since about 1506, much to the wrath of that serious-minded artist.

Romano duly finished the Vatican murals and returned to Mantua. Raimondi started selling his engravings so eagerly and indiscreetly that they soon fell into the hands of people who strongly objected to them. Their protests led to the engraver's arrest and imprisonment by the papal authorities. Pietro, was well acquainted with Raimondi, who had painted his portrait. He protested with a great show of virtuous indignation against puritanical interference with his friend's art. He had the nerve to go straight to Clement over the Datary's head and actually succeeded, at a somewhat later date, in getting Raimondi released. One can only suppose that Pietro's tactful and eloquent representations to the cautious pontiff, grateful perhaps for having been left alone for so long by his trouble-some devotee, suggested that Raimondi's technical skill out-weighed the peccadillo of the subjects he had chosen to illus-trate it. After all, worse things had been carved and drawn in the not so distant Middle Ages, he may have urged. They could be seen in cathedrals and missals to this day, uncondemned by any responsible priest. Surely Marcantonio, a simple sort of chap, would be sufficiently punished by a few days more in gaol?

But whatever arguments Pietro may have used with his patron, their success proves that the Pope still considered him a potentially useful adherent. Giberti thought otherwise. He remained determined to show up his former flatterer as a vulgar, unscrupulous conspirator against Clement's best interests. To the grim Datary's triumphant delight the prospective victim played right into his hands.

Pietro had been carried beyond the bounds of discretion, by winning the first round, when he bypassed the Datary to a gratifying interview with the Pope. The poet now circulated in manuscript copies sixteen unprintable sonnets he had scribbled for the sixteen scabrous sketches by Romano. The sonnets found their way by a malicious hand, perhaps that of Francesco Berni, the Datary's secretary and Pietro's sworn enemy, to Giberti's desk.

Metrically these verses were not in the strict sonnet form but in a Spanish variant of it, which had a *coda* of three lines after the usual fourteen, this final tercet beginning with a hemistich rhyming with the last line of the preceding tercet. For example, in Sonnet III the male speaker declares in line twelve, which would normally begin the last tercet of a sonnet in conventional form:

'Let him who hath it small play sodomite.
But one like mine, both pitiless and proud,
should never leave the female nest of joy.'

His partner replies, in the *coda*:

'Ay, but we girls, boy,
so greedy are of what we hold so glad
a thruster that we'd take him whole behind.'

In each poem courtesan and client mutually urge each other
in the crudest terms and in diverse detail, to make the most of
whatever form of sexual congress is being indulged in. They
also express at frequent intervals their delight in it.

Rabelais, in this connection, helped himself to the last verse
of Sonnet V when he made Panurge (*Gargantua*, *IV*, 4), in
writing to his father Gargantua, refer to the 'Stoics who say that
there are three parts in a benefit, one being that of the giver,
one of the receiver and one of the remunerator.' Pietro's lines,
spoken by the male partner, bid the woman not only accept but
repay with interest the act of fornication. Like D. H. Lawrence
in *Lady Chatterley's Lover* he calls the respective sex organs by
their colloquial names and refers graphically to their respective
functions.

Sometimes the names of well known Roman courtesans or
lechers are invoked, not always to their credit. Once (in Sonnet
XI) the dialogue is interrupted by an old woman who, aghast
at the behaviour of the couple, 'partly on floor and partly on
bed', threatens to beat the girl. The latter, however, is more than
a match for her senior, treating the interloper to a flood of
obscene abuse as 'rotten with pox' and proclaiming her own
susceptibility to this 'arch-perfect joy' and her habit of experi-
encing orgasm at the mere sight of a 'noble organ male'. In the
last sonnet the lovers copulate beside the cradle of the prostitute's new-born infant, which she rocks with her foot, 'thus
pleasing of us all the three'.

These sonnets have no literary touches, unlike the author's
later pornography. The wit is coarse and blunt, meant to shock
like a blow in the face, an almost exact analogue of talk among
the more ferocious and facetious inmates of a modern boarding-
school dormitory or barrack-room. Pietro's own defence of

these brutally exuberant appendages to Raimondi's engravings is contained in a letter he wrote at the time to a physician, one Battista Zatti.

'When I obtained from Pope Clement the release of Marcantonio, who had been imprisoned on account of his engravings, there came over me a wish to see the figures which caused that busybody Giberti to exclaim that the good craftsman should be hanged and drawn. Seeing them, I was inspired by the same spirit that caused Giulio Romano to execute them. And since it is well known that the poets and sculptors, ancient and modern, saw no harm in allowing their genius to entertain by writing or carving once in a while such lewd trifles as the marble satyr trying to violate a boy which is in the Chigi palace, I amused myself by writing the sonnets which you can now see under each picture. I dedicate their indecencies to all hypocrites, for I am quite out of patience with their scurvy strictures and that foul convention by which eyes are forbidden to look on that which they most delight to see. What harm is there in beholding a man possess a woman? Are the very beasts more free than we are? It seems to me that images of the organ which nature gives us for our preservation should be worn round the neck as a pendant and in the hat as a medal. It is that which has made you, who are the first of physicians. It has produced the Bembos, the Sansovinos, the Titians and the Michelangelos. It has generated popes, emperors and kings. It has begotten the loveliest of children, the most beautiful women, the holiest of saints. The hands might well be hidden. For they gamble money away, are raised to give false witness, lend at extortionate interest, make insulting gestures, pull and tear, strike, wound and slay. As for the mouth, well, doesn't it spit in your face, gourmandise, drink to excess and vomit?'

This letter seems to garble the apparent order of events in the affair. Pietro, as a close friend of Giulio Romano, whom he must have met and found a congenial spirit at Mantua, can hardly have been excluded from the circle round which the pictures passed before they were engraved. He probably jotted down most of the sonnets there and then. It is true that Sonnet IV refers to the captivity of Francis after the battle of Pavia and must therefore be dated 1525. But Pietro for some reason of his own tells Zatti that all the sonnets were written after both Pietro himself and Giberti had seen the engravings and after Raimondi had been released. That would have been an act of such open defiance of both Clement and the Datary that it hardly seems credible even in so reckless a character as Pietro Aretino.

But it scarcely matters whether he was simply careless or had some ulterior motive in so describing the sequence of events to Dr. Zatti. The Datary now had proof that the scurrilous poet was a corrupting influence in the Holy City and would, if he, the Datary, was to have his way, be wiped off the map by arrest or assassination in a matter of hours.

Pietro realised that he had miscalculated. He should have stuck to that powerful and vindictive francophile. But it was too late now; nothing but instant flight would serve. Already, with a heartfelt shudder, he felt gaol-fever and the rack remorselessly heaving at his big wrists and ankles.

Physically frightened but morally undefeated, he made for his birthplace by way of Spoleto, Assisi and Perugia. He felt safe at Arezzo, so far north of Rome, since no one in his native city seemed particularly interested in him. But for that very reason, and probably for the first time in his life, he also felt unhappy. For Pietro's main problem at this stage seems always to have been how to evade obscurity without courting acute material discomfort, torture and violent death.

A letter he received at Arezzo heartened him greatly. It had been written in a crabbed fist by a loyal friend – Giovanni delle Bande Nere.

'On receipt of these lines' – wrote the commander who was beginning to be called, not only by his official enemies, the 'Great Devil' – 'I beg you to leave Arezzo and to come to me. This is something I desire greatly. I admit I should not do this, but should really be angry with you. For in turning to the party of Fra Nicholas' – Schomberg – 'and Vaison' – Girolamo Schio, Bishop of Vaison in south-eastern France, who was Schomberg's right-hand man – 'you have lost Giovanmatteo and consequently also lost the Pope. So doing, you who could give laws to the world have ruined your own prospects. You have harmed me too, for while you were at

the Roman court I had a friend there who would defend with
all his heart the rightness of what I was doing, what I had
already done and what I might do. Yet I do wish to see you
and very much. Here is probably the reason. The very foolish
thing you have done was done through bad judgment but
in sincere good faith. For I am able to give you this praise,
that while everyone calculates from time to time you never
do.'

This last opinion could scarcely have been more mistaken.
But the downright young soldier, since he took little interest in
political intrigue, must have paid far more attention to his
friend's congenial impetuosity than to his talent for elaborate
scheming which, moreover, Pietro would hardly care to reveal
in such impatient company as Giovanni's.

Giovanni, it appeared, was at Fano on the Adriatic, between
Pesaro and Ancona. He had taken to piracy in order to pay the
debts incurred owing to the parsimony of those who had been
employing him, on behalf of Charles, on land. But by the time
Pietro joined him – galloping most of the way down from the
Apennines to the sea – there was better news. Clement had
agreed that, since the imperial generals declined to maintain
Giovanni's Black Bands, he might take service with Francis.

That energetic sovereign had already quite enough on his
hands, not only with the rebellion of his Constable, the Duke
of Bourbon, who had the year before joined the Emperor,
Francis's great rival for European dominion, but also with
German and English invaders. Yet the King remained obstinately determined to seize Milan as a first step in wresting the
control of Italy from Charles. Bourbon threw the royal forces
back from the city at the bloody battle of Romagnano in
northern Piedmont, where the greatest French soldier of the
day, Pierre Terrail, Lord of Bayard, known as *le chevalier sans
peur et sans reproche* 'knight fearless and blameless'), lost his life.
That was in April 1524, while Pietro was in Rome courting the
francophile papal Datary Giberti and the Hispano-German
Schomberg by just such nicely calculated shifts of emphasis as
Giovanni de' Medici had declared that Pietro Aretino never
employed.

In the following September Francis in his turn sent the Constable flying back from Marseilles. By mid-October, the King

was capturing certain outworks of the Milan defences, though the citadel still held out against him. After losing Bayard he had no commander capable of outwitting the combined Spanish, Swiss, Venetian and other Italian generals opposing him. He would be lucky if he could get the invincible Giovanni delle Bande Nere to help him.

Pietro and Giovanni galloped north. The future 'Scourge of Princes', on his best behaviour, made a hit with Francis, who soon admitted him to a certain intimacy. Pietro's candid jocularity – obviously natural to him and just as obviously not the heartiness of a dullard, since he was never at a loss for a smart repartee or an amusing, usually scandalous anecdote and never said anything really stupid – always greatly entertained persons who bore heavy political or social burdens.

Not even the uneasiest crowned head, not even the Pope himself, could ever be wholly convinced of Pietro's insincerity, however black things looked against him. He seemed invariably to blurt out, like his formidable 'brother' Giovanni, whatever came into his head. And what he had to say was generally either witty or indulgent. Even his frequent floods of abuse made the magnates laugh, as though these sallies had been a professional jester's. Moreover, the 'princes' often wondered at his charity, in words at any rate. Unlike the majority of his contemporaries Pietro never paraded out of season his affection for his patrons or pretended seriously to hate their enemies. He simply appeared to feel sorry for such wrong-headed antagonists in their ridiculous pretensions. Above all, he gave the impression of being genuinely delighted with those who were delighted with him.

On paper it was different, as Francis was to find out before long. When Pietro Aretino used a pen for complimentary effusions – almost always as a matter of policy, hardly ever from the heart – his real megalomania tended to erupt into pomposity and his real ambition to spread itself in a sticky flow of obsequiousness. Modern Russians in the top flight of politics or espionage often display characteristics closely similar to Pietro's in these respects. *Pravda* journalists, for instance, when commanded to set up an attractive image of this or that public figure, often dispense a distinct whiff of such Aretine incense.

Both Francis and Giovanni promised to make their favourite's fortune. They meant what they said and were capable, with luck, of fulfilling their intentions. But Pietro could never fancy himself as a third musketeer between these two born men of action. They were both actually his juniors, not only in years but also in knowledge of the world beyond their camps and council-chambers. It was that world, the world of backstairs court intrigue, in which Pietro felt most at home. He was determined to return to it, but now at the highest possible level – the Papal.

He composed two fulsome odes in praise of Clement VII. Then he coolly issued a third, almost equally honeyed, in honour of Giovanmatteo Giberti whom he had attacked so recently and who had so promptly and disastrously counter-attacked him. As usual, Pietro's medicine proved irresistible. As early as November 1524 he returned from Francis's camp to Rome, where he received an interesting letter from the Marquess of Mantua.

'To our great pleasure and content we have been informed by persons worthy of credit and likewise we have learned from the letters of Messer Francesco Gonzaga, our most dear ambassador, that you have been talking so honourably of us that it seems there is nothing you do with such readiness. Your praise has reached the most frequented places of Rome and even His Holiness himself. So we are greatly obliged to you. For we cannot deny that it delights us to be lauded by skilled writers. Theirs, we think, is the one true and solid praise. And yours in particular we so estimate, for we never urged you to any such thing, which would be contrary to your character.'

Clement, for his part, made Pietro a Knight of Rhodes. Papal policy was now, under Giberti's influence, more distinctly favourable to France and the poet's gracious reception by the king of that country could not be ignored at the Vatican. Giovanmatteo's secretary, Francesco Berni, later to come prominently into notice as a dangerous rival to Pietro Aretino himself, wrote, with less malice than might have been expected:

'He now walks through Rome dressed like a duke. He takes part in all the wild doings of the lords. He pays his way with insults couched in decorative words. He talks well and he knows all the scandal of the city. He hobnobs with Estes and Gonzagas. Them he treats with respect, others with arrogance. He lives on what the former give him. He is feared for his satiric wit and enjoys hearing people call him a cynical, impudent slanderer. The Pope has bestowed on him a fixed pension as the reward for having dedicated certain mediocre verses to His Holiness.'

One sentence in this letter throws light upon the otherwise not easily intelligible change of front in the austere Giberti. 'He is feared for his satiric wit'. This is the master-key to the mysterious problem of how the big, blustering civilian from Arezzo, for all his fine airs by no means so much of an intellectual as to counter-balance in that way his humble birth, uselessness in war and flagrant impiety, managed to get so many people who did not trust him to keep him in luxury.

To an outsider there was always something comic about the methods of this highly effective blackmailer. Everyone except the victim laughed over them, including the operator himself. An early case in point at about this time, where the penalty involved nothing more serious than the shame of appearing to be ungentlemanly, happens to be well documented.

Pope Clement, owing to his frequent and incalculable shifts of policy, was being called by the Roman gossips a 'chameleon'. By way of insurance against the pontiff's impending changes of colour, Pietro proceeded to make it practically impossible for the Marquess in his turn to modify his recently expressed grateful attitude. *Noblesse oblige!* It was Pietro's opinion that you couldn't go far wrong if you remembered that principle when exerting pressure on your social superiors. No doubt his present behaviour had been planned when he first realised, during his stay at the Mantuan court, that Federigo might some time need a sharp rap over his grasping knuckles for his meanness.

'Messer Pietro Aretino' – wrote Francesco Gonzaga, the Mantuan ambassador in Rome, to his cousin the Marquess – 'told me that while talking to the Pope three evenings ago he informed His Holiness that you had lately mentioned your keen desire to have the picture by that great artist, recently deceased, Raphael of Urbino, which is now in Florence, representing the late Pope Leo of blessed memory, our present Pope himself and certain others, all as large as life. The Pope has ordered this picture to be sent to you at Mantua and says he would gladly do more to give you pleasure.'

The picture, however, did not turn up at Mantua within a reasonable time. Francesco Gonzaga, at the Marquess's urgent request, asked Pietro to investigate. Pietro reported that Clement had commanded 'a certain excellent painter in Florence' to make a copy, which His Holiness wished to keep in memory of Pope Leo, and that as soon as the copy was finished the original would be sent to the Marquess. It would be accompanied, Pietro went on, by an ode which he had composed in honour of the Marquess. Francesco added, faithfully transcribing the intermediary's demands in detail: 'I would pray your Excellency to have sent to the Aretine two pairs of shirts worked with gold in the style now in use and two other pairs of shirts worked in silk, together with two golden caps.'

But Federigo never got his Raphael. The sly Pope sent him the copy (by Andrea del Sarto), correctly anticipating that the recipient would be none the wiser. Pietro was luckier than his patron. He got his shirts, if only after typically Aretinian negotiations.

By the end of a month the shirts had still not arrived. Pietro pressed Francesco Gonzaga in the bluntest terms to do something about their delay, which 'annoyed' him. The ambassador dutifully applied to the Marquess's secretary. But another six weeks went by and there was still no sign of the shirts. Francesco then wrote to his cousin direct, as sharply as he dared, but enclosing by way of bait a poem by Pietro in praise of Giovan-matteo. It would be followed, the Roman envoy announced, by another in celebration of Mantua, plus a lifesize plaster copy of the famous 'Laocoon' preserved in the Belvedere gallery, a group representing the priest Laocoon and his sons being strangled by serpents, executed in the last half of the first century B.C. by Agesander, Polydorus and Athernodorus of Rhodes. Some genuine antique portrait heads in marble, Francesco added, would accompany the Laocoon sculpture.

But none of these gifts was enough to stir up the 'nobility' of Federigo. Two days later Pietro burst into the Mantuan Embassy in a tearing passion, blaspheming against God, Whose existence, he swore, he would deny if the shirts were still to be withheld from him. Immediately afterwards, with a further cascade of oaths, he declared that he didn't want those wretched garments any more. The ambassador suggested, with what diplomacy he could muster, that the delay might be due to the negligence or previous commitments of the women embroiderers. After a long dispute Pietro grudgingly admitted that the fault might not be the Marquess's own but his servants' and flung out of the Embassy as furiously as he had entered it.

A week later, Francesco wrote to his cousin: 'Regarding the shirts of the Aretine, your Excellency has seen how much I have written about them . . . he does not want to make peace, since the Carnival has passed without his having had them. Your Excellency knows his tongue. Therefore I will say no more.'

Now at last they were down to brass tacks. The Marquess simply could not afford to have satires on himself by so ruthless a hand circulating among his friends, least of all his enemies. He wrote promptly to the ambassador:

'We send you by Paolo Bondi, our familiar, the shirts and the caps which we have had made for Messer Pietro Aretino. There are four shirts worked in gold and four of silk' – twice the number, therefore, which the Scourge had demanded – 'and a pair of gold caps and a pair of silk ones. Have them brought to him as coming from us and excuse the delay as best you can. Certainly we are greatly displeased that the matter has taken so long. But we have had to deal with persons whom we could not command . . . even though they were paid. The holy sisters will not work except at their own hours and convenience.'

Federigo's fright at what so popular a writer might say of him and the alleged indifference of the local nunnery to the urgent and apparently tactful prayers of their Marquess are both highly significant. Pietro, after all, despite his literary merits, was more of a man about town than a revered scholar or artist of genius. Moreover, the spiritual authority of monks and nuns had declined, to say the least, very considerably since medieval times. Federigo Gonzaga, one of the most important noblemen in Italy, could have browbeaten the abbess and shut the mouth of his importunate friend if he had cared to make use of his sovereign position. Other rulers of the day might not have hesitated. If the Marquess did, it was almost certainly because he had something to conceal which Pietro knew of and the disobliging abbess might find out. In other words, so far as Pietro was concerned, his favourite weapon of blackmail may reasonably be assumed to have been at work.

However that may be, Pietro closed the affair with a polite but not effusive letter of thanks to his anxious patron, who may have thought himself lucky to have got off so lightly. Pietro's epistle had a characteristic sting in the tail; a veiled reference to what might have happened.

'I have had the ancient Laocoon of the Belvedere copied in stucco ... in the opinion of the Pope and of all the sculptors in Rome nothing was ever better copied. It was done by a certain Jacopo Sansovino ... it took him all the winter and the Pope often went to the Belvedere to watch him at work ... I will send it to you within ten days, accompanied by many other new things ... The Pope told me yesterday that the painting by Raphael is almost copied. He will send it to Your Excellency soon. They are going to celebrate Master Pasquino in my name this year and he will make a fortune. God protect every faithful Christian from the evil tongues of poets!'

The business of the shirts had been dexterously managed by Pietro. He was now in a stronger position with Federigo Gonzaga, Marquess of Mantua, than ever before. He had shown that nobleman that the low-born Pietro of Arezzo could be a generous friend to any protector, however rich and powerful. The shoemaker's son, as notable for getting into scrapes as for getting out of them, was soon to need every bit of backing he could conjure up from the Marquess.

Francis, one of Pietro's most important patrons, was disastrously defeated at the battle of Pavia on February 25, 1525. The King had failed to capture Milan and moved south to besiege Pavia, some twenty odd miles from Milan. He meant to use the city of Pavia as a base for more elaborate operations against Milan. But Pavia, defended by the excellent Spanish general Antonio de Leyva, held out stubbornly. By the middle of January Francis had made no progress and Giovanni delle

Bande Nere, hit in the leg by an arquebus ball during a skirmish, lay seriously wounded at Piacenza.

Then Charles de Lannoy, Viceroy of Naples under the Emperor, moved to the relief of Pavia. He was accompanied by the Marquess of Pescara and the Constable. On February 25 the imperial forces were at first pushed back by a skilful deployment of the French artillery. Francis, as Rupert, but not the better soldier Giovanni would have done, at once charged the disorganised attacking column for all he was worth, himself riding at the head of his lancers. But the Marquess of Pescara, Vittoria Colonna's husband, met this charge on Lannoy's side with fifteen hundred Spanish arquebusiers. They were the most expert infantry of the day, trained to wheel on their own initiative with astonishing rapidity so as to direct their fire wherever assault appeared heaviest.

The King's French, German and Italian lancers and their supporting Swiss pikemen were brought to a standstill by this system of defence, exceptionally mobile for those days. The French cannon could not fire over the heads of their pinned troops, closely engaged as these were with the enemy. Then the Pavia garrison in Francis's rear sallied. Lannoy charged in his turn. The King was caught between these two attacks, surrounded and captured. Pescara's Spaniards, combining individual enterprise with steady discipline and using the arquebus with as devastating effect as the English archers had used the longbow at Agincourt, won the day.

It was unfortunate for Francis that his newly engaged and most up-to-date mercenary just then lay wounded at Piacenza. Giovanni had faced the arquebus before, to his cost, and knew that it could only be countered by artillery fire. He would have brought up the guns before charging, if he had been allowed to do any such thing by the impetuous young monarch.

The King himself, in one of the few isolated groups which had not surrendered to Lannoy's final charge, had stood almost alone, unhorsed, wounded in the head and arm, in a ring of corpses and carcases. Yet he still thrust and slashed this way and that with a lightning sword few men in that age of practised duellists ever cared to confront, even in sport. Giovanni would have admired him at that moment. It was only when the viceroy in person rode up and named himself that Francis dropped his weapon, wrenched off his right-hand gauntlet and held out these two symbols of submission, the blade with its pommel outwards, to the opposing commander-in-chief, who instantly dismounted, falling upon one knee to receive the tokens of his victory. In the imperial camp that night the bandaged and respectfully attended captive sovereign had every excuse for writing to his mother, Louise of Savoy, 'All is lost but honour'.

The French defeat was bad news for Pietro, to whom Francis had shown so many marks of favour. On April 24, 1525 Pietro characteristically wrote a long, ostentatious letter of condolence to the royal prisoner, a letter of which he kept several copies for immediate publication in the form of pamphlets to be sold in bookshops and in the street.

'I don't know' – he observed – 'whether the conquered or the conqueror deserves more praise. For Francis, thus entrapped by fate, has freed his mind of any doubt that fate could ever imprison a king, while Charles, by his good fortune, has been made to realise that an emperor too might suffer the same mischance ... I believe that fate, in perceiving that others pardon those whom they have defeated and that your loss is thus your gain, would scorn to triumph over you who triumph over her, since necessity, which guides her, though intent upon precipitating you into the abyss, has on the contrary raised you to the skies. That is obvious from your endurance of your fate, whence you learn to protect yourself against it and to understand that its disappointments are lights upon the life of him who is not lost when he loses ... More praise is deserved by those who are able to endure misfortunes than by those who are never satisfied. A noble heart should tolerate calamities, not flee them, for it is in toleration that grandeur of soul becomes apparent, while flight calls attention only to unworthy circumstance ... but whoever heard of so great a king performing, in the unexpected reversal of the fortunes of battle, such feats in his own person as would have been the duty of captains, knights and common foot-soldiers? It would have well become the dignity of all your royal accoutrements on the field if you had then and there, your sword still reeking with the blood of the enemy, forced fate to confess that she had made prisoner a combatant, not one who ordered others to enter into combat for him.

Victories are the ruin of those who gain them and the salvation of those who suffer defeat. For conquerors, blinded by
the exultation of their pride, forget God and remember only
themselves, while those who lose the day, enlightened by the
modesty of humility, forget their own condition and are
recalled to consciousness of God. May the disaster that has
befallen you act as a brake upon rash thoughts and enter-
prises undertaken without due prudence since a time will
come when the recollection of your present plight will be a
source of advantage and delight to you . . . If it has pleased
Christ that your Majesty should lie at the mercy of your
adversary, it has only been so that you might recognise yourself to be but a man, as indeed he is also. If you were to
measure your respective shadows, you would find them
neither greater nor less than before it was fated that one
should be conquered and the other victorious.'

After the issue of this carefully calculated sermon in the full
antithetical style of the contemporary pulpit, the versatile
Pietro's next move involved a persistent series of written attacks,
lasting from Messer Pasquino's Day in April on through the
May and June of 1525, against the long-suffering Giovanmatteo Giberti, who in fact really stood, like his master Clement,
for the French alliance. But it seemed that for Pietro personal
admiration of a Frenchman was one thing and toleration of
French policy in Rome by an Italian quite another. It may have
been now, too, that, by way of further defiance of the Datary,
the author of the *Sonetti Lussuriosi* revised some of them, including the fourth, which refers to Francis's captivity.

Giberti waited for reaction to the news of Pavia to die down
a little before he hit back. He meant his retaliation, when it
came, to be a knock-out blow.

At about two o'clock of a still, dark July morning, the 28th
of the month, Pietro was riding home alone from a late session
with friends when a masked man on foot, flourishing an eighteen-
inch dagger, seized his bridle, stabbed him twice in the chest
and fled. Pietro squealed with pain and panic. For the blade,
in its second, fiercer thrust had severed two fingers of his right
hand. He toppled from his horse with blood streaming from hand
and chest. The watch that picked him up a few minutes later
found him unconscious; for some days he was not expected to live.

As soon as it was reported that he was recovering, a young Bolognese poet called Della Volta came to visit the invalid in the latter's own quarters. Pietro knew him slightly; they had both been lovers of one of Giberti's cookmaids called Lucrezia. Della Volta showed Pietro a paper.

'Did you write this?'

It was a satirical sonnet addressed to or about the pretty Lucrezia.

'Of course. Could anyone but I have written so excellently?'

'It's certainly a decent enough piece of work,' the boy admitted, rather sourly. 'But you couldn't expect me to ignore it, could you?'

'Oh, I don't know,' groaned the wounded man. 'I don't keep your conscience, do I? Go to your confessor.'

'I have done so,' retorted Della Volta sullenly. 'He sent me to you.'

'To me?'

'To beg your forgiveness for stabbing you that night, in my jealousy. And to hope that you will swiftly recover. Now I have done that. I have only to say thirty paternosters and I shall be able to attend mass tomorrow. Do you forgive me, Messer Pietro?'

Pietro stared sombrely at him.

'I forgive your jealousy, man. If it exists, which I doubt. What I don't forgive is that you took money from Giberti to kill me.'

Della Volta jumped up, glaring in his turn, but not very convincingly.

'Are you mad, *messero*? Were I a hired bravo, would I come to visit you?'

'Quite possibly. If Giberti ordered you to do so. You are too fond of ducats, Achille. And you are ashamed of being so. If I were as young as you and as good a swordsman, I wouldn't hesitate to kill if I were well paid for it. What else do our great captains, even my glorious lord Giovanni of the Black Bands himself? But I would never deny that I had done so. I fear you are a hypocrite, Achille. Think better of it. And do not try to deceive me again. On the contrary, imitate me. After all, I was your successful rival in love. If you think well over what I have just told you, I'm sure that Lucrezia will smile upon you as she has smiled upon me. In fact, if I recover from these accursed wounds inflicted by you upon my sacred person – they call me Divine, do they not? – I shall tell her to watch you very carefully and report to me if she catches you out in any more lies. Now go. I'm tired and sick. I don't want to see you again until I am resurrected.'

Weeks passed. Doctors, friends and even enemies came regularly to visit the prostrate and bandaged high priest of Messer Pasquino. The doctors ruined his digestion and bled him white both literally and metaphorically. Friends paced his bedchamber proclaiming vengeance. Enemies drowned him in compliments and never stopped grinning.

Pietro took little notice of any of them. He was concentrating on learning to write with his left hand. After a fortnight he found he could use the thumb and the last two fingers of his right almost as well as his left. A few days later, a new salve applied by a Greek physician began rapidly to heal the incisions made by Della Volta's blade in his chest.

Pietro rose, bathed, perfumed himself, donned his most gorgeous garments and wrote some eloquent letters to the Roman magistrates, demanding the arrest of both Della Volta and Giberti. This was a mere stylistic exercise; for naturally, in view of Giberti's official rank, the letters were all ignored. But these compositions greatly refreshed Pietro's literary energy. He turned to more serious work, the revision of his first comedy, *La Cortegiana* ('Court Life'), improving it a good deal with dialogue that reflected his recent adventures.

In the Prologue of this blackest, most bitterly savage of all Pietro's comedies, a Gentleman gives an account to a Foreigner of the exceedingly complex plot. The events narrated all take place in consequence of the ambition of a Sienese visitor to the papal court who wishes to become a cardinal. The ensuing episodes are of such a vile and mean character, so compact of fraud and treachery, that the Foreigner, when told that all this 'fun' happens in Rome, exclaims in stupefaction: 'Rome! Rome? Good heavens, I should never have recognised the place!'

'Don't send your son to Court,' says a new personage, introduced at this date, the autumn of 1525. Successful as both man of the world and as man of letters, this character, named Flaminio, transparently disguises the author himself. 'He'll only turn into a rogue there.'

'A rogue?' asks the father in surprise. 'What sort of a rogue, then?'

'The old sort. Liar and thief. But there'll be worse to come. Treachery and villainy. For he'll find that if he's enough of a hypocrite he can literally get away with murder.'

Eventually Flaminio, weary of the worthless world he knows so well, decides to go to Mantua to die. For there 'the kind-hearted Marquess Federigo denies bread to no one'.

In real life, Flaminio, the Divine Pietro Aretino himself, left Rome on October 13, 1525 for the Marquess's court, where he expected, so far from dying, to be beyond the reach of Giberti and his bravos. At Mantua he would not be tempted, either, to try further conclusions with the slippery Pope, whom he had helped so much in the past, whom he was to help even more in the future and who had yet so often cheated him and would do so again.

The equally slippery German agent of the Emperor Charles V in Rome, Nicholas Schomberg, Archbishop of Capua, wrote to the Marquess: 'The Pope has asked me to recommend Messer Pietro Aretino to you most strongly . . .' The letter is peppered with the words 'love', 'loyal service' and 'warmth of heart'. It is clear that Clement VII remained as determined as ever to go on hunting with the hare his own hounds were so persistently trying to bring down. The Pope was to find, in the terrible year 1527, that this policy paid off. But even so he was lucky. For Pietro Aretino really seems to have been the only man of importance in Italy at that date who never bore malice or made a study of that leading preoccupation of Italians, revenge.

A Hero Falls

MANTUA, AS USUAL, bored Pietro. He spent a dull winter there, in spite of the presence of the affable and versatile Giulio Romano, now official architect to the hospitable but otherwise uninteresting Marquess. In the spring, as happened regularly during these years, there were rumours of war. Francis had been released from his captivity by Charles after the prisoner had signed away Burgundy to the Empire. But the King of France was now preparing to go back on his commitments and counter-attack his old enemy.

In May Charles refused to join the League of Cognac formed by Francis with the exiled Duke of Milan – that city being still a Spanish dependency – Venice and the Papal States. The object of the League, ostensibly, was to 'protect the peace of Christendom'. But really the signatories intended to recover Milan and Burgundy for France, that country then appearing to both Clement and Venice to be less dangerous to their independence than the generally victorious Empire.

The Pope's military contingent consisted of some ten thousand men, of whom four thousand were commanded by Giovanni delle Bande Nere, now recovered from the serious leg-wound received in Francis's service. This last item of news definitely meant that great events were pending. The restless Pietro rode off from Mantua in June to rejoin his friend.

They met at Marignano, the strategically important village near Milan where the King had won a great victory over the Swiss eleven years before. Giovanni was in jubilant spirits.

'If I live through this year, Pietro,' he said, 'I'll make you Marquess of Arezzo.'

It was the sort of prospect the *condottiere's* unmilitary friend had counted on. The two friends slapped each other's shoulders, laughed and gossiped. Then Pietro, more experienced in politics than the younger man, grew serious.

'Don't rely too much on your cousin in the Vatican, Giovanni.'

'You mean Clement?'

'Yes. He's a weathercock, a chameleon. Too clever by half.'

'Damn all courtiers! I've got one stuck on my back at this moment. My darling chief, the Duke of Urbino. He's no more a fool than my holy cousin. But he acts too much like one, and like a coward too, for my taste. If only I could get him, for once, to act like a soldier!'

But he could not. Urbino had twice as strong a force as the imperial generals holding Milan commanded. Yet he did nothing but skirmish, alleging that it would be dangerous to attack the city in strength until his Swiss mercenaries arrived. Even when they did, a bold sortie from Milan sent him flying in retreat. It is hard for historians to avoid the suspicion that he saw no reason why he should defend Clement, a Medici whose family had deprived the Duke, both by fraud and by violence, of much of his property.

Giovanni did not join in the panic of the main army. He fought on until almost surrounded, then withdrew, cursing but in good order. Pietro's sarcasms about the Duke of Urbino kept him laughing. He was also agreeably surprised to find his friend, a self-confessed craven among hard knocks, so steady under the fire of cannon and arquebus. It was really Giovanni's own perfect coolness under all circumstances of warfare, even in one of his hell-for-leather charges, that had influenced Pietro. He would have run like a rabbit from the side of any other commander, however steadfast, than the man he loved more than any other human being he had ever met or ever would meet.

But Pietro could never stand field service for long. He easily convinced his friend that a capacity more useful to the young commander would be that of ambassador to the various important persons who ought to be persuaded that Giovanni delle Bande Nere rather than Francesco Maria della Rovere, Duke of Urbino, should be Italy's true champion and paid accordingly. In any case, owing to the Duke's vacillations or deliberate blocking of all schemes in the Medicean interest, no more serious fighting occurred that summer.

Giovanni went off to Mantua to look up one of his special girl-friends, the courtesan Paola, so respectfully eulogised by Pietro in his list of the *condottiere's* mistresses. At Mantua the Great Devil received a letter from his industrious ambassador. It was dated from Reggio and contained little diplomatic news but a lot about another courtesan who, however, was not named. The phrasing of the letter renders it unlikely that the writer exercised this discretion because she was a married woman of rank or at any rate of decent social position. Prominent courtesans were as jealous of one another and as reckless in their revenges as so many great lords; the coupling of this woman's name with Giovanni's might have got her into serious trouble with her local rivals for the favour of so famous a captain if documentary evidence of it fell into the wrong hands. It might easily do so in view of the competition for any scrap of writing by such a notable scribbler as Pietro Aretino, who was moreover far too experienced a whoremonger, as well as being a naturally good-natured one, to offend such useful allies as ladies who sold their favours at a high price to influential magnates.

'The endless enquiries' – he began, with ostentatious tact – 'by people of both sexes in Reggio as to when you may be expected to return here oblige me, most illustrious patron, to tell you that the Messiah was never awaited by the humblest Roman with such eagerness. Your long absence has widowed the town. Your unhappy feminine slave mourns you so greatly' – Giovanni must have known perfectly well whom he meant – 'that I'm sure you'll soon hear some terrible news about her. My lord, I swear to you by my own heartfelt servitude and absolute loyalty to your magnanimous valour that I don't believe any woman in the world could be so devoted to you. Her state of mind would arouse pity, I don't say in any man, but in cruelty itself. By God, the very women who used to envy her for having the invincible Giovanni de' Medici for a lover now feel something more than compassion for the wretched and comfortless life she leads. You're getting a reputation for pigheadedness, almost for ingratitude. For you alone awakened love in that chilly heart of hers, which had formerly yielded to no other. Her angelic face is no longer that of a woman, but more like that of a buried corpse. Tears, sighs and vain invocations of your name are all she feeds on. If she were sure that you were not coming back for a long time I wouldn't give much for her life . . . Do write her an occasional line . . . and come back here soon to live with her. You won't regret it, for I can assure you that no danger or disgrace or anything else will ever henceforward prevent her from pleasing you. If you do that, I'm certain that all the local gossip and the distress that afflicts you both will come quietly to an end. I'm also sure that you will suffer most unwontedly if you try to forget the time you spent in loving her, especially since you got nothing by it. I repeat once more that she is ready to reveal not only her body but also her soul for your delight. So please behave like a constant and serious lover. Put an end to all this trouble by lavishing your most tender affection on her.'

No doubt Pietro was well paid in cash or kind for these representations on behalf of a lovelorn client. But it is obvious enough that all he really wanted as a result of all this sentimental special pleading in favour of a courtesan who had apparently turned the great Giovanni down was to get his friend back for more revels in Reggio. He proved this by adding four lines of sheer barrack-room obscenity, homosexual at that, to the jovially honest tone of the rest of the letter.

The Great Devil did not comply with his friend's urgent request. He was soon back on active service in the approaches to Milan, but as hard up as ever for funds to pay his 'Bands' and as furious about it. King Francis begged him frequently not to risk his life, expressed the greatest confidence in his prowess but made no attempt to pay his debts as agreed.

That August Niccolo Machiavelli, always on the look-out for a hero 'to save Italy', came to see his latest candidate for this operation. Niccolo had now been restored to Medicean favour and was in Lombardy in attendance on the historian Francesco Guicciardini, who was acting as a lieutenant-general in the papal army. Giovanni had heard of his visitor's reputation as a writer on the theory of war but probably knew little of his other books. Machiavelli's analysis, in 'The Prince', of the methods by which an able, ambitious and unscrupulous man may rise to sovereign power, had been completed in 1513 and was probably known to Pietro, who must also have studied the Florentine author's *Mandragola*, the most brilliant comedy in the Italian language, which had been printed in 1524.

The social personality of the bright-eyed, sharp-featured, bustling little man, whose conversation so readily fell into obscene jesting, could certainly not have failed to amuse both his boisterous hosts on this occasion – Pietro having now rejoined his friend in the field – whatever reservations Giovanni might have felt about a man who merely talked about soldiering without participating in it and however Pietro may have despised one who had made such a mess of his own attempts to meddle in high politics.

'Like to take a parade, Messer Niccolo?' the *condottiere* asked him maliciously. 'I promise you I won't interrupt.'

The distinguished author bowed, beaming, but with condescension in every line of the lean, sallow features under the straight black fringe of hair. He was fifty-seven, an old man by Renaissance standards, and was to die suddenly in the following year. But no one could have been more active in mind and body in that summer of 1526, though the two incorrigible jokers who were entertaining him regarded him as a superannuated patriarch.

'You are too good, my lord. I shall be delighted.'

For two long hours, in scorching heat, the great political philosopher and dramatist squealed his orders for march and counter-march to Giovanni's three thousand veterans, till the files fell into utter confusion.

The Great Devil managed to keep a straight face for all that time. But at last he felt he must speak or die of laughter.

'Perhaps, *messere*, I might now take over?'

Niccolo Machiavelli, sweating and reeling with fatigue, almost fell on the renowned commander's neck.

'Perhaps you should, my lord – I – the men—'

The other's dreaded voice pealed across the parade-ground, ordering the drummers to beat one tattoo after another. After a few perfectly executed evolutions the troops were stood easy, then dismissed. At supper that night Messer Niccolo, whose manners, when required, were always excellent and whose sense of the ridiculous never failed him, apologised and laughed at himself. The other two let him down lightly.

Pietro filled in this period of enforced leisure by finishing off the comedy *La Cortegiana* which he had been revising in Rome, and also by writing letters, including many to the Marquess of Mantua. That nobleman replied effusively and kept his correspondent provided with clothing and horses in return for the manuscripts, among them that of the *Cortegiana*, which the poet regularly sent him.

'Your learned comedy has now arrived,' Federigo wrote

towards the end of August, 'and is filling me with delight. It is the true mirror of the modern court and of present-day life.'

Meanwhile the Emperor, encouraged by Urbino's vacillation or treachery, was seeking reinforcements in Germany, by then a mainly Protestant area. An outstanding soldier of fortune, Georg Frundsberg, who had fought for the Emperor at Pavia in the previous year, promised him thirteen or fourteen thousand lancers if Charles would give him a free hand to teach the Pope a lesson. The Spaniard was now as angry with Clement, for his precious League of Cognac, as with the 'false Frenchman', Francis, for initiating it. He agreed to Frundsberg's terms, especially as the latter guaranteed to pay the fanatical *Landsknechte* out of his own pocket, being as ferocious a Lutheran himself as any of the men.

By October 1526 the Germans had crossed the Alps and were descending into the Po valley. Frundsberg boasted, like any Attila, that he was bringing halters of 'brocade enriched with gold' with which to hang Clement and the cardinals. The whole history-conscious peninsula trembled. Only Giovanni delle Bande Nere rode off with a substantial force, perhaps ten thousand men, to face the invaders. Urbino had at last given him permission to act alone, probably hoping in this way to get rid of the hated 'Chameleon's' last serious defender. Pietro, certain now of his friend's rising star, rode with the *condottiere* to the darkening north-east.

No one, least of all Duke Francesco Maria della Rovere, could for a moment doubt the headlong courage and tactical mastery in the field of 'Giovanni d'Italia'. But the young champion had more than once threatened to cease serving a Pope and a King who kept the Black Bands so short of pay. Only the indefatigable diplomacy of Pietro, who knew Giovanni to be the only soldier standing between Rome and ruin, kept the Great Devil facing the Spaniards and the Germans.

Nothing is more touching in the life of so coolly dishonest a busybody and self-seeker as Pietro than his immediate recognition of and permanent admiration for the honest idealism in the dark and dreaded Medici, martinet and roisterer, still little more than a boy, who terrified everyone else by his violent and incalculable fits of temper. Pietro never deserted or doubted Giovanni. He remained determined to stick to this unpopular character, whom only his Bands adored, to the very end, an end the despiser of princes could only envisage as the unification of Italy under this explosive but just despot.

The historian Francesco Guiccardini, the Medici commander's lieutenant-general, expressed his gratitude for Pietro's loyal services to this aim in a letter dated November 14, 1526, written with obvious relief and much more cordiality than was usual in the case of that austere analyser of fallible human nature:

'Del Caccia and the man I sent down to the camp to appease the wrath of the Lord Giovanni have told me that you have persuaded him not to go to Milan' – to join the Spaniards – 'If he had done so it would have made him most unhappy. For he would have inflicted injury on his rank, his renown, his duty and all he holds dear. It would be well for him if he always had such a man as Pietro Aretino at his side. I don't write this to encourage you to go on representing yourself as what the whole world knows you to be. I merely express the pleasure I feel at so laudable a service, which I have reported to the benevolence of his Holiness so warmly and sincerely that I trust in God I shall soon see you reconciled with him to the extent that your talents deserve. I greet you as a brother.'

Perhaps Pietro touched up this letter slightly before publication. But the substance of it rings natural enough in the political circumstances of the time and Guiccardini's own known view of them. He had already written to Rome:

'Is it my fault if the Lord Giovanni keeps his infantry at work while Rangone' – another of Urbino's generals – 'lets his sleep? Is it my fault if the Lord Giovanni, who hourly exposes himself to danger, wishes his companies to be commanded by captains who really fight like soldiers? And if that other fellow has only, with one or two exceptions, men under him of no military capacity, with neither creditable reputation nor valour? Or that he employs them not as commanders but rather as courtiers to adorn his table and crowd after him wherever he goes in the camp? Or if the Lord Giovanni is ever with his foot-soldiers, seeing to their weapons, clothing and good discipline? And if that other fellow never sees his own troops or thinks of their comfort, arms or control, so that his men are worth more the first time that he pays them than ever afterwards? If he doesn't rob them himself, and I don't know that he does, he lets his captains rob them without the slightest compunction, so openly that it is a perfect scandal. Such are my reasons for not having reduced the strength of the Lord Giovanni's two thousand infantry. On the contrary, if it had not been for my expectation of an outcry by that other fellow, I would have increased their numbers and dismissed the contingents under other commanders, as my terms of reference entitle me to do.'

But at this very moment of genuine support for Pietro's plans by some of the most eminent Italians personally in touch with him the greatest tragedy of that enterprising schemer's mainly comic life was closing in on him. Alfonso d'Este, Duke of Ferrara, shared the Duke of Urbino's detestation of the Pope. Alfonso, among his other hobbies, was deeply interested in the relatively new process of casting cannon. His big bronze guns, firing cast-iron shot of six pounds in weight, were already famous. He sent four in secret up the river Po to Frundsberg, who had none.

Giovanni found the Germans entrenched at Governolo, a small town about eight miles south-east of Mantua, with the river Po on one side and its tributary, the Mincio, on another. A line of lime-kilns covered the front facing the Italians.

'Charge!' roared their commander, whipping out his long sword. So far as he knew, the enemy in the trenches behind the kilns had no artillery. But as his troops drove in the German outposts a ball from one of Alfonso's 'falconets', so called because the projectile's flight was supposed to resemble that of a hawk, broke the Great Devil's right thigh at the very place where it had been struck during the Pavia campaign.

Giovanni, to his men's consternation, fell from his horse and lost consciousness. The attack was at once broken off. The wounded man was carried from the field, where snow was beginning to fall, first to the village of San Nicola, then seven or eight miles on, as the snowstorm thickened, to Mantua itself. There, in the palace of Luigi Gonzaga, the Marquess and even the Duke of Urbino hastened to make much of the stricken general. He recovered consciousness, jested in his pain and submitted with iron fortitude to the necessary amputation – without anaesthetics – of his gangrened right leg. It was only during that fearful period that Pietro, unable to endure the spectacle of his beloved hero under torture, left his bedside for an hour or so. The agony did not kill him until the night of November 29/30. He had laughed, threatened his enemies and cursed his bandages to the last. Even in death, wrote one witness, he retained his fierce and proud looks, just as when going into battle. But no modern description of the death of Giovanni delle Bande Nere can equal that in the letter his closest friend despatched to Francesco degli Albizzi, secretary to the dead man's son, on the subject. This prose, for once, is sincere and thoroughly objective, noble in its expression of the deepest sorrow Pietro was ever to know.

'When the hour drew near which the Fates, with the consent of God, had appointed for the death of our commander, His Highness was assaulting, with his usual dreadful energy, the town of Governolo, around which the enemy had entrenched themselves. While thus engaged a cannon ball broke the leg which had been previously wounded by an arquebus. As soon as he felt the blow fear and melancholy descended upon the army. Ardour and joy died in all hearts. Not a man but forgot himself and wept, complaining bitterly of the fate that had so blindly brought to death the noblest and most excellent general in the memory of centuries at the very beginning of superhuman achievements and in the hour of Italy's direst need.

'The captains, who followed him with love and veneration, blamed fortune and his temerity for their loss. They spoke of his vigorous youth, ripened to bear fatigue, sufficient and apt for every difficulty. They sighed over the greatness of his thoughts and the wildness of his valour. They could not control their voices in remembering the good fellowship which allowed them to be his companions and even to share his cloak. They could not forget his foresight and the acuteness of his genius. They warmed with the fire of their lamentations the snow which was falling heavily as they carried him to Mantua, bearing him in a litter to the house of the Lord Luigi Gonzaga.

'There, that same evening, the Duke of Urbino came to

him and seeing the situation said: "It is not enough for you to be great and glorious in arms if you do not also distinguish your name by observing the rites of that religion under the sacraments of which we are born." And Giovanni, understanding that these words referred to the confession of sins required from those in danger of death, answered: "I have done my duty in all things. If need be I will do it in this also." Then, after the Duke had departed, he set himself to talk with me, calling with great affection for Ser Antonio' – this was Lucantonio Cuppano, Giovanni's favourite lieutenant – 'and when I said that we would send for him, he answered: "Would you dare to summon such a warrior to leave the battlefield for visitation of the sick?"

'Then he remembered the Count of San Secondo, his nephew, saying: "I wish he were here to replace me." Sometimes he scratched his head with his finger-nails or chewed one of them, muttering: "What will happen?" and often repeating: "I have nothing to repent of."

'Then, by the wishes of the doctors, I went to him and said: "It would be an insult to your soul if I tried to persuade you that death is the cure of all ills and is made heavy only by our fears. But because it is the highest happiness to do everything of our own free will, you should let the surgeons cut off that leg wrecked by artillery. Then in eight days you will be able to make of Italy, now a slave, a queen. And your lameness will serve instead of the royal Order" ' – offered to Giovanni by Francis – ' "which you have always refused to wear round your neck. For wounds and the loss of limbs are the true medals of the friends of Mars."

' "Let them do it at once," he answered. At that moment the doctors came in, praised the firmness of his resolution and ended their services for the night by giving him some medicine. Then they went to prepare their instruments. It was already the hour to eat when he was seized by a violent nausea. Then he said to me: "Such was the omen that warned Caesar. I must now think of something other than life." He folded his hands and made a vow to go on pilgrimage to the shrine of St James at Compostella. When the time was come and the surgeons entered with their instruments they asked for eight or ten assistants, strong men to hold him down while the terrible sawing lasted.

Portrait of Pietro Aretino by Titian (Galleria Pitti, Florence)

Detail from portrait of Pope Leo X and Cardinals Giulio de' Medici
and Luigi de' Rossi by Raphael (Galleria Palatina, Florence)

Portrait of Federigo II, Marquess of Mantua by Titian (Prado, Madrid)

Detail from portrait of pope Clement VII by Sebastiano del Piombo
(Gallerie Nazionali di Capodimonte, Naples)

Portrait of Giovanni delle Bande Nere by A. Bronzino (Palazzo Riccardi, Florence)

Detail from portrait of King Francis I by Titian (Louvre, Paris)

Detail from portrait of Emperor Charles V by Titian (Prado, Madrid)

Self-portrait by Titian, 1550 (Gemäldegalerie, Berlin)

'He smiled and said: "Twenty could not hold me." Then he sat up with a perfectly calm countenance, taking the candle in his hand to light the doctors to their work himself. I ran out of the room and put my fingers in my ears. I heard only two cries. Then he called me. When I came to him he said: "I am cured." He turned about in all directions with every sign of great rejoicing. If the Duke of Urbino had not stopped him, he would have had them bring in his foot, with the piece of his leg adhering to it, for us to look at, laughing at us because we could not bear to behold what he had suffered. Yet his sufferings were far greater than those of Alexander and Trajan, when the former smiled as the tiny arrowhead was pulled out and the latter laughed as he severed his own nerve.

'But finally, two hours before daybreak the pain, which had left him, returned, inflicting every kind of torment on him. I heard him beating the wall of his room wildly. The sounds stabbed me to the heart. In an instant I was dressed and ran to him. As soon as he saw me he exclaimed that the thought of cowards caused him more displeasure than the pain of his wound. By talking thus lightly with me and so disregarding his misfortune, he hoped to set free his spirit, tangled in the ambush of death. But as day dawned the torture grew so much worse that he made his will, dividing the worth of many thousands of *scudi* in money and goods among those who had served him and leaving only four *giulii* for his funeral. He named the Duke of Urbino as his executor. Then he turned, in a most Christian mood, to his last confession. When he saw the friar he said: "Father, I have followed the profession of arms and lived according to the customs of soldiers. I should have lived like a monk if I had assumed the habit you wear. If it were lawful, I would confess before everyone. For I have never done anything unworthy of myself."

'It was after Vespers when the Marquess of Mantua came to his bedside ... He kissed the wounded man tenderly and spoke words which I should never have believed any prince ... would have known how to utter. His Excellency ended his address by saying: "Your noble pride has always hitherto forbidden you to take advantage of any offer that I made you lest it should be said that you had yielded to my will. Ask me now one favour that shall do honour to us both.'

'Giovanni replied: "Love me when I am dead."

' "That heroism," answered the Marquess, "by which you have gained such glory will make you not merely loved but adored by myself as by all others."

'When the Marquess had withdrawn Giovanni turned to me and said I must ask his wife to send his son Cosimo to him. At that moment death, calling him to the underworld, redoubled his sufferings. All the household, without thought of the respect due to rank, came crowding to his bed, mingling with his chief officers. Shadowed with chill sadness, they wept for the sustenance, the hope and the service they were losing with their master. Each tried to catch his eye with a glance to show the sorrow and love that moved them. Thus surrounded, he took the hand of the Duke, saying: "You are losing today the greatest friend and the best servant you have ever had."

'His Excellency, lending his face an appearance of false joy and his tongue the tones of encouragement, tried to make him believe that he would recover. But he, who had no fear of death even when he was certain of it, began to discuss the progress of the war with the Duke, putting forward proposals which would have been most admirable had he been in full health instead of on the point of death. His mind remained thus active until about the ninth hour of the night, that being the eve of the feast of St Andrew. Then, because his suffering was very great, he begged me to put him to sleep by reading to him. I did so. He seemed to sink from sleep to deeper sleep. Yet after some fifteen minutes of such dozing he awoke and said: "I dreamed I was making my will. Yet here I am cured. If I continue to make such progress I shall yet be able to teach the Germans how to make war and show them the nature of my vengeance!" Even as he said this the lamp of his spirit, which had deceived his bodily eye, began to yield to perpetual darkness. Wherefore of his own accord he asked for extreme unction.

'Having received the sacraments he murmured: "I will not to die among all this linen." So we brought a camp-bed and laid him on it. There, while his mind slept, death took him.

'So perished the great Giovanni de' Medici, gifted from

his cradle with as much amplitude of soul as any man that ever lived.

'The vigour of his spirit was incredible. Liberality meant more to him than power. He gave more to his soldiers than he kept for himself, though he too was a soldier. He endured hardship with patience and grace. He could always control his anger. All that he said he would do he did.

'He valued brave men more than riches. In fact he only desired the latter in order to keep the valiant, who served him, from going hungry. There was nothing about his men's lodging or their conduct in action that he did not know of, for in battle he fought side by side with them in the ranks and in time of peace he made no distinction between himself and others. The very clothes he wore proved it. They were worn and shabby, like those of common soldiers, stained from armour on the legs, arms and chest. He was eager above all to win praise and glory. He pretended to despise such honours. But really he coveted them. Most of all did he win the hearts of his men by calling upon them to follow rather than precede him into peril.

'His virtues were his own, his faults those of youth. God knows that if he had lived into age all would have known of his bounty, as I myself already had experienced it. Truly he was the most generous friend that ever a man could have. He sought only honour, not his own interest. I speak not in flattery, for he sold all his possessions to his son for money to pay the overdue wages of his men. In the field he was always the first to mount his charger and the last to dismount. His boldness loved to play a lone hand. He could plan a campaign as well as fight it. Yet in councils he never proudly proclaimed that those who knew their trade the best should order affairs. All he would try to arrange was that those who sat at the council table understood the business of warfare.

'He showed wonderful skill in reconciling quarrels between his men. He knew exactly when, to keep control over them, he should make them love or fear him, expect punishment or reward. No one knew better than he when to use deception and when force in an attack. He never deafened the ears of his troops with lies and boasting, but always inspired them with the astonishing fervour of his own native daring. Above all things he hated indolence. He was the first to use the Arab steed in war. He was the first to insist upon comfortable clothing for his soldiers. He delighted in seeing them eat and drink well. But his own habits were frugal. He quenched his thirst with water merely tinged with wine. In short, all were obliged to envy him and none could imitate him.

'I only wish I were lying when I state that Florence and Rome will soon find what it means not to have this man among the living. Yet methinks I can already hear the Pope rejoice. He believes himself better off for having lost so great a hero.'

The reckless bitterness of the last paragraph proves the depth of Pietro's grief and rage. He was defying the most powerful man in all Italy, the head of all Christendom, accusing him, in effect, of betraying his trust by disgraceful irresolution in the face of deadly danger. Instead of launching his full force against the Lutheran invaders, as many of his firmer predecessors would have done, under the best commander available, he had allowed that commander to be held in check by an inferior soldier, or at any rate one who had his own reasons for wishing to frustrate the ambition of a Medici, though in this case that ambition was a noble one. Its realisation might well have saved Italy from miserable servitude and Clement himself from the dishonour of capitulation. Thus the Pope had sent his only effective defender to a wretched death in what was little more than a raid on Ferrara's guns.

There is of course strong personal bias in Pietro's stern judgment of Clement's timidity and indecision. His best friend had fallen as a result of the Pope's shiftiness, fallen almost alone in the defence of a cowardly time-server, just as the critic himself had very nearly died – so he was now convinced – at the hands of the pontiff's hired assassins. History confirms beyond doubt that Clement's outlook, though far from being that of a scoundrel, remained also far from adequate to the duties of his exalted office. The cause of Catholic Christianity, shaken to its foundations by the Reformation, imperatively demanded his whole attention. But he acted in this crisis very much more like a secular prince concerned chiefly with promoting the interests of his family, though unfortunately not those of the best man among them, than like a pope in charge of the spiritual salvation of mankind.

The pontiff was to pay dearly for his narrow-minded selfishness within the next few months, as Pietro prophesied in his letter to Francesco degli Albizzi. That composition, perhaps the finest and sincerest that he ever wrote, clearly owes something in its style to a reading – in translation of course – of Pliny and Tacitus. But again and again the rounded phrases and periods in this antique mode give place to characteristically vivid touches of the closest observation and the keenest insight, as in every one of Giovanni's brief exclamations on his death-bed, reflecting his changes of mood from vigorous hope to austere resignation or from bold jesting to proud humility. Pietro's instinctive pictorial faculty, his ability to set a scene impressively before the reader without the slightest tedious detail, is here at its best.

On the Grand Canal

PERSONAL MOURNING FOR the death of Pietro's passionately adored *alter ego*, for the two men were as much alike as any born soldier and born writer can be, was sharpened by the check this tragedy administered to the survivor's material prospects – he did not admit the possibility of any other kind. The poet was now approaching middle age without yet having achieved anything like the ultimate goal he had set himself, nothing less than literary domination of the peninsula. Moreover, he was an extremely impatient man.

There was only one Italian at this stage of his career who might be induced and trusted to help him. This was a character Pietro did not think very highly of, whom he had often – at second or third hand – peremptorily reprimanded and more than once cavalierly rejected, and yet who continued to bombard him with extravagant protestations of friendship. Pietro and the Marquess of Mantua were just then actually living together under one roof, Pietro having since Giovanni's death been the guest of this powerful, wealthy and usually amiable nobleman. The most influential man in Italy was of course still Clement VII, whom Pietro now really hated as ultimately responsible for all his misfortunes of the last three years. But Pietro, realist that he was, and though he knew perfectly well that the Pope must be by this time or would very shortly be his determined enemy, had by no means given up hope of nobbling him. The pontiff, however, could only be approached through the Marquess of Mantua.

After the funeral accorded to Giovanni delle Bande Nere on November 30, Pietro asked for a private interview with Federigo Gonzaga. The upshot was a letter from the Marquess to Francesco Guicciardini, lieutenant-general of the papal forces. Guicciardini, now in his early forties, was not a popular man in society. Cynically ambitious and morally unscrupulous, with cold and pedantic manners, he was nevertheless respected as an

outstanding intellectual. He was eventually to prove himself
capable of a masterpiece, the *Storia d' Italia*, published post-
humously during the period 1561–4, but dealing only with the
writer's own time, 1494–1532.

'I would be very ungrateful' – wrote Federigo – 'to the
devotion which Messer Pietro Aretino has always shown me
and I would scarcely act as a friend of genius, if I did not in
every way try to make the world pleasant for this unique
man. I have myself seen him perform miracles. In a month he
has composed more verse and prose than all the talents of
Italy have in ten years. For that reason and also because that
excellent man has spent half his life in the service of two Popes,
with what affection and loyalty everyone knows, I feel
obliged to do what I can for him. If the Pope does not choose
to listen to me in this very vital matter, I can only suppose
that I am utterly out of favour with him. Yet if Messer Pietro
were not the most humble servant of His Holiness, I would,
so far from coming to his aid, dismiss him from my company
as a scoundrel.

'The object of my application is the restoration of Pietro
to the Pope's goodwill and that of his respected Datary. Such
an event would be as important to me as the appointment
of my brother to be a cardinal. Messer Pietro does not ask to
be allowed to return to Rome but only for proof that his
services to His Holiness have not been wasted. The ignoring
of his petition can reflect little credit upon either the Pope
or his Datary. In present circumstances general approval of
their policy is more than ever necessary and everyone knows
that the Aretine has good grounds for his feelings of resent-
ment. For myself, I would rather fail to promote my own
interests than those of Messer Pietro. But I am acting in this
matter as much for the honour of His Holiness as for the
advantage of the Aretine. I intend to address both the Pope
and the Datary on the subject and I would be most grateful
if you too would write to them about it in whatever sense
your wisdom may suggest. I shall be glad to hear from you
what steps you see fit to take in this affair and on receipt of
your reply I will act accordingly.'

From internal evidence there seems little doubt that this

letter was practically dictated by the Marquess's aggrieved
guest. The addressee, however, answered discouragingly,
though in polite terms. 'The mere memory,' he wrote, 'of one
of the Aretine's offences will outweigh any argument I can
offer.'

The offender in a rage at this dry rejoinder, dashed off an
embittered sonnet.

'Seven false and futile years I've flung away,
four with Pope Leo, with Messer Clement three.
And if I thus made an enemy,
their fault it surely was, not mine, I say.
And for all this I've had so little pay
that poor as threadbare mountebank I be.
Ay, just as so much wind have blown away
all hopes I had of any papacy.
Scars I still bear upon my hands and face
because five times a day I did defend
the honour of my patrons and their fame.
But rank and benefice and salary and place
to bastards only come and men of shame.
Clement rewards but those who Clement rend.'

In a 'Complaint' he actually called the Pope 'a sorrier wretch
than Adrian'. Worst of all, he forced even this pace with a
giudizio or 'prognostication' for the year 1527 which he called
'The Prophecy of Messer Pasquino, the Fifth Evangelist'. There
was a great demand for such 'prognostications' by the princes of
the day, who were practically all devotees of astrology. Their
lives were so precarious that most of them suffered from persecu-
tion mania and felt themselves to be the prey of vindictive fate.
They wanted to know how their wars and treaties would turn
out, whether their syphilis would be cured and what their
children would be like. The supply equalled the demand. But
the tipsters hedged as shamelessly as the ancient oracle at
Delphi.

Pietro's *giudizio* for 1527, which so angered Clement, unfortunately exists only in fragments. It was his first, and perhaps
less menacing than that of 1534, which has been preserved and
will be quoted later in these pages. But the earlier 'Prophecy
of Messer Pasquino' seems to have predicted, and with satanic

relish, the dreadful sack of Rome by Charles's mercenaries which duly occurred in May 1527.

The Pope was not amused.

'Yesterday' – wrote the Mantuan ambassador at Rome to his overlord the Marquess – 'a Franciscan friar who is the Pope's confessor came to see me. He said that his business was of no small importance to Your Lordship. A little book by Pietro Aretino has just appeared in Rome. It is full of slander and deals principally with the Pope, the cardinals and the other prelates of this court. It is dedicated to Your Lordship. This fact has caused a great deal of scandal among the persons concerned. It is thought strange that in view of your relations with the Pope and his cardinals as a Captain General of the Church you should allow such a book to be brought out in Mantua under your auspices and name. For that reason, said the friar, and because he was urged to do so by a person who loves Your Lordship's honour and wishes Your Lordship to remain in favour with His Holiness, he had come to give me this information in confidence. He suggested that I should write to Your Excellency and beg you to dismiss the Aretine from Mantua and deprive him of your grace. If you do so, he said, His Holiness and the prelates affected will have no reason to believe that Your Excellency knew of and was privy to such villainies, which you may rest assured they despise thoroughly and will requite as befits those who esteem their honour.'

Federigo obsequiously ordered his ambassador to let everyone in Rome know that in sheltering Pietro Aretino he had supposed him a close friend of the late Giovanni de' Medici of the Black Bands, and to be equally in favour with the Pope. But now, wrote the Marquess, who had been frightened by his envoy's communication, he had 'come to know the fellow's true character and commanded him to leave his dominions, despite the blackguard's threats to slander him, and finally the brute had 'slunk off like a beaten dog.'

'Of the fact' – the ambassador was instructed to add – 'that the Aretine dedicated the book to the Marquess, His Excellency knows nothing. The obvious deduction therefore, which should be made known, is that His Excellency could not have consented to the said maledictions. If His Holiness should not consider it enough for the Marquess to have dismissed the Aretine from his court, the Pope should inform the Marquess what further steps ought to be taken. In that event the Aretine would not escape the Marquess as he has escaped others. The necessary measures will be adopted by the Marquess in such a way that no one will be able to guess who ordered the matter to be arranged.'

This typical piece of Renaissance princely rascality, actually ending with an offer in transparently veiled language to assassinate a formerly honoured guest, was quite probably read out by its perpetrator, with the necessary explanations, to the prospective victim himself. For it is most unlikely that the Marquess intended to alienate permanently, much less murder, so useful a supporter of his reputation, and one who might so easily severely damage it.

At any rate the two men parted amicably enough, Pietro with a hundred crowns in his pocket by way of travelling expenses.

' "I shall go to Venice" ' – he told the Machiavellian Marquess, quoting a speech by Flaminio in the *Cortegiana* – ' "I shall enrich my poverty with her liberty. For there at least poor men are not ruined at the whim of any male or female favourite. Only in Venice does justice hold the scales with an even balance. There only fear of disgrace does not force you to adore someone who was in the gutter only yesterday. Surely Venice is a holy city and the earthly paradise." '

Flaminio, in the comedy, says he has already been to Venice. But there is no evidence that Pietro was ever there before March 1527, though he talks confidently of the city's constitution and social habits. These were no doubt at this date, as they had been for a long time, common gossip all over the peninsula, since Venice was unique in several respects. The city had been regarded throughout its history, like England after the rise of tyrannies in Europe, as a refuge for those politically or otherwise discontented with their native circumstances.

The Venetian State had originated under Byzantine protection early in the 11th century. By 1400 the city's peculiar geographical situation and enormous wealth derived from trade with the East had rendered the so called Serene Republic practically invincible. Its constitution was strictly oligarchical, the Council of Ten wielding absolute authority and the Doge being little more than a respected figurehead. During the first half of the sixteenth century Venetian political power, maintained by a most able and widely dispersed diplomatic corps, had scarcely yet begun to decline. Venice was then enjoying, like Britain in the early nineteen hundreds, a glorious afterglow, that of the moral and intellectual confidence, the luxury and the gaiety of an imperial past still believed immortal. Verona, Vicenza, Padua, Bergamo, Brescia, Treviso and even Ravenna were administered by the Council. In literature the editions of contemporary classics issued by the Aldine Press, one of some two hundred other presses founded at Venice in the latter half of the fifteenth century, were already famous, as were the masterpieces of the painters of the Bellini and Vivarini families, of Carpaccio, of Giorgione and of Titian. So cultivated, cosmopolitan and materially splendid a haven of sensuality and aesthetic vision could not fail to attract the temporarily baffled but still exuberant poet and art critic Messer Pietro of Arezzo.

Pietro landed at the jetty opposite the Doge's palace on March 27, 1527, accompanied by a single attendant, a young groom who had been a member of the Black Bands. Five weeks later his *giudizio* prophecy came true. Charles's German and Spanish troops burst into Rome and imprisoned Clement in the castle of San Angelo.

Pietro was now thirty-five years old, with his restless youth, beset by maddening failures as well as by ephemeral triumphs, behind him. His mental pattern, however, had long been set; he was never to vary from it. Psychologically though not physically a reckless daring, carried out with a peculiar kind of humorous arrogance, predominated. An innate creative originality, not only in the literary sense, distinguished him from other typical Italian Renaissance adventurers who ran truer to the national failings – from a north European point of view – of unscrupulous cynicism, over-sharp practice, remorseless cruelty when their material interests seemed to demand it, and persistent ostentation. In Pietro all these traits were evident enough, but they were regularly modified, often even completely countered, by a humanity generous to the point of gullibility and a lack of common prudence which again and again got him into unnecessary trouble, where more cautious swindlers like the Marquess of Mantua would easily have evaded the consequences.

Like many men of humble birth beginning to make their way in society, Pietro cultivated an appearance of aristocratic magnanimity and sensibility. But he was by nature incapable of refinement, as his facile poetry proves, to say nothing of his greedy, indiscriminate sensual appetites and extravagantly pretentious dress and bearing. He had, however, many of the virtues often considered plebeian or middle-class, such as loyalty to friends even when they cheated him, indomitable industry, a sturdily honest pride in his talents and, above all, the ability to get on wonderfully well with all sorts of men and women not in the least like himself.

There was one particular respect in which he had tackled his problems just like any other ambitious and hard-up provincial citizen of his day. He deliberately set out, first to attract attention, and then to attach himself to a patron. In the rigidly organised, hierarchical society of the sixteenth century sheer merit and hard work got you nowhere. Pietro did not consciously intend to change this situation; he was no social revolutionary. But in the freer Venetian atmosphere, oligarchical and commercial rather than aristocratic, scholarly, martial and priest-ridden, he found after a while that even without prior acquaintance with any person of official consequence in the city he could make people listen to him and respect him.

Other writers, though for some time only theologians, were to do the same in the interval before the 1770s. But it can fairly be claimed that Pietro Aretino, when he first came to Venice in 1527, was ready to become the leading publicist of Christian Europe. For the rest of his life he occupied this position, so far as secular affairs were concerned. Since the collapse of the civilisation of ancient Rome no private individual had exercised so considerable an influence on politics and social behaviour both by his written work and the force of his personality. Nor did any of his untitled contemporaries achieve equal effects in either field, though many tried to do so.

In March 1527 he came to Venice more as a refugee than as a voluntary visitor on business or pleasure. Venice was no longer, as it had been a century before, the centre of an empire. Pietro meant primarily to hide from his enemies in the rest of Italy, with Clement in Rome at their head. But he did not intend simply to go to ground like a hunted animal. He saw himself rather in the character of robber baron in ambush poised to swoop with blistering battalions of words upon the prelates and princes whose bravos and *condottieri* could only repel others like them. They would be incapable, he had good reason to believe, of dealing with the devastating paper squadrons of eloquent blackmail.

He discovered that the Venetians, in their military decline, enjoyed hearing other people abused. They listened with malicious grins to Pietro's stories of corruption in the rest of the peninsula and with proud smiles to his equally blazing and much more sincere eulogies of their own beloved republic.

'You may believe me' – he wrote to his 'half-brother' Francesco Bacci – 'when I say that those who have never seen Rome or Venice have missed two marvellous sights. But they are marvellous in entirely different ways. For in Rome the insolence of undeserved fortune struts up and down, whereas here you may see the grave demeanour of just dominion. It is strange to behold the confusion of the Roman Holy See. But it is splendid to observe the singleness of purpose in the Venetian State. Even if you should let your imagination soar to heaven you would never be able to picture in your mind the evasions of the former and the calm deliberation of the latter as it goes about its business. They are both immense edifices. But the one contains turmoil and the other tranquillity. One day a Mantuan citizen, I can't remember who it was, wanted to show us how Venice stands in the sea. He split some walnuts and set the halved shells floating in a basin of water. "That's what it's like," said he. Another time, so I have heard, a preacher somewhere or other, wishing to describe the papal court and not want ing to get clergyman's throat over it, simply showed his congregation a painting of hell. Go to Venice and you will

find that other cities, in comparison, seem like paupers'
settlements.'

To the Doge himself Pietro proclaimed:

'Here treason has no place. Here favour in high circles does
no wrong to be set right. Here no cruel mistress reigns. Here
the insolent and effeminate give no commands. Here no one
robs, coerces or murders. O hostelry of all the dispersed and
exiled, how much greater would be the woes of Italy if your
bounty were any the less! Here stands a refuge for all her
nations. Here her wealth may be kept in safety. Venice opens
her arms to all whom others shun. She lifts up all whom
others abase. She welcomes those whom others persecute.
She cheers the mourner in his grief and defends the despised
and the destitute with charity and love. And so I bow to
Venice with good reason. She is a living reproach to Rome.'

Pietro informed another correspondent, a priest:

'I am now in carefree, liberal and just Venice, where neither
sickness, death, hunger nor war oppresses the citizens. It is
my opinion that if Eden, where Adam dwelt with Eve, had
resembled Venice she would have had a hard time trying to
tempt him out of that earthly paradise with her fruit. For to
lose a place like Venice, where so much is lovely, would be
a very different matter from losing the Garden of Eden, for
all its figs, melons and grapes. For my part, as I have said
before, I should wish God to change me into a gondola when
I die, or else into its canopy, or if that is considered beyond
my deserts into one of its oars, rowlocks or cleaning rags.
Even a baling scoop would do. A sponge would be still more
appropriate. And I would love, just so as not to have to leave
Venice, to become one of those little copper coins with which
people here pay the ferrymen. If I were a rat that feeds in
the Venetian Treasury I would feel like one of heaven's
cherubim. Nor would I change my condition for that which
popes are said to have in paradise, though I doubt whether
any are really there, if I could only be the door leading into
the Tower of St Mark. For, to sum up, Venice is not only
more eternal than or rather as eternal as the world itself but

also the refuge, the delight and the consolation of all who live there.'

He added that he thought anyone who left Venice would be no better than one of those poor, foolish animals which refused to enter Noah's Ark when the flood rose. As for the Venetian gondola, he fell in love with it at first sight.

'What a heartfelt pleasure it is to get right away from everyone in a gondola! Carriages for those that like them! Litters too! Away with horseback! The first are likely to break down, the second bury you alive and the third bounce your bones, flesh and guts all over the place. But the dear little gondola rests, soothes and consoles the mind, the limbs and the whole body. Truth, wisdom and certainty are its gifts. Charon had good reason to take it as a model for his bark. He knew very well what he was doing when he copied it and needed its comfort for his task!'

So enthusiastic, verbose and versatile a foreign citizen – since all foreigners, if they flattered Venice, were welcome there – could not long remain a beggar after Federigo Gonzaga's hundred crowns were gone. Somehow or other – no doubt the proceeds of the *giudizio* for 1527 continued to be substantial – living on his tongue and his wits, Pietro maintained himself in ever growing affluence until, by 1529, he was able to take a long lease of a fine *palazzo* on the Grand Canal, at the point where the rio San Giovanni Cristostomo runs into it and the Canal turns north-west, above the Rialto bridge.

His landlord, the Bishop and Patrician Domenico Bolani, received a long letter from his new tenant, which is worth quoting. It is a superb piece of *reportage* and might well be regarded as equivalent to a year's rent in literary terms. It is in fact doubtful whether Pietro ever did pay any rent in cash for his grand accommodation.

'It seems to me, Honoured Sir, that I would commit the sin of ingratitude if I did not repay with praise some part of the debt which I owe to the heavenly situation of your house. I now dwell in it with the greatest pleasure that I have ever had in my life. For it is so placed that neither above it nor below it, in no part of it, is there room for the slightest improvement. Consequently I am almost as afraid to start my eulogy of it as I would be to start one upon the Emperor. Certainly its builder chose the finest position on the Canal. And since that Canal is the patriarch of all others and since Venice is a female pope among cities, I can truthfully say that I enjoy both the fairest highway and the most joyous view in all the world.

'Whenever I look out of my windows at that time when the merchants foregather I see a thousand persons in as many gondolas. The squares to my right are those of the butchers' and fishmongers' markets. To my left I behold the much frequented Bridge and the warehouses of the German traders. There are grapes in the barges below, game of all kinds in the shops and vegetables laid out on the pavements. There is no need for me to long for meadows watered by streams when I can marvel at dawn over waters covered with an endless variety of merchandise, each article in its due season.

'What sport it is to watch those who bring in great quantities of fruit and vegetables handing them out to others who carry them to their appointed places! All is tumult and bustle, except where about a score of sailing-boats laden with melons are moored together, making a sort of island to which crowds hurry off to count, sniff and weigh, so as to test the quality of the goods. Of the ladies, gleaming in gold and silk and jewels, though they are mere housewives, I will not speak, lest I grow tedious with the description of such pomp and circumstance. But what makes me roar with laughter are the whistles, catcalls and jeers directed by the boatmen at those whose rowers are not equipped with scarlet hose.

'And who would not laugh till he cried at the sight of a boatload of Germans who had just reeled out of a tavern being capsized into the chilly waters of the Canal? I can tell you that Giulio Camillo and I did. He is that same good fellow who once wittily compared the land entrance to this habitation of mine, since the portico is dark, badly designed and gives on to a most shocking stairway, with the dreaded name I have acquired for spitting out the truth. He added however that anyone who persisted in dealing with me would find, in my disinterested, frank and natural friendship, the

same serene delight that one encounters after leaving the
portico and coming out on the balcony above.

'Next, so that nothing should be lacking to please my eye,
I can gaze in one direction upon the orange trees that gild
the base of the Palazzo de' Camerlinghi and in another on
the rio San Giovanni Crisostomo and its bridge. Even the
burning winter sun never rises without first sending word of
its arrival to my bedroom, my study, my other private apartments and my great hall . . .

'And what of the lights, which after nightfall resemble
stars scattered over the places where all that is necessary for
our feasts and banquets is sold? Or the music which in the
dark reaches my ears with soothing harmonies?

'Nor must I forget the great foreign lords of the world who
often pass me at the entrance to my palace nor the pride that
lifts me to heaven when I see the Bucentaur' – the Venetian
State Barge – 'plying hither and thither, nor the triumphant
festivities continually in progress over that part of the Canal
dominated by my windows.

'I could more easily describe the profound wisdom of your
judgments of literature and politics than I could give a com-
prehensive account of all the entrancing sights that meet my
view.

'Therefore, if any breath of genius is wafted from the
trifles which I have written, it comes not from the light or
the shade, not from the violet or the green, but from the
grace bestowed upon me by the airy happiness in this mansion
of yours. May God grant that I spend here, in health and
vigour, all the years which may justly be allotted to one who
ever strives to do what is right.'

Pietro was writing to an aristocratic sixteenth-century Italian
bishop accustomed to be addressed with florid compliments and
in an unctuous tone. This style is evident enough in the above
passages. But what makes them unlike the letters written at that
time to such personages as Domenico Bolani is the vivid touch.
The boatload of drunken Germans being capsized, orange
trees gilding a *palazzo*, and lamps scattered like stars over the
market-stalls – only Pietro Aretino's pen could have lavished
such colourful details on an ecclesiastical landlord.

The man 'who ever strives to do right' at a later date

persuaded Jacopo Tintoretto to paint a ceiling for him. As time went on, Sansovino and Vasari, Titian and Sebastiano del Piombo contributed to the decorations of the interior of the palace. At the front door, on a pedestal, stood a marble bust of the tenant himself, heavy-shouldered, with strong, confident features and a splendidly flowing beard. In the main reception room, roofed with a glass dome, a big ebony filing-cabinet contained communications from princes, prelates, military commanders, painters, poets, musicians, great ladies and merchant bankers. In each compartment of the cabinet the most important of these documents were conspicuously displayed. Other chambers were adorned by gifts, many forcibly exacted, of tapestries, chests, beds, desks, armchairs and other furniture sent to Pietro from every corner of Europe. He was living in such splendour through his pen alone, and was almost certainly the first man in Christian Europe to do so.

The man's unique style in both prose and verse enthralled burghers in Amsterdam and counts in Hungary. Germans and Spaniards, Frenchmen and Greeks, even Turks and Persians, joined Italians in hailing the writer as the most brilliant commentator on both public and private events their age had ever known. His letters and poems, comedies and narratives flashed with wit and picturesque detail scarcely found at all in the laborious compositions of his more sober-sided literary colleagues. Machiavelli alone was capable of something similar, but he only used such language in his comedies. In general the ambitious sixteenth-century writer aimed at fame through dignity and erudition rather than jocularity and savage sarcasm.

Yet in the Casa Aretino there were only a few books. It was one of this tireless scribbler's most amusing affectations to pretend that he did not care for reading and knew little or nothing of the literature produced by other people. He really knew a great deal, of course, both in Italian and in translations, mainly from Latin, still the *lingua franca* at that time. His printer and publisher in Venice, one Marcolini, penned, probably at his author's suggestion, the following 'blurb' to boost the books under the Divine Aretino's name which now began to appear. The advertisement took the form of a letter to Pietro himself.

'If a poor man or poor woman of your acquaintance falls

sick, you send a doctor to him or her at once. You pay for the drugs required and provide enough food for both the invalid and those in charge of him. Often you even pay the rent of his lodging. Even if you don't know him and he is merely recommended to you, you do the same. If a brat is born in poverty, the family come to you for help in attending both mother and child. If some needy person dies in the street you live in or even elsewhere, your charity will often bear the cost of his burial. As for prisoners, I know only too many to whose aid you have come. For example, Cavorlini, that worthy man, still sings your praises for bailing him out of gaol, for which purpose you raised fifty ducats in two days, extorting contributions from Don Diego de Mendoza, Cardinal Ravenna, the Lord Girolamo Martinengo and the ambassador Benedetto Agnello.

'Yet what you force others to do, when you cannot do anything yourself, is as nothing to what you take from your own emergency storehouse. You pay travelling expenses for traders, come to the assistance of unmarried mothers who have been deserted, advise and help women whose husbands ill-treat them and see to it that orphans are placed in suitable asylums. You clothe the destitute beggars who come to you, taking the hose off your legs, the shirt off your back and your very doublet to fit them out decently. I've seen you even give them shoes. I was told by Dragoncino that he actually did not have an old pair from you, but new ones, which you took off your own feet.

'You aid even the poor gondoliers. It is a fact that I know fifty to whose children you have stood godfather, giving each of them a handful not of coppers but of silver *scudi*. You are so well known for this habit that, when your gondola passes, the embankments and bridges are packed with boys, girls and elderly people who owe their daily bread to you.

'Furthermore, the reports of your generosity have brought into being a whole tribe of impostors. Bareheaded and barefooted, they besiege your dwelling. They pretend to be starving and their tears extort presents on your usual scale. I can't help smiling at the trick played on your good nature by one such rogue. He emptied your purse by telling you that a nice girl, who used to be one of your neighbours, had just died and money was needed for her burial. But a few days later her brother turned up, begging you to provide her with a dowry. Before he could even open his mouth you went to him with outspread arms, embraced him and condoled with him on the death of his sister. "My lord," exclaimed the young man in amazement, "If she hasn't died during the last half hour she is alive and perfectly healthy!" But you wouldn't believe him until he went and fetched her. She arrived so poorly clothed as to be almost naked. But she departed with a pretty dress and the promise that you would see to her dowry. And you not only in fact paid it but also stood godfather to her first son. I firmly believe that God will reward you for all these good deeds.

'Another tale which amused me very much has become quite celebrated. As you dispense endless hospitality and keep open house, it was no wonder that on May Day, 1533, a group of foreigners passing by and seeing numbers of men coming out of your door and declaring that they had just tasted the best wine in Venice, thought your palace was a tavern. So they mounted the stairs and sat down at a table. They called for a salad and much else and when they had been served with all these things and were ready to go they took your servant Mazzone, since he is a tall, fair, handsome young man, very gay and pleasant, for the host. They asked him for the reckoning. Mazzone was offended by their treating him like an innkeeper and thought they were making fun of him. So he fell upon them with his fists. But when you came up and cursed him and struck him four hearty blows, the boisterous revellers realised that you were the master of the house and not just some important guest, as they had hitherto supposed. They found that they had eaten and drunk like emperors for nothing but a "Thanks!" and a "Good luck to you!". So they departed very merrily. But first they bowed low to you, with many compliments.'

Marcolini's extravagant exaggerations in this puff do not conceal the underlying truth of his anecdotes. Pietro's impulsive generosity is well documented from other sources and so is the extensive scale on which the poor were allowed to exploit the rich in sixteenth-century Italian society. Pietro himself wryly comments, in a letter to the Spanish officer Don Lope de Soria, on the automatic way in which those who fell sick or were wounded in the streets were carried into the Casa Aretino as if it were a hospital. 'So you can see why it is,' he added, 'that I am always complaining of being hard up.'

It was part of Pietro's policy to recount such tales, whether true or false, to excuse his own persistent exactions from wealthy patrons. He deposed, for example, that he had spent a thousand crowns a year during the first decade of his sojourn at Venice, as compared with the hundred he had started with. 'I drew my livelihood,' he confessed with candid arrogance, 'with pen and paper from the heart of avarice'. The phrase certainly dresses up his habitual blackmail in the cloth of gold he was so fond of wearing.

But much of the money and more of the gifts he received were bestowed on him freely by those who wished to curry favour with so prominent a figure or were grateful to him for past generosity. Many of his dazzling letters of thanks for quite trifling donations are addressed to obscure priests, soldiers or petty landowners. But he could sharply rebuke mean offerings to his shrine. 'On the Thursday after Carnival,' he exclaims to Girolamo Agnelli in 1529, 'there was presented to me a leg of veal which was such a miserable specimen that I gave it to a dog to break his fast on. If he could speak as well as he can bark, he would tell you just what he thought of so lean a gift.'

Pietro's notoriety made it easy for him to obtain the information he used as a weapon to menace the great and rich. He writes to the scholar Francesco Alunno:

'It must be that I have become an oracle of truth, since everyone comes to me to tell of the wrong done to me by such and such a prince or such and such a prelate. So many gentlemen give me headaches with their calls upon me that my stairs are as worn down by their tramping as is the pavement of the Capitol by the wheels of triumphal cars. Nor do I believe that Rome ever heard such a mixture of languages as resounds in my house. Turks and Jews, Indians and Frenchmen, Germans and Spaniards, come to see me. So you can imagine how many Italian visitors I have as well.'

Pietro's informants would be even freer with accounts of the wrongs done to themselves. In any case his native shrewdness generally demanded colourable proof of the allegations before he struck, though he rarely troubled mere beggars with such enquiries. In the same letter to Alunno he wrote:

'I need not refer to the lowest class of my visitors. But I can tell you that it would be easier to detach you from your allegiance to the Emperor than to see me for a single instant unaccompanied by soldiers, poor scholars and priests . . . so that I am become the world's secretary' – he means 'depository of the world's secrets' – 'and thus they call me in their superscriptions.'

He could only escape from such importunities by taking a gondola to the house of a friend.

As well as being an 'oracle' Pietro had achieved the status of a fashionable institution. A friend at Mantua notified him:

'Here there is a fine race of horses known as the Aretines. They are much in demand and are descended from your palfrey. If I go to Murano' – an island off that on which Venice is situated – 'I am presented with certain handsome vases of crystal, in the very latest style. They, too, are known as Aretines. If anyone asks where you live, he is told, "In the Casa Aretino, situated in the Calle dell' Aretino, on the rio dell' Aretino." Many good-looking women call themselves Aretines. When I asked one I met the other night her name, she replied: "L' Aretina". "Well," I said. "I'm an Aretine too. So we're bound to get on famously together!" '

But this remarkable popularity had been preceded by circumstances which repeatedly verged upon the sordid. For some time after reaching Venice Pietro bombarded the Marquess of Mantua and other officials in power at the Vatican with requests for favour and support which read rather pathetically, as though he were more anxious that no one should think ill of him than that everyone should contribute to his well-being. The dreadful news of the 'Spanish Fury' – it was really the fanatical German mercenaries of the new religion who behaved worst, since the Spaniards, after all, were Catholics – at the sack of Rome on May 5, 1527, though at first it shocked Pietro, in the end improved his prospects with Clement.

'The year 1527,' wrote Guiccardini, 'was to be filled with

horrors of a kind unheard of for very many years. Revolutions broke out in State after State. Cities were looted amid scenes of atrocious violence. Famine and pestilence reigned. Death, hordes of refugees, brutish devastation and plunder became the common order of the day.' The great historian might almost be describing the fatal years 1940–45, marking the culmination of a dreary and shameful decline in European civilisation that may almost be said to have begun in his time, with its rising scale of national ambition and population.

Georg Frundsberg had retired sick some six weeks before the invading troops reached Rome, while Pietro was still in Mantua. The Constable of France, Charles Duke of Bourbon, still the enemy of King Francis, took over command. But on the fatal 5th of May he was killed on one of the first scaling-ladders by a shot which that great artist and incorrigible liar and boaster Benvenuto Cellini declares was fired by himself.

'Aiming my arquebus' – he writes in chapter 34 of his memoirs – 'where I saw the enemy was thickest, I discharged the weapon at a man I beheld standing above the rest. The cloud of smoke prevented me from seeing whether he was on horseback or on foot. Turning hastily to Alessandro and Cecchino' – two companions who had gone with Benvenuto to the walls – 'I bade them also fire their guns and showed them how to escape a return shot from the enemy outside. When we had each fired twice I crept stealthily up to the wall and saw an extraordinary tumult among the enemy. For one of our bullets had knocked over Bourbon. So far as I could hear afterwards he it was whom I had seen raised above the others.'

Cellini's eyewitness description of the sack is rivalled by Pietro's own, given through the mouth of the old bawd Nanna in his famous dialogue known as *I Ragionamenti* ('Discussions') written about this time, though not published until long afterwards. In the second part of this composition, which is divided into three 'Days', Nanna is instructing her daughter Pippa, on the Second Day, in the wiles practised by men upon silly credulous women. Pippa is being prepared for her future profession as a harlot. Nanna instances the way in which a certain baron, by his eloquence on the subject of the sack of Rome, made a conquest of a noble and respectable lady.

'He had escaped' – says Nanna – 'like a rat, through some hole or other in the walls of the city, taken ship and been wrecked close to a great city, ruled over by a lady whose name I cannot tell you. She happened to be taking a walk when she came upon the poor man lying on the beach drenched, bruised, pale as death and all dishevelled. – Pietro evidently recalls here the story of Odysseus and Nausicaa – 'He looked more like the image of fear than modern courts look like the image of roguery. Worse still, the peasants, thinking that he was some great Spaniard, had gathered round him, intending him such mischief as footpads plan for some poor weaponless wretch who has lost his way. But the lady saved him from the noose they were preparing for his neck, comforted him, gave orders for his ship to be repaired and lavishly entertained him and his sailors in her palace.

'When he was quite restored to health she visited him and listened attentively to his elaborate, verbose and moralising account of his adventures, he preluding his tale with an oath that he would only forget her courtesy when rivers began to run upstream. While he talked of treacherous, lying and false-hearted men, she, the poor, simple innocent, had eyes only for his gallant person, his broad chest and shoulders, his dignified features and frank gaze, which entirely deceived her . . .

'When he mentioned the Pope and the cardinals she asked him how it could be that priestly craft should ever have fallen as a prey to such evilly disposed men. He answered, in his anxiety to meet her wishes, by heaving just such a sigh as rises in rascally fashion from the guts of a whore when she sees a well filled purse.

' "Madam," said he, "Since Your Highness wishes me to remember that which makes me hate the fact that I can remember it, I will tell you how the empress of the world became slave to the Spaniards and all the woe I have witnessed. But what scoundrel, German or Jew, could relate such horrors without tears?"

'He began by describing the panic of the citizens when they heard of the *Lanzknechte* and braggadocios of Spain who were coming in pitiless bands to render Rome the backside of the world. "Take up your goods and flee!" was all the cry. Everyone would indeed have done so, he continued, if that gang of brigands, with their hanging customs, had not burst in upon them so soon. As it was, after these tidings the terrified citizens started hiding their money, their silver, their jewels, their necklaces and their garments, everything of value. Little groups of men would gather, scatter and then assemble again in every direction, with every sign of terror of what they imagined would befall.

'Meanwhile, the district leaders and their pestilential hangers-on came buzzing after the regular files of foot-soldiers and, of a truth, if valour could reside in fine doublets and hose and gilded swords alone, the Spaniards and Germans would have caught it hot.

'A certain hermit, the baron went on, paced the streets crying, "Repent, ye priests! Repent, robbers, and implore the mercy of God, for the hour of your punishment is at hand!" But the pride of the citizens had no ears. And accordingly, quoth the baron, when the Scribes and Pharisees appeared at the cross-roads of Monte Mario outside the city and the sun glittered on their weapons, that dreadful dazzle struck more terror into the simpletons gathered on the walls than if it had been the flash of thunder.

'Then few thought any longer of how to hold the coming assault, but most looked for somewhere to hide. Yet the roar of conflict now rose to the heights of the Hill of the Holy Spirit and in the square our fine fellows, in the first rush, bore themselves like men who will never fight so well again. They slew the Duke of Bourbon and captured I don't know how many standards, which they carried to the *palazzo* with such shouts of victory as deafened heaven and earth. It seemed that they had gained the day. But then the barricades round the Hill were stormed and the enemy, after making mince-meat of many non-combatants, charged on into the Borgo. Some crossed the bridge and got as far as the quarter of the bankers, but then returned. I heard it said that the Castle of San Angelo, into which our friend the Pope had fled, did not fire on the assailants for two reasons, one, that the defenders were too mean to spend powder and shot, and two, that they didn't want to increase the rage of their adversaries just at the moment when ropes were being let down to haul up into sanctuary a batch of fat pedants who were already feeling pins and needles in their backsides.

'At nightfall the troops guarding the Sistine Bridge were put to flight and the whole army of the invaders poured over from Trastevere into the city. Screams rose to high heaven, doors were beaten in, the whole population took to its heels, weeping and trying to hide. Blood flowed over the pavements, people were being slaughtered, the tortured shrieked, prisoners begged for mercy, women tore their hair, old men quaked, and the whole city was turned upside down. Those who died at once were happy, so too those who in a lingering agony found someone to despatch them. The horrors that took place that night are indescribable. Friars, monks, chaplains and the rest of that crew, whether armed or unarmed. took refuge in the tombs more dead than alive. Not a cave nor a pit nor a well nor a tower nor a cellar nor any secret place but was crammed by all sorts of people.

'Respectable men were cudgelled, their clothes were torn off their backs and they were derided and spat upon. No church, hospital, house or any other building but was invaded. The soldiers even broke into those places never entered by men and in scorn drove the women into places where women are excommunicated for going. It was pitiful to see fire consuming gilded loggias and painted palaces. It cut one to the heart to see husbands reddened with the blood from their own wounds calling for their lost wives in voices that would have made the solid marble block of the Coliseum weep.

'Such was the narrative the baron told that lady, describing also the lamentations of the Pope in the Castle of Sant' Angelo, cursing I don't know whom for his betrayal and shedding so many tears that they nearly drowned him, till he became perfectly speechless with rage and grief.'

It is impossible to render in English the peculiarly cynical flavour of this vivid report. It conforms perfectly with the character of the bawd who is talking. Proletarian mispronunciations and colloquialisms are frequent. But Nanna's contempt for wealthy cowards and priests, including the Pope himself, is the author's own. So is her genuine compassion for the disaster so far as it affected the common people. The dramatist-novelist in Pietro here reaches a high degree of accomplishment, perhaps his highest; it is as though he were whispering his own fluently literate and striking sentences in Nanna's ear and she were instantaneously translating them into the rude, pungent dialect of the Roman streets.

In Pietro-Nanna's tale, based on information Pietro received at the time from Sebastiano del Piombo and other Roman residents or refugees about the sack of the metropolis, echoes of the story which Virgil makes Aeneas relate to the Carthaginian queen Dido about the fall of Troy are just as evident as those the author derives from the Homeric episode of Odysseus and Nausicaa when the old bawd's narrative begins. Like Aeneas the Romagna baron soon deserts his infatuated listener and in the end she kills herself. Pietro's contempt for Aeneas, the alleged founder of Rome, is unmistakable. He had long since come to hate the city in which he had failed to make his fortune; he could not forget his ignominious exile from it in 1525, when wounded physically as well as mentally by its fraudulent violence. Pietro here uses history and legend in the Balzacian manner for the purposes of satire.

Clement grew a long beard in captivity and never shaved again. Among other matters that he repented of in the Castle was his treatment of Pietro. According to Sebastiano del Piombo, who shared the pontiff's imprisonment, he wished he could have had the Divine One's advice before landing himself in this mess. Again, when he ordered the poet Tebaldeo to write a letter to the Emperor calling upon that ruler to restrain his 'Spanish Fury', the unhappy Pope lamented that Pietro was not at hand to do the job properly.

Clement was now a changed man in all respects but his restlessness. He even reproached Giberti for giving him disastrous counsel and said that Aretino would have been better worth listening to.

Pietro, when he heard this heartening news, at once dashed off a letter to no less a personage than His Imperial Majesty Charles V, the mightiest autocrat in all Europe. This missive, dated only a fortnight after the Roman catastrophe, referred to the Emperor's 'clemency' in releasing Francis I and putting faith in 'the promises, the instability and the pride of a vanquished prince, since it is the habit of princes who have been defeated to devote soul and body, not to say wealth and whole nations, to the study of revenge.' But another 'crown of generosity', he added, was now Charles's to command 'and so put into operation that blessed clemency of which I have spoken. Without it fame has no wing – feathers and glory are burnt out. Mercy is the triumphal crown of him who triumphs and the reasons which lead him to grant pardon are of greater worth than the virtues to which he owes his conquest. Indeed, that victory may be called a defeat which is not accompanied by mercy.'

The letter continued:

'Release the Pope! Give back to Christ His Vicar in return for the favour of conquest that He granted you. Do not consent that the joy of victory should change your godlike custom. For then certainly, among all the prizes which you have already acquired and which God and the Fates owe you during the remainder of your illustrious life, none other will be more worthy of admiration. But who would not set his hopes upon the excellent, courteous and religious majesty of Charles the Fifth? He is ever Caesar and ever august.'

It must be admitted that this communication was not a prose masterpiece. The phrases, with one or two exceptions, are hackneyed and the sentiments ring hollow to modern ears. But the advice given to Charles was sound and sensible. To keep the Pope a prisoner would certainly not be good policy. All the same, Pietro's real object in writing to the Emperor was to strike Clement while Clement was hot. If Charles had immediately acted as his correspondent wished, the restored pontiff could not have avoided restoring Pietro Aretino to power and opening the door to a career for the 'Scourge of Princes' which might have led to a cardinalate and possibly to the Chair of St Peter itself.

But it was typical of Pietro's incapacity to let well alone and also of his arrogance that he proceeded to lecture the Pope direct. He spoke in a letter to Clement of May 30, 1527 of 'hatred' and 'perfidy', which should yield to 'piety' and 'generosity', strongly hinting that the Vicar of Christ had in the past been more conspicuous for the vices named than for the opposing virtues. He ended by recommending total submission to the Emperor.

'Therefore to Him Who has power over all things yield all things and in so yielding them thank Him that, since the Emperor is the foundation of that faith of which you are the father, God has delivered you into his hands. For you can now cause papal and imperial policy to agree and by such action your glory will be so greatly increased as to shine out throughout the entire world. Consider that Charles's generosity has benevolently restored you to your former estate. He stands before you in the humility which befits both him who occupies the seat of Christ and him who holds the rank of Caesar. In his majesty there is no arrogance. Captivate him, therefore, with the arms of that power which comes from above. Turn his Catholic sword against the bosom of the East and so transform him into the agent of your designs. Thus, from the sorry state into which you fell through the sins of the clergy you will rise to receive the reward of all your patience.'

The Pope, as so often before with this egregious counsellor, was not amused by the sanctimonious and perhaps ironic advice proffered. The moment Charles allowed him to 'escape' – in December 1527 – he set his favourite poets on Pietro's track. Francesco Berni, still the Datary's secretary, was particularly abusive.

'You say so much and do so many things
with your foul tongue that has no salt of wit
that in the end a blade will silence it
sharper than that of Achille, with more stings.
The Pope's still Pope and you are a vile thief
nourished by others' bread and words of scorn.
You live in a brothel, in the slums were born,
O cripple ignorant and proud beyond belief!

Giovanmatteo and those men, his friends,
who, thanks to God, are living sound and sane,
one day in cesspool deep will drown your praise

unless, O filthy rogue, your life amends.
If you must chatter, of yourself complain
as on your head and chest and hands you gaze.'

'Like a dog's are your ways
which beaten strongly with most fierce endeavour
cringe and then whining are more tame than ever.

Will you shame never
O puffed-up monster, swine by fame unsung,
at whom are bitter words and hunger flung?

Know then a pile of dung
awaits you, scurvy wretch, whom scourges chide
when you shall die with sisters at your side,

those two who are the pride
of an Arezzo brothel, where they gain
applause for capers to lewd songs' refrain.

Of these, I tell you plain,
should be your stinking sonnets and low tales,
not of Sangallo, who had no such females.

From these, when your wit fails,
comes that from which you live in style so grand
and not from my lord Mantua's generous hand.

Since every place and land
you have polluted, man and beast make prayer,
God and the devil too, for your ill-fare.

Those ducal robes you wear,
of ducal thefts or ducal charities,
upon your back with such an awkward ease

to hard blows' melodies
shall be snatched off your shoulders ere you die
by reverend father hangman swung on high

to our great revelry
upon a gallows swaying to and fro
with quarterers attending down below

and sycophants you know
chanting for you the "May he rest in peace!"

So go, but pray decrease
your dirt till knife or well or noose
binds your vile tongue and never lets it loose.'

Such ingeniously laboured invective in one of Pietro's
favourite metres, the sonnet with a prolonged *coda*, did not dis-
concert him in the slightest. Though it is technically superior
to most of the other attacks on him, he could easily have
bettered it himself. But he decided to ignore it and go several
lengths further by appearing before the world as, of all things,
an epic poet. Then everyone, he reasoned, including even the
supercilious Clement, would have to respect him. His only
rival in this sort of narrative composition would be the great
but modest Ludovico Ariosto, diplomat, wit and the kindest of
men as well as the most exquisite Italian stylist in verse since
Dante. But Ariosto would not be jealous. He had already hailed
Pietro as the 'Scourge of Princes', those fraudulent patrons
whom the indigent author of *Orlando Furioso* hated as much as
their 'scourge' did.

Ariosto lived at Ferrara, in his own words 'in a small house,
but bought with my own money'. He had continued the
Orlando Innamorato by the Ferrarese Count Matteo Maria
Boiardo (1434–94), a somewhat cumbrous poem, though skilful
in construction and not without some vivid naturalism in the
characters. But Ariosto's *Furioso*, published in 1516, so far surpassed the Count's effort that he, like Pietro, acquired the nickname of 'divine'. The *Furioso* instantly became an Italian
classic, strongly influencing Spenser in particular and in general
all Europeans since then who have seriously aspired to this
form of metrical story-telling.

Pietro, it seems, thought that if the Divine Ludovico so
brilliantly extended Boiardo's *Innamorato*, he in his turn would
even more brilliantly extend the *Furioso*. He announced that he
would take up the story where Ariosto dropped it and that the

title of his new epic would be *Marfisa*, the name of a much tried but glorious heroine, a female knight also invented by Boiardo, who represented her as a paladin equal in skill and valour to any of those she meets. Ariosto greatly improved this character in general psychological interest when he brought her into the *Furioso*.

By 1529 the ingenious Messer Pietro had enough stanzas ready to make a short book. He proceeded with characteristic originality and business acumen to secure copyright, an unheard of privilege at the time, by requesting the Marquess of Mantua, to whom he dedicated the work, to get the Pope and the Emperor to forbid publication in their territories for ten years. The poem would then, for that period, be issued in Venice alone, so that only the author and his publisher Marcolini could draw the profits from the huge sales expected. Equally typically Pietro added in his letter to Federigo Gonzaga: 'If they are not willing, I will write twenty stanzas in the manner of Master Pasquino in which I will speak so scandalously that anyone who prints them will be excommunicated. And for that I will not need brief or privilege.'

But this well tried approach had been ill-timed. Charles was just then perfectly indifferent to the master scribbler, whose letter of 1527 he had ignored. Clement, for his part, saw no reason why he should not follow the Emperor's suit, especially as he had not forgotten the future epic poet's lecture to him in his captivity. The Mantuan ambassador at Bologna, where the Pope was about to crown his new friend Holy Roman Emperor, reported that 'the Aretine is in worse grace than ever, for in addition to his former offences he has just written a "Last Will and Testament" in which he speaks very scornfully of Charles and Clement.'

Pietro sharply denied the authorship of the piece referred to by the ambassador. He told the Marquess finally:

'I never repented more of anything than of asking you that favour. Your ambassador will testify that I had hardly sent the letter when I desired to recall it. I admit that I have written of the Pope with little affection. But had I not good reason to do so? As to the "Testament", I never saw it, nor has anyone here. You can tell your nuncio that it is not mine. What I have done is a series of eight sonnets on the coming of the Emperor to Italy and this year's *giudizio* in favour of both the Pope and the Emperor. I want no brief or privilege from anybody. They will soon enough find out who Pietro Aretino is. The works of genius are not subject to the favour or disfavour of princes. The Pope may not think that I deserve gratitude. But the world does not agree with him. He does know, however, that when I was with him I pleased him and that I am an uncommon and straightforward man. One day his eyes will be opened to my glory.'

These grandiloquent phrases were not entirely expressions of arrogance. Pietro was concerned to impress upon the somewhat naïve Federigo that the latter would gain very great prestige by having a 'genius' in his pocket. In any case, despite his disclaimers, Pietro returned tirelessly to the charge, actually seizing the opportunity to present himself to his old enemy Giberti, now Bishop of Verona and visiting Venice. The indefatigable author reported exultantly to the Marquess that the Bishop had received him 'cordially':

'I must tell you that, moved by almost divine inspiration, I have made peace with his reverence the Datary. If I have correctly interpreted the expression of his features they indicated cordiality and affection. I could not be more pleased with this reception and venture to hope that he will be so good as to return what he took away from me. Consequently I trust that Your Excellency, to me ever godlike, will inform the Datary with what pleasure you have learned that I now resume my service to him and with what still greater pleasure you will hear that I have been duly rewarded by him for doing so.'

The Marquess, as so often before, did as he was bid. The subtle Bishop replied urbanely that he had never really had anything against Pietro.

'There is one phrase in your letter that I cannot allow to pass without comment. I beg you to be as certain as you are that I am your humble servant that if anything was undertaken against Messer Pietro I gave no order for it and knew nothing of it. I was so much displeased, in fact, by what occurred that

only repeated requests prevented me from taking more
drastic steps than I did.'

This was pretty cool, even from a bishop whom no one below
the rank of cardinal would venture to contradict. But Giberti's
calm lie had been deliberately calculated. For his new diocese
of Verona was part of the Venetian Republic and the Doge
himself had now, rather unexpectedly, come out on the side of
Pietro Aretino.

The ruler in question, Andrea Gritti, a remarkably resolute
and circumspect statesman, saw dangerous times ahead for the
Serene Republic. The French wolf and the Spanish lion, to say
nothing of the Turkish sea-mastiff, coveted that still lovely, self-
willed heiress, the Queen of the Adriatic. They were strong
enough to get her if they could agree among themselves, and
unless Venice could find a powerful friend elsewhere. There
was only one such star still in the ascendant, Pope Clement VII.
He was unlikely to listen to the Doge himself. Would he listen
to the most prominent foreigner now resident in the city?

Gritti sent for Pietro and had a confidential chat with him.
They reached a 'gentleman's agreement'. Pietro was to stop
lecturing, slandering and bullying the Pope and instead praise
him to the skies. The head of the Serene Republic, on his part,
would recommend Clement to adopt a more reasonable attitude
to the penman whose weapon was mightier than any sword in
Europe and could therefore serve the Vicar of Christ, for certain
considerations, better than any diplomat or soldier available to
the Papal States.

With the Doge behind him, Pietro felt he could let himself go.
It was now that he began to hold high festival in his rented
palace on the Canal. He engaged five servants, dressed them
in gorgeous liveries and revelled democratically with the
carnival crowds in the streets and on the waters. Yet when Lent
came, the Mantuan ambassador to Venice reported to his
overlord:

'Yesterday I saw Messer Pietro Aretino with a written confession in his hand and tears in his eyes. He told me that he
knew God would never forsake him, but would treat him
better than he deserved, though hitherto he had been a great
sinner. He said he was determined now to live a different sort

of life altogether, that he was going to lay aside rancour and hate and all the other wickedness people so gossiped about. He repented of it with all his heart, he said, and was now going to confession and mass with his entire household, a thing he had not done for many years.'

This alleged reform, despite the unctuous sentimentality with which he expressed it to the Mantuan and no doubt to anyone else he thought might believe in it, soon bore fruit, especially as it was adorned with panegyrics of the Pope that now once more poured from his desk. In May 1530 Clement promised to send him five hundred crowns, adding that he would sign the copyright brief soon. In September the document in question, together with a gold collar instead of the five hundred crowns, actually arrived. The recipient, who had probably been losing patience, replied with formal courtesy but not much humility.

'Your majordomo, Monsignor Girolamo da Vicenza, Bishop of Vaison' – in south-eastern France, near Avignon – 'has delivered your brief to me. He handed me the document in the house of the Queen of Cyprus here. In accordance with your instructions he told me that neither your elevation from the rank of a mere Knight of Rhodes to the papacy nor your transfer from that office to a prison has astonished you so much as my attacks upon you in writing, especially since I knew why you did not punish anyone for the attempt made upon my life. Holy Father, in everything I have ever said or written I have always expressed what I felt. As for attacks upon your honour, as your loyal servant I could not be blamed for reproving you. Yet I do repent and am ashamed of having censured a Pope whose glory I valued more than my own life. I am also ashamed that since I could not help finding fault with you I did so at the lowest ebb in your fortunes. I thank God that He has taken from your mind the harshness of contempt and from my pen the sweetness of revenge. From now on I shall be the good servant I was when my talents, fed by your appreciation, armed themselves against all Rome during the vacancy of the throne of Leo.'

The issue of the privilege may have been largely due to

Andrea Gritti's pressure on Clement. At any rate Pietro wrote more graciously to the Doge, keeping copies, of course, for immediate publication.

'Sublime prince, I have two reasons for being grateful to Christ ... In the first place He guided me to this city and secondly He assured your interest in me. Consequently I hereby acknowledge that you have saved both my life and my honour. The faith that I had in the good name of this city and in the glorious reputation of its Doge has now reaped its reward. I therefore owe a double debt of gratitude, to the city for its generous welcome to me and to yourself for defending me against my persecutors and restoring me to the good graces of Clement. You bore in mind both the exasperation of His Holiness and the justice of my case, which was indeed so just that when the papal promises were not kept I held my peace in accordance with the command of Your Serenity. Such is the difference between the good faith of a loyal subject and the word of a sovereign.

'I have learnt to be free on the soil of the Venetian Republic. I shall never return to the life of courts. I shall devote the rest of my life to my home here ... I who once terrified the great and encouraged the good am come to serve you, who are the father of your people, the brother of your subordinates and the beloved son of truth ... Accept my homage ... Ah, Venice, whom all may call fatherland, where freedom reigns and wanderers find lodging, how much greater would be the sorrows of Italy if your courage were any less!'

Pietro was in fact sincerely enough attached to the Venetian republican ideal as represented by Gritti, especially as republicanism in this case went hand in hand with a love of what Baudelaire, echoed by Matisse, was long afterwards to call '*luxe, calme et volupté*', a tripartite atmosphere more often breathed, since the days of Pericles, under benevolent despotisms than under oligarchies. The last sentence in his letter, repeated almost word for word from an earlier address to the Doge (see page 117) includes Venice in Italy. This idea would not have appealed to many Italian politicians of the period, with the possible exception of Machiavelli. It perhaps indicates that

Pietro could see a unified Italy ahead, once the Habsburg dynasty had been expelled. Such prescience would not at all be surprising in a man so often ideologically in advance of his age.

Meanwhile the Habsburgs were still very much in the saddle. Yet to the Emperor's offer of a knighthood, communicated to Pietro about this time by the Bishop of Vaison, he snappishly quoted a line from one of his own comedies, the *Marescalco* ('Master of the Horse'), published that year: 'A knight without revenue is like a wall without a prohibitive notice on it. Everyone commits nuisances there.'

Pietro was now living in such open extravagance and dissipation in the Case Aretino, though he always watered his wine and would not allow playing-cards or dice in the palace, that both his most intimate friends, Titian and Sansovino, constantly reproved him for his prodigality. He had rarely been so sure of himself. 'I enjoy being abused by dull people,' he said at this time. 'For if they praised me it would look as if I were like them. The envious who attack my morals also prove to me that I must be famous, since I am envied. If they swear I'm in debt and really a pauper, I'm equally pleased. For only the poor are good.'

The Master of Masters

NEITHER CLEMENT NOR the Emperor nor the Doge had shown any palpable enthusiasm for the *Marfisa* epic still in preparation. Now that the author had his copyright, the poem had to be launched somehow, by some rich man. The Marquess of Mantua, to whom it was to be addressed, was obviously the target. He had no literary judgment whatever, but he had plenty of personal and family conceit. He had liked very much, he said, the abominably pretentious preliminary stanzas, all in praise of himself and his ancestors, which Pietro had sent him.

'I have read the fine stanzas you have sent me and I know that you have completed them in less time than most people would have taken to begin them. Yet they could not be more fair and learned than if you had worked on them for twenty-five years. I am intensely desirous for you to finish them. I give you infinite thanks for the great honour you have done me in writing them especially for me and thank you equally for the compliments to myself that they contain.'

It would be simple enough to put Federigo under such an obligation to the writer that he could not refuse to bear all the expenses of publication and promotion. The old technique which had brought Pietro those embroidered shirts a few years ago would have to be tried again. But this time the tactics must be carried out on a grander scale and without untrustworthy intermediaries.

The sculptor Jacopo Sansovino, then in his middle forties, whom Pietro had known in Rome, had fled to Venice, like other Roman artists, on the sack of that city in May 1527. He soon foregathered with his old friend and introduced him to Titian, who was greatly taken with the poet's striking appearance and painted his portrait (now lost) in the following month. Pietro persuaded Messer Tiziano, then at the height of his fame, though barely forty, to send the picture free of charge to the Marquess of Mantua as an investment in the well known liberality of that nobleman.

'In the end you'll get more out of him than any price you could dare to name for the portrait alone. And besides, he'll make you known to all Italy.'

Sansovino also promised, at Pietro's suggestion, to send Federigo a statue of Venus he had nearly finished.

'Just the thing for that young lecher!'

Titian, moreover, happened to have on hand the portrait of a deceased gentleman named Adorno, who had been friendly with the Marquess.

'Send that too!'

The recipient expressed his gratitude in the following letter.

'I have just received the two handsome works by Titian which were brought to me. They are dear to me not only because I have always wanted to have a picture by that excellent painter, but also because one of them is a portrait of your talented self and the other of Signor Hieronimo Adorno, whom I loved much while he was alive. Please thank the said Titian in my name as cordially as you can and tell him that I will shortly make him such a present that he will realise how grateful I am. I would not want to accept the pictures without giving him the reward they deserve.'

Sansovino's statue is not mentioned in this letter. But there is other evidence that it was equally well received by the Marquess. So far so good! Further gifts to Federigo from Venice followed, in the shape of glass, a saddle and a dagger, all by famous Venetian craftsmen. As regards the dagger, it seems that Pietro got it for nothing. At any rate he told the Marquess that work on it was being delayed because the maker was worried by the predicament of a son-in-law imprisoned at Mantua. The captive had not been able to pay a fine imposed on him for some reason, possibly wool smuggling. Federigo immediately had him released. In these circumstances the grateful father-in-law could hardly dun Pietro, his benefactor in this matter, for the price of the weapon ordered. It had appeared to the worthy artisan that Pietro's intervention on the prisoner's behalf had been nothing short of miraculous.

There are several other cases at this time of the Lord of
Mantua's exercising his power in order to comply with one of
Pietro's requests. The Marquess, for instance, freed an old
soldier of the Black Bands charged with murder. Federigo also
managed to divert the imperial forces from Arezzo.

'So that Pietro Aretino can have the necessary peace of mind
to go on with his writings and studies' – Federigo wrote to
his brother in Charles's army – 'I beg you to free the
Aretines from any of the inconveniences of war and to give
them the same protection that you would if Arezzo were
part of my own dominions. Tell the citizens that your favour
arises from my intercession, to which I have in my turn been
urged by Messer Pietro.'

Again, the Marquess kept Pietro in the good graces of a
Mantuan lady with whom the petitioner had been intimate
and whose favour he did not want to lose. She may have been
in a position to promote Pietro's interests in some way; she
may have been reproaching him for deserting her; or he may,
perhaps, have wanted her to join him in Venice. In any case
the Mantuan ruler promised to do what he could for Pietro
with Isabella Sforza.

But in another matter the great man declined positively to
act as a pander for Pietro. The latter had asked him to plead
with an obstinate youth named Bianchino, since the boy had
incomprehensibly repelled the giant writer's embraces. 'I
could not command him,' wrote the decidedly heterosexual
Federigo with unwonted austerity. 'For in such affairs to
command is neither right nor decent.' Pietro, always tactful in
love if not in hate, did not press his patron for compliance in
this direction.

The poet, like many Italians of his day, had a taste for both
sexes. He had no objection whatever to occasional acts of
sodomy, though his enemies and censors never ceased, nor have
they ever ceased down to the present day, to accuse him of the
regular practice of 'unnatural vice'. Even Swinburne of all
people, who loved to whip boys, attacked John Addington
Symonds, the nineteenth-century authority on the Italian
Renaissance period, as 'the Platonic amorist of blue-breeched
gondoliers who is now in Aretino's bosom', as if Aretino's chief

claim to distinction were that of a seducer of young boatmen.

But apart from the occasional case like this of the beloved Bianchino the Scourge of Princes did not spare the lash in his dealings with the nobleman whom he had promised to immortalise in the *Marfisa* epic. Federigo had more than enough excuse for getting sick of his petitioner, whose inordinate demands now rose month by month. The Marquess began to show a certain asperity after reading a *giudizio* for 1529 which contained scathing remarks about some of his friends. He told his ambassador to inform Pietro that owing to the war the revenues of the Mantuan State were declining and its ruler was becoming hard up.

Pietro retorted by announcing through a third party that he was about to leave Italy for good. After his departure, he added vindictively, he would take his revenge upon those high and mighty ones who had refused to help him. He would at last 'tell the truth about them'. Then he arranged for Malatesta, the Mantuan ambassador, to overhear him reciting sarcastic epigrams about Federigo Gonzaga to a distinguished audience which included the Florentine envoy. Malatesta warned him haughtily that his master knew how to resent insults from greater men than Pietro. Pietro appeared quite abashed by this menace. He apologised profusely and wrote one of his expertly fulsome letters to the Marquess, who remained for the time being guardedly gracious.

'For ten years, with the greatest ardour, I have advertised, exalted and celebrated the name of your Excellency. For but one hour, moved by over-impulsive love for you, I have assailed what you hold dear. Since I have not been rewarded with your usual royal generosity for my best efforts on your behalf, I surely do not deserve to be punished for my worst indiscretions with such severity as would reflect upon your honour.

'I, Pietro Aretino, serve you out of true affection, not fraudulent design. A warm regard, not a cold servitude, renders me your friend. If tongues could weary, mine would be entirely worn out with praising you. If your angelic benevolence turns to hatred and cruelty it necessarily assaults its own glory with such sentiments.

'No King nor Emperor nor Pope, only the Marquess of

Mantua, whom I love, causes me to humiliate my pride in this way, not in fear for my own life but in affectionate recognition of your outstanding merits.

'I kiss your hands if I am worthy to do so.'

Medieval Christianity, in which fierce intolerance of heresy and luxury played so conspicuous a part, rendered people much steadier in their loves and hates than they had ever been before, with the result that the pagan *Pax Romana* vanished for ever from Europe, while implacable adversaries fought one another to the death all over the continent. But in the Renaissance period with the revival of classical culture and the development of a self-conscious refinement of manners, involving a certain growth of moral scepticism, the age-old subtleties in negotiation, often introducing a 'phony' character into warfare, once more became fashionable. This was especially the case in Italy where Machiavelli rose to be the chief prophet of such manoeuvres.

Pietro arrived at the crafty Florentine's principles independently, by sheer native intuition and the cool courage to practise what it told him. He carried such exercises to amazing lengths in his dealings with Clement, who had himself once been a Machiavellian 'chameleon', and particularly with the relatively innocent Marquess of Mantua. Such letters as those already quoted show Pietro again and again not only moving in a flash from insolent reprimand to sentimental adoration, but even combining these two attitudes in one communication. The correspondence with the Marquess continued with many shifts of mood on both sides.

But in December 1529 Pietro's tone sharpens dangerously.

'Most honoured lord, can it be possible that you who have been so courteous, not to say prodigal, to all men, should show avarice only to me, your adorer? When did I receive my last crust from you? After my death you will regret that you permitted a work celebrating the glory of your house to be pawned for a paltry two hundred crowns. Are you so anxious to punish me for a couple of words spoken in criticism of you that you do not reward me for a whole book composed in your honour? By the body of St Francis, I would burn it if it were still in my possession, which it is not, since you have not paid me for it. Even after all this time I don't suppose I will ever get a single shirt from you!'

But the bass note elicited no more response than the treble. In January Pietro was pathetically pleading, through the Mantuan ambassador, for fifty crowns, and at the same time, sending the Marquess his latest comedy, *Il Marescalco* ('The Master of the Horse'). The central figure of this lewd skit had been modelled from a real person, a well known homosexual at the Mantuan court. In the play he believes, to his horror, that he will be obliged to marry and then finds to his delight that the wife forced upon him is after all a boy.

Pietro got his fifty crowns for providing a mainly heterosexual court with such congenial amusement. He thanked the Marquess obsequiously. But a couple of months later he was whining in much the same tone as before, lying for all he was worth about the length of time during which he had 'served' Federigo, the poor acknowledgment he had obtained for his 'services' and the contrasting generosity of people who hardly knew him. The Lord of Mantua, now created a duke, was not impressed by such exaggerations. But his new rank – *noblesse oblige* again – stirred his conscience to the extent of despatching a robe of 'night-hued velvet' to the author in return for further stanzas celebrating the Gonzaga dynasty.

Nevertheless, towards the end of 1530 a definite break occurred. The patron wrote that a benefice Pietro had demanded from him had already been given to another petitioner. The poet, in a fury, openly threatened the Duke with written slander. The magnate answered through his envoy Malatesta that if he had any further cause to complain of the Scourge's conduct he would have him stabbed 'in the middle of the Rialto'. The reprisal to this communication was the beating up and robbery of a Mantuan nobleman in the streets of Venice by armed bravos who called to their victim as they retreated, 'We do this at the behest of Pietro Aretino!'

Next, the author offered his *Marfisa* to Alessandro de' Medici, Duke of Florence, substituting eulogies of the latter's family for that of the Mantuan, which at the same time, in the same laboured stanzas, he depreciated. Alessandro courteously declined the honour. But the Marquess of Vasto, as vain and pompous as Federigo Gonzaga, if perhaps rather more intelligent, accepted it. His decision was probably taken more because he wanted people to talk about him than because he thought highly of the poem in a literary sense. *Marfisa* was duly published, dedicated to Vasto, in 1532.

But this marquess, compared with the 'princes' at whom the Scourge was really aiming, amounted to very little as a patron; certainly far less than the Mantuan ruler had once meant to Pietro. So Pietro turned to his own and Giovanni's former protector, the King of France, peppering that sovereign with all sorts of communications, laudatory or covertly censorious, for nearly three years. Francis, a more typical man of the Renaissance than even Pietro Aretino himself, sincerely loved literature and art as well as violent exercise and complacent women. He entertained many Italians of genius at his court, notably the turbulent metal worker and sculptor Benvenuto Cellini, with whom he had much in common. Pietro reminded the monarch that in the latter's darkest hours after the battle of Pavia in 1525 almost his only defender in public had been his present correspondent and that furthermore, in 1528, he, Pietro Aretino, had called upon the French king to save Italy from the 'Spanish Fury'.

It was some time, as usual, before Francis took any notice of these appeals. But when he did, it was with characteristic wit and generosity. In November 1533 he sent the Scourge of Princes a massive gold chain valued at six hundred crowns. It included many little pendants enamelled in vermilion, as though 'poisoned', and shaped like tongues. Each was inscribed with a Biblical text in Latin. 'His tongue uttereth great lies'. This playful motto could mean that the recipient was one of the biggest liars in Italy, which was perfectly true. In that case it could be taken in good part as the blunt statement of an intimate and otherwise highly appreciative friend, recording a well known fact which neither party regarded seriously. But an equally obvious interpretation might be that a great man – Francis – was deprecating the extravagant flatteries rained upon him so persistently and at such enormous length by his eloquent petitioner. Pietro was delighted with the present and the ambiguity of the inscription, but he intimated in his habitual style that he considered this regal gift only a beginning. He wrote to Francis:

'I suppose that if I told you that you are to your people what God is to the world, and what a father is to his sons, I should be lying, should I not? And if I informed you that you have all the rare virtues, courage, justice, mercy, magnanimity and wisdom, should I be lying then? And should I not be telling the truth if I declared that you know how to rule your own passions to the amazement of all? And if I stated that your subjects feel your power more in the benefits they receive than in the injuries they endure, should I be speaking ill of you? And would I not speak well if I said that you are the father of virtue and the eldest son of faith? And if I proclaim that love of others has led you to inherit your kingdom, will you still deny me?

'But it is true that if I should boast of the gift of this collar I should lie. For that cannot be called a gift which the hope of ever seeing it has devoured and which is sold almost before it has been seen.' – This hint of his poverty did not in fact prevent Pietro from keeping the chain until the very day of his death – 'For that reason, if I did not know that the goodness of your heart is immeasurable and had no part in the delay, I would tear off all these linked tongues and make them ring so loud that the ministers of your royal treasury would hear them for days to come. Then they might learn to send in haste what their king gives so promptly. But since there is no deceit in your royal character, it is my duty now to refrain from employing my talents in the scorn of others but on the contrary to turn them ever to the humble chronicling of your Majesty's ineffable benignity, in the favour of which I pray that Christ may always keep me.'

The King, however, did not rise to this broad insinuation. Pietro, as in the case of the similar snub received from the Marquess of Mantua some years previously, petulantly announced that he . as about to go into exile. It was now, moreover, that he dedicated to Francis I the striking 1534 *giudizio* referred to in the last chapter in connection with the prognostication of 1526.

'If God Almighty had not poured down His grace upon those idiotic prophets and sibyls, they would have conjured

up the same kind of chimerical drivel about Christ's Coming
as their successors did about what was going to happen at
Marseilles.'

Charles and Clement had recently held a conference at that
city to decide upon measures in the interests of peace in
Europe, but this much publicised and optimistically reported
event had about as much practical effect as the somewhat
similar discussions at Munich in 1938.

'But because the Holy Spirit' – continues Master Pasquino –
'descended upon those prophets and sibyls, just as French
amity did upon Clement, they forecast correctly that He
would be born in a manger and thus a poor silly sheep
bleated and "behold, He was made man".'

'I must tell you, however, that the cow Gaurico and those
other wandering oxen, the astrologers, since nothing rained
down on them from heaven but claptrap, have got everything wrong. When they predict peace for Milan war breaks
out. When they foretell freedom for Genoa, that city is
enslaved. When they say the Pope will die he looks younger
every day. And so they go on with their endless erroneous
guesses about both good and bad fortune, all the result of
that pitiful stargazing of theirs.

'Just as I was inspired to forecast the ruin of Rome, that
backside of the world, so now I have calculated a prophecy,
based upon the revered lives of princes, for this present year.
And since Your Majesty has prudently yoked the necks of
the treacherous stars, the robber planets and their drunken
emanations, causing all to tremble before your wisdom, I
address this prophecy to yourself. I am certain that the
Crab, the Scorpion, the Balance and the Twins, with the
rest of the scribes and pharisees of the zodiac, will let fall
upon me the secrets of the universe, just as they have
showered that herd of cattle, the lords, with meanness,
cowardice, ingratitude, ignorance, villainy, evil thoughts and
heresy, and made you yourself generous, honourable, appreciative, skilled, courteous, upright and most Christian.

'And since it is the sky that has rendered those others
fools base-minded and blackguardly, why should the lords
of Ferrara, Milan, Mantua, Florence and Savoy, who are

Dukes in name only, call me to account? Is it my fault that the Emperor is a tight-lipped miser? Did I advise England to seek a new bed-companion? If the god of war abandons the troops of Federigo Gonzaga, am I responsible? If the Fishes incite Alfonso d'Este to salt his eels, blame him for it and not Pietro Aretino. If the Twins link Cardinal Cibo with his sister-in-law, must I be threatened by the bold Lord Lorenzo? If the Goat stamps the forehead of a count, a marquess, a duke or a prince with his device am I their villainous instigator? If the Crab' – i.e. syphilis – 'eats the bones of Antonio de Leyva, it is through his own misdeeds, not mine.

'The Voyevoda' – title of an East European ruler – 're-nounces Christ and would I am sure, if asked why, declare that he was impelled to do so by fate. Ferdinand, who is about to turn Lutheran, will give the same reason for his apostasy. So will the Pope for his break with the Emperor. The truth is that all these great lords do such great wrongs because they were clumsy donkeys from birth and then charge me with causing their misbehaviour, just because I publicly relate their public acts.

'And if the King of France has followed such men in committing the sins of avarice and stupidity, neither his gilding of my tongue nor the gold chains he put upon me will prevent me from saying the same of His Majesty – whose liberal hands I kiss – as I have said of all the lords and prelates who imitate Catholic and Apostolic stinginess instead of the generosity of Cardinals Lorraine and Medici, who shame their colleagues by being too good for this scurvy century, which suits the Duke of Ferrara as well as the Golden Age suited Saturn . . .

'In this present year of 1534, the Marquess of Vasto being Lord of the Ascendant and sitting in the centre of the zodiac between Maramaldo and Tucca, the former buffoon and falconer, respectively, of the Duke of Mantua, many re-nowned Generals, as for instance the Duke of Malfi, stallion-in-chief to the women of Siena, will take to perfumes and embroidery . . .

'In the autumn the Bull (according to the Bishop of Lodi, alchemist and wizard) or the Goat (according to Taccuino) will break their tethers and with their horns gore and bring to earth certain members of that useless tribe, the Cardinals, to wit, lousy Trani, rascally Gaddi, boorish Cesi, thick-headed Spinola, thievish Bari, Valle the pot-belly, bestial Santi Quattro, Accolti the idiot, the wretch Palmieri, drunken Trincaforte' – i.e. 'toss-pot', not of course the real name of the cardinal in question – 'and good-for-nothing Mantua . . .

'Winter will be chillier than spring and autumn. Conse-quently, all the lords of Lombardy will take their cousins, their sisters-in-law and their sisters to bed with them, in accordance with the local custom, so as not to die of cold. If censured for this conduct they will quote the example of the Emperor, who in Bologna, with the consent of the Pope, lay with his own sister-in-law . . .'

The *giudizio* calls Clement a liar by punning on his name, *Clemente* becoming *Chi mente* ('He who lies') and adds again that Charles will turn Protestant. The author gives Henry VIII of England the motto of *Omnia vincit amor*, which also applies to the Duke of Mantua and priests and friars in general, except that the latter are also much too fond of their own sex. The author further wonders why Clement refused Henry a divorce when he granted one to the Duke of Mantua, who himself had not allowed two young wives to separate from their husbands. 'And if I had not taken a vow to speak nothing more of his Holiness I would quote his depriving Madonna Giovanmattea' – Giovanmatteo Giberti is thus accused of pathic homosexuality – 'of her consort, now in a Veronese monastery . . . The cardinals, in a word, are safer from the evil influences of the stars than is genius, thanks to King Francis, from poverty. For there is no star so wicked as even to think of a cardinal . . .'

The prophet ended his public prognostications with a typically sly jest, no doubt much appreciated by the addressee:

'The Lord God, with the consent of all the planets, stars, signs and heavenly bodies, has resolved that this year the sons of King Francis, on whom have been rained so many virtues that paradise is running short of them, will be healthy, happy and much beloved. The Dauphin in par-ticular, since he has followed his father's footsteps in benevolence, courtesy and valour, will not abandon them in the field of Venus either. This year he will have dealings with women.'

Francis the Dauphin was in fact to die two years later at the age of twenty-one.

The last paragraph refers to the poet's own decision, already announced elsewhere, to leave Italy.

'Pietro Aretino, who has in the ascendant Luke, John, Matthew and Mark, so that the Arctic and Antarctic stars give him the same liberty of speech that all foreigners have in this dear Venice, has broken with all lords, whether of the Church or the anti-clerical party. In the latter part of December he has found the liberality of the great Doge Luigi Gritti appearing in the most remote parts of the zodiac. So, to the infinite discredit of their most excellent and reverend lordships, Pietro Aretino will then turn his steps towards Constantinople. And at every step he takes he will preach the charity of Christian princes who, in order to exalt the seven deadly sins, constrain poor men of merit to go to Turkey, where they will find more courtesy and more piety than they find cruelty and asininity here. Thus the Aretinos of this world are forced to worship pashas and janissaries.'

Pietro was not talking idly. The Venetian ambassador in Constantinople had informed him that he would be welcome there. The Grand Vizier had seen a portrait of him and had asked of what country that magnificent-looking personage was king. Khair-ed-Din ('Barbarossa'), regent of Algiers and formidable corsair, also wanted to see this 'writer with the face of a soldier'. The Divine One was also talked of, so he heard, in Cairo and even in Teheran. He would not have been the first or the last European to have judged life in the East, with its elaborate dignity, noble charity, automatic harems and utter indifference to the conventions of Christian morality, more congenial than the more slapdash, mean and hypocritical society of the West.

But in the end the pull of Venice, itself half Oriental, proved too strong. After all, though Clement VII died this year (1534),

Pietro had not yet exhausted the supply of possible patrons in the form of marquesses, dukes and even monarchs. He still had great hopes of Francis I. He had reason, as time went on, to proclaim on a medal he commissioned for himself that 'the princes who are paid tribute by the people pay tribute to their slaves.' This was not altogether ironical. The Scourge could be as servile, when it suited him, as any lackey; he had, after all, spent much of his early life in that capacity. But since he had many masters, he could play off one against another and turn his back on any of them whenever he pleased. In a very real sense, he was able to master his masters.

'My detractors,' he had once said, 'reproach me for some-times lauding princes to the skies and at other times precip-itating them into the depths. I am accused, accordingly, of judging like a fool, though my critics themselves have nothing of the judge in them but their wordiness, while I, Pietro Aretino, when I censure princes, show them what they are, and when I praise them teach them what they ought to be.'

A Private Room at the Top

PIETRO NOW HAD a palace of his own in the most luxury-loving and amorous city in the Christian world, with a greater population of courtesans in proportion to its size than Rome or Paris. Most adventurous young males in both the French and the papal metropolis longed for the embraces of a Venetian courtesan. Pietro, when not engaged in his regular business of blackmail, did not neglect the erotic field.

He had read both *Of The Beauty Of Women* by his old friend Angelo Firenzuola and the treatises on sexual love by his new friend the Venetian scholar and future cardinal Pietro Bembo, at this time official historiographer to his native city and also the librarian of St Mark's Church. Bembo's rapier of wit, on occasion, could cut even deeper than Pietro's combination of axe, cudgel and mace. 'We shall call you Cicero,' said an obsequious friend to the exquisite exponent of Tuscan dialect (though Bembo was born a Venetian) in classical Latin style, 'and him' – Pietro – 'Pliny'. 'So long as Pietro doesn't object,' came the instant rejoinder.

It was the gay Bembo, rather than the grave Plato, who first clearly distinguished between the sensual and the intellectual elements in the intimacies of men with women. Titian, who could be both gay and grave, was to paint them as 'profane' and 'sacred' respectively. 'Being by nature rational,' wrote the worldly-wise Bembo, 'man can at pleasure turn his desires now in the one direction and now in the other, and in these two ways desire beauty, which universal name applies to all things, whether natural or artificial, that are formed in due measure and in good proportion, according to their nature.'

The scholarly librarian, as his position demanded, proceeded to advocate the 'sacred' approach to love.

'Let the lover therefore' – he wrote on – 'shun the blind judgment of the senses, except in so far as he may with his eyes enjoy the physical glories of his lady, her grace, amorous looks, laughter, mannerisms and all the agreeable ornaments of her charm. Likewise with his ears he may enjoy the sweetness of her voice, the harmonies of her speech and of her music, if she playeth upon any instrument. Thus, by means of these two senses he will feed his spirit upon the pleasantest of nourishment, they having little of corporeal appetite in them and being ministers of reason, so that they will prevent his desire for the body to descend to any improperly lascivious sentiment.

'Next, let him obey, please and honour his lady with all reverence, hold her dearer than himself and prefer her convenience and gratification to his own, loving in her no less beauty of mind than of flesh. Let him take care, therefore, not to allow her to fall into any kind of error, but always seek, by prudent warning and good counsel, to lead her into the ways of modesty, temperance and true chastity, seeing to it that no thoughts but those that are pure and free from the least stain of vice find any place in her understanding. By thus sowing virtue in that fair garden of her spirit he will also gather fruits of most admirable behaviour in his beloved and taste them with extreme delight. This will be the genuine procreation of beauty in beauty, which by some is said to be the end of love.'

This was literature. In life Cardinal Bembo was no more 'intellectual' in his dealings with lovely and light-minded ladies than any marquess or *condottiere*. His language closely approximates to that of the 'romantic school' of German philosophers and poets of the first half of the nineteenth century, Hölderlin, the Schlegel brothers, 'Novalis', Fichte, Schelling and Schleiermacher. Bembo, however, had much less influence on the erotic practice of his time and that of the next fifty years than had the predecessors of Schopenhauer, Theodor Storm and Gottfried Keller.

Firenzuola, for his part, opted both in literature and in life for the frankly sensual. Though a churchman, he was a mere abbot and had consequently less to lose by public declarations of susceptibility in this line than an ecclesiastical 'prince'. But he still took the trouble to quote Plato in justification of his amorous transports.

Pietro appreciated the rhetoric of Bembo and Firenzuola. But he remained a far more uncompromising realist than either. He told the philosophic tragedian Speroni:

'I who am no philosopher have again read the discourse which you have philosophically composed on the subject of how harmful it is to do what we wish to do. So far as your argument is concerned with love I will answer it. To those who assert that in following sensual appetite we hasten death I reply that a man prolongs his life precisely in proportion to the extent that he satisfies his desires. And it is I who say that, not Plato!'

It is doubtful whether any other author of the day had the nerve to cast off in this cool fashion the mighty intellectual despot of sixteenth-century lay philosophers. For Plato's reputation overshadowed the High Renaissance in almost every direction taken by scholars, including theology. Even Rabelais spoke against him only through the burlesque characters of *Gargantua*. Here in the sexual context, as in so many others, Pietro often speaks with the very accent of mid-twentieth-century anti-Establishment rebels.

He informed the somewhat dull poet Bernardo Tasso, pedestrian father of the brilliant Torquato, who was to startle all Italy with his literary genius in the 1560s: 'Now comes a second love-affair.'

'It follows on the heels of the first, just as a fourth will come after the third. One's added to another like those mounting debts of mine. Of a truth, some tender fury dwells in my eyes that draws every fair beauty to me and cannot ever be satisfied.'

To another correspondent he wrote, with equally boastful complacency:

'Titian, who is as much our brother as we are his, spoke truly when he said that I am living as gay a life as if my beard were sprouting black from my chin instead of my hair hanging pure white from my temples. I know, of course, that the philosophic wiseacres declare that I lack both decorum and prudence. But you can tell them that they are wrong. For to me it seems that every hour which I spend in youthful ardours takes half a ton off the burden of my age. I do not deny that there are steers of the breed of Plato who do not allow themselves more than one love-affair a year. But for my part if I didn't have forty a month I should really feel worried about my health and believe it to be declining.'

Such jocular exaggerations were of course deliberately calculated not only to shock sober lawyers, doctors or statesmen, but also to raise a laugh from festive artists or soldiers. Pietro's letters are often as specific in the details of his erotic exploits as the autobiographies of twelfth-century troubadours or the memoirs of Cellini or Casanova. A measure of typical Mediterranean bluster must be allowed for, but it is certain that he kept at least a dozen girls, who all appear to have been quite contented with their lot, for a reasonable time at least, at the Casa Aretino.

Their names are recorded at this date as Pocofila, Cecilia, Tina, who was an ash-blonde, Maria Basciadonna, who had prudish manners, Lucrezia Squarcia, Franceschina, who sang like a nightingale, Paolina, with intensely black hair and eyes and a vile temper, Cassandra, Giulia and Marietta d'Oro. Then there was La Zufolina, a nickname which means 'chatterbox'. This animated young woman reflected the twentieth-century taste which her protector so frequently showed, especially later in life, by being a boyish type. Her prattle, he said, resembled 'marchpane and honey on the comb and pinecone tartlets'. Duke Alessandro de' Medici, the far from jealous Pietro swore, had started an affair with her simply to discover whether she was a man or a woman.

Others mentioned from time to time include Angela Sara, whom Pietro first saw as she passed under his balcony in her gondola, where she 'burned' him with her beauty, 'splendidly lascivious, proud and passionate'. She was 'always handsome as the moon and genial as the warming sun'. To Angela Zaffeta, one of Titian's favourite models and reputedly the most beautiful woman in Venice, the great word-manipulator exclaimed: 'I give you the palm among all those who have lived your sort of life. Licence with you wears the mask of decency. You do not make use of your wiles in order to betray men, as most harlots do, but on the contrary fascinate your lovers to such effect that he who spends money on you swears he is the gainer. You distribute your kisses, caresses and nights of love so skilfully that no one is jealous of you and quarrels and complaints never come your way.' Lorenzo Veniero, one of Pietro's more presentable 'secretaries', describes in a poem, (not the first of its kind) a 'symposium' at which Angela Zaffeta is said to have taken on thirty-one lovers consecutively (see page 175).

Certain top-ranking courtesans in the big cities of Renaissance Italy were apt, especially in Venice, to be as difficult of access and as capricious when their favours were ultimately gained as any Hollywood star of the twentieth century. A rejected suitor or one who had been dropped after failure to pass gruelling tests of his generosity or good-nature would sometimes invite the offending lady, in the politest terms, to attend a banquet at his house in her honour. If she were so rash as to accept this compliment, the lavish repast offered would be followed by an orgy in which her person would be forcibly violated by every male guest present in order of social seniority and without the slightest remuneration. She would have no redress in law for such assaults, having regard to her profession, for the participants would take care not to cause her any serious physical injury.

No one who heard of these affairs, not even a magistrate or duly accredited lover, did anything but laugh at them. To take private vengeance on the culprits would be as impracticable as to arrest them. One could not very well poison or beat up such a large number of shameless midnight copulators with a prostitute who had, after all, been stood a first-rate supper beforehand. For the number of the sinners was always exaggerated above the traditional figure of thirty-one; Veniero in the poem just mentioned refers to no less than eighty.

Like Byron in the same city after him, Pietro also greatly relished the company of the excitable and choleric wives of gondoliers and 'servant-girls of twenty-five carats', who were to be found in the streets. From these, and from pseudo-respectable spouses of tradesmen and merchants, from famous and wealthy courtesans and, on occasion, from the aristocracy, he recruited housekeepers and housemaids, cooks and cupbearers, who all became his mistresses sooner or later, as well as those, now and again, of his male servants and friends.

Children were born, stayed on or disappeared. Pietro could not have cared less who might have been their real father. Shrill feminine disputes broke out which he was never at a loss to settle. The Casa was more like an aviary of tropical parakeets than a writer's mansion. He enjoyed the noise, the bright colours, the incessant agitation, not unlike his own prose in effect. And by merely watching and questioning these exuberant females, with his tireless curiosity, he became an authority on hairdressing, cosmetics, false bosoms, high heels and other aids to allurement of the male.

He kept all these resident women well supplied with gold ornaments, silk gowns, red stockings and sweetmeats. They had to be a credit to him when important visitors came, as they did every day. But he rarely paid the recipients of his momentary favours in cash, even the prostitutes. They all knew who he was and felt themselves sufficiently remunerated just by being seen with such an almighty scoundrel as gossip reported Pietro Aretino to be. A reputation for successful swindling, or even more serious crime, could then as now often be a better passport to intimacy with the other sex than mere good looks or well deserved fame and charm. Pietro only possessed, beyond any reservation, charm.

There is evidence, however, that this apparently indiscriminate debauchee experienced a true and deep passion for at least three of his mistresses not named in the above catalogue. In the first place the auburn-haired Caterina Sandella, endowed with a figure which neither Titian nor Tintoretto could resist, acted for ten years as queen of his seraglio. She had married a gay young nobleman named Polo Bartolo, who had a highly developed taste for courtesans. Her complaints on this score to Pietro caused him first to lecture the errant husband and then to counsel Christian resignation to the hitherto faithful wife. The third step he took, naturally, was into Caterina's bed – that is, one he fixed up for her at the Casa.

Bartolo made a fuss to begin with and talked of taking legal action. But he had really lost interest in his consort by this time and was weak enough to allow Pietro's long tongue to persuade him that all was for the best, especially as Caterina's imposing lover not only always treated her with great respect, as befitted her rank, but also introduced her delinquent spouse to lots of other pretty girls not required for the moment by the master of the Casa Aretino.

In 1537 Caterina Sandella bore Pietro a dark-haired daughter. He asked his old friend the painter Sebastiano del Piombo to act as godfather. The child was called Adria, after the Adriatic Sea. A new side to Pietro's character, though not an altogether unexpected one in view of his native geniality, appears in a letter he wrote that year to Sebastiano, who had grown lazy and self-indulgent and had just quarrelled with his former idol Michelangelo.

'It has pleased God that my child should be a girl. Like most fathers I had hoped for a son. Yet is it not the truth that daughters, unless there is some doubt as to their virtue, which we must guard carefully, are the greater consolation? For at about his twelfth or thirteenth year a boy begins to strain at the parental bridle. He runs away from school, refuses to obey and makes those who begot him sorry they did so. His father and mother are lucky if the mischief and threats of mischief with which he assails them night and day go no further. Sometimes his conduct is such that they fear the intervention of the law or of heaven itself. But a daughter is a couch on which those who brought her into the world can take their repose when their hair is turning white. Not an hour passes in which she does not bring pleasure to her parents with her gentle ways and sweet, affectionate care for their needs.

'So as soon as I saw this child, created in my own image, I forgot all my disappointment that she was not a male. I was so overcome by a natural tenderness that I experienced all the joys of fatherhood. I had her baptised in the house because we feared she might die before she had lived many days. A certain gentleman acted as your proxy and held her in his arms in accordance with the Christian custom. The affair was contrived rather hastily, for we thought from hour to hour that she might fly to paradise. But Christ has preserved her to be the pleasure of my later years and a symbol of the life which I received from others and which in turn I pass on to her. For this boon I give Him thanks, praying only that I may live to see her married.

'Meanwhile I must submit to being her plaything. For what are we fathers but our childrens' clowns? The little innocents trample us underfoot, pull at our beards, beat our faces with their tiny fists and rumple our hair. It is for such coin that they sell us the kisses and embraces that bind us to them. Nor could any delight be compared to the pleasure we so obtain, if we were not constantly plagued by the fear that some misfortune might happen to them.

'Each tear they shed, each cry they utter, each sigh that escapes them, cuts us to the heart. Not a leaf falls, not a shred of down floats through the air, but seems a leaden weight that might strike and crush their childish heads. We tremble for their health whenever they are afflicted with the common ailments of nature and are restless at night or lose their appetites. In this way sweetness is mingled with bitterness. The prettier they are, the greater our fear of losing them. So may God preserve my little daughter for me. She is the most engaging creature in the world and I would die to save her pain, let alone real injury. . . .'

It is impossible to imagine that the man who wrote these heartfelt lines was the lecherous and fraudulent monster of legend. Pietro's sensual appetites – except for wine – were certainly enormous and he despised moral restraint on principle. Yet if he never disciplined his passionate impulsiveness, he rarely allowed the natural extravagance of his prose to get out of hand. There is nothing sentimental in the expression of his transports over little Adria. Though barbarous and primitive in his emotions as any savage – except that he never committed physical violence throughout his life – he nearly always controlled his intelligence in the interests of a remorseless realism. He was more remarkable for the amount of contemporary nonsense that he saw through than for any great debauchery or trickery, in which fields many other Italians of his day rivalled or surpassed him.

A certain writer named Antonio Francesco Doni, whom Pietro had befriended and who became unbalanced in his later years, brought to the Casa one day, when Adria was three or four years old, an acquaintance who had expressed a desire to see 'this great man'. Doni, entering the living-room ahead of his companion, was scandalised to see the hoary-bearded colossus rolling on the floor with so young a female. But the visitor soon realised, from the exclamations of the couple, their true relationship. He held back the man behind him with outstretched arm, not wishing the stranger to see their far-famed host in so undignified a posture.

'He has no children of his own,' Doni explained to Pietro. 'He'll think you have gone out of your mind.' 'So I have!' roared Pietro, sitting up and brushing his hair out of his eyes. 'And glad of it, too! That's the best thing children do for us fathers. They prevent us fearing to look silly!'

On another occasion he solemnly lectured Caterina on the bringing up of offspring. She had borne him another daughter, called Austria, in honour of the dominions of the Emperor Charles V of Habsburg with whom he was then on good terms.

'All good qualities are the fruit of the words that define them. They are nourished through the ears which hear their names and the fame of those who are rich in them. Take care, therefore, that if Adria learns less virtue than we should like she at least acquires as much as she can. Then everyone will praise her and she will please everyone.

'My dear Caterina, I beg you not to beg me, I counsel you not to counsel me and I command you not to command me to give Austria to the nurse you first suggested nor Adria to the governess you now mention. The first lacks milk and the second character. Let both my daughters stay in my own home.

'It is wise to take faults in hand before they grow too serious. So please stop Adria being so obstinate. That is the reason why she is so naughty just now. Reprove her gently for it and you will succeed, since she is naturally docile and affectionate, in eradicating her contempt for those paternal and maternal caresses we have hitherto lavished upon her.'

But Pietro, despite his behaviour as a family man, resolutely declined to marry Caterina. He told well-meaning friends that there would be no point in any such ceremony. 'She and her daughters are legitimate in my own heart and that is enough.' Pietro's detestation of all authority, whether secular or spiritual, is once more evident here, again relating him much more closely to the independent mentality of the twentieth century than to the highly legalistic and superstitious, if no longer feudal, society of the sixteenth.

His second serious love-affair, which had a less happy issue, concerned a certain Perina Riccia. She appealed to him not so much as a consort like Caterina, but more as a passionately adored plaything. He compared her with a dryad, a fawn and a nestling chick. So close an observer of appearances could not have been at fault in these images. No doubt she looked something like that. But the implacably realistic lover did not realise for a long time that Perina was at heart nothing more than a shallow, scheming little gold-digger.

They had met either in the spring of 1537, before Adria was born, when Caterina may have required extra female attendance, or else in the summer of 1538, while Pietro was living in temporary exile from Venice at his villa on the Brenta, about twenty miles from the city. Authorities differ, but on the whole the former hypothesis appears the more likely. For a letter dated March 1537 from Pietro to a general's wife named Barbara Rangone, thanking her for the gift of a doublet, announces:

'I am going to give it to Perina Riccia, the wife of one of my young men. She is no less virtuous than if she had been brought up by angels in paradise. She calls me her father and mother and in truth I am both to her. Indeed, I have adopted her. I am keeping her to care for me in my old age, for which there is no cure.'

It is evident that Pietro's latent paternal instincts were already aroused in the case of this extremely young matron. Perina had been married at fourteen, an age regarded as unquestionably nubile in sixteenth-century Italy. Her husband dealt, like many Venetians, in cotton and pepper, 'the white and the black', as the trade was called in Venice. He, like Caterina's spouse, was also called Polo and, by an even stranger coincidence, surnamed Bartolini. He also resembled Polo Bartolo in his vain, frivolous character. All three names were pretty common at this time and place. Nevertheless, the two Polos have caused some confusion among biographers. It is not always clear from Pietro's letters which one he is talking about. But there is much more record of the second Polo –

Bartolini – who actually lived at the Casa with his wife Perina after she had become the master's mistress, or at any rate so great a favourite with him that tongues were wagging.

But the fragile little blonde's health had always been poor, both in Venice's foggy winter and its oppressive summer. August 1537 appears to be the most likely date at which Pietro packed her off, to the villa at Gambarara on the Brenta, accompanied by her ne'er-do-well husband, Caterina Sandella, with whom she – like everyone else – got on very well, and some servants. She had scarcely been gone a week before Pietro asked her to return.

'The gossips' proverb, my dear daughter, tells us that what's done can't be undone. You yourself, Messer Polo and Catherine all asked me to let you stay in the country for eight days. Now ten days have passed and it seems to me almost your duty to come home. I am glad your mother was so pleased to be able to show those simple peasants' – possibly Perina's own friends and relatives – 'her handsome and refined son-in-law and that you were praised for having chosen him for your husband quite of your own accord. I am also glad that you could show off the fine clothes in which you and your husband were dressed, since it is a proof that both of you deserve what you had from me. But now you had better return, unless the Gambararians appeal more to you than the Venetians and the Brenta more than the Grand Canal. I'd never dream myself of staying in the country more than a week . . . otherwise the initial pleasure of finding onself there would soon turn to boredom. . . . So I await you. . . . Your unvarying good-nature, my dear daughter, provides the sweet support of my declining years. Your natural honesty and prudence refresh me after the difficulties I encounter in earning the hundred crowns a month which is all, thank God, we need for living expenses. . . .'

This tactful but firm letter, praising both her and her husband, while reminding them that they both depended upon his earning power, which in its turn depended upon Perina's presence, brought the couple back in a few days. But Perina immediately developed a feverish cough and had to go to bed, where her anxious adorer nursed her devotedly.

The girl's family, however, were by now growing uneasy, both on the score of the young wife's health and her equivocal relations with a quadragenarian employer who had just begun to dye his beard and had a reputation, even in Venice, for promiscuity. Pietro hastened to assure Polo Bartolini's mother that all was well, that her son had nothing to fear in respect of his wife's fidelity, that the young couple got on like a house on fire. . . . But in fact Polo and Perina – shallow young people who married without thinking twice about it – were now quarrelling incessantly. Nevertheless, Pietro was determined to make a go of this rickety set-up. He told one Francesco, a priest who passed as Perina's uncle and perhaps really was:

'God did more for the friendship between you and me when He ordained that Perina should live in my house than even the Bishop of Verona' – Giberti – 'did when he introduced me to you. For if you summed up all the love that four fathers have for their children you would not have even a small fraction of that I bear towards this lively and pretty young woman.'

To still another correspondent he wrote:

'There is no one like her. Her innate goodness causes her ever to live chastely. Yet the pretty child accompanies her virtue with such tact and gaiety that I weep for joy merely to think of it. I swear to you that I have never seen anyone with so sweet a nature. I wish to God the gratitude she shows to me for the little I do for her were shared by some of those I really help. She knows she can have everything I own. And yet she does not put on airs for that reason. Best of all, she and Caterina always walk with their arms around each other.'

It is impossible to suspect Pietro of sentimentality in the case of this cunning little baggage. He was simply besotted for four years by perfectly genuine emotion. He always had an inexhaustible supply of all kinds of feelings except the insincere.

The other two sides of this unstable triangle, however, were more shakily drawn. As Perina's health improved and Bartolini was more and more often away 'on business', she began, naturally enough, to flirt with younger, simpler and slenderer Don Juans than her weighty and sophisticated admirer, whose funds of wit and experience were quite beyond her powers of appreciation. Pietro understood the danger only too well. He redoubled his efforts at a complete physical conquest of the girl, no doubt hoping that his renowned amorous prowess might save her from inferior junior practitioners. To his surprise Perina, with her newly awakened erotic proclivities – Bartolini, it seems, had never been much use to her in bed – yielded almost at once.

But soon afterwards – the exact chronology of all these events is not easy to establish from the conflicting evidence available – young Polo Bartolini disappeared. So did Marietta d'Oro, one of the married kitchenmaids and probably to be included in the list of the poet's casual concubines. So did a lot of silk, damask and ducats. Pietro cursed heartily, then laughed, feeling, no doubt, that he was well rid of such a pair of rogues. But he found Perina in tears. A true Venetian, she howled for days on end from wounded vanity. It was then, perhaps, that the usually ruthless and cynical master of the house, in his pity for her wretchedness, fell much too seriously in love with her. Almost at the same moment she became infected with tuberculosis.

Pietro stopped writing, nursed her personally, and slept at her bedside. She grew steadily worse. The doctors recommended country air. He took her once again to his villa on the Brenta – where according to some authorities they had first met – though in that reedy valley the air was not much better than in damp and feverish Venice. The river Brenta runs into the Lagoon and can be negotiated by gondola from it. Pietro visited his sick mistress constantly all through the winter, that of 1539/40, which happened to be very wet and cold. But he wrote, 'I was no more troubled by the rains which descended on my head, the snow that drifted round me and the winds that moaned than if those sheets of water, curtains of snow and furious gales had been drops of dew, clusters of flowers and gentle zephyrs.'

Eventually Perina was pronounced cured and brought back to Venice. She was nineteen, he forty-eight. They enjoyed a renewed 'honeymoon'. But on a certain morning in July 1541 he awoke to be faced with an example of one of the oldest dramas in the world. Perina was gone. So was one Marco, a handsome, muscular young gondolier[1] he had often employed. Youth must be served and Pietro's beard, despite the dye, was more silver than black now. Perina, in questions of sexual passion, was by this time, more on Firenzuola's side than Bembo's or Plato's.

Pietro may or may not have remembered that he had once agreed cordially with Firenzuola. But outwardly at least he maintained his dignity. In a letter written at this time he declared: 'I blush at my own stupidity just as she should blush for her iniquity'. As for the new lover, 'I pity him'. But he added at an unguarded moment, though with his usual acute prescience: 'I have no water to put out the fire of her love,' — i.e. her love for Marco – 'But perhaps it will go out of its own accord when she realises how unworthy the object of it is.'

On August 1, 1541 Pietro wrote to a sympathetic military friend, Captain Adriano da Perugia:

'I thank you, my dear brother, for offering to regain my beloved mistress for me and chastise her wretched companion. My gratitude is as warm as the friendship which inspired you to make the offer. But I cannot agree to either of its parts. It is my duty to refuse the first and I do not desire the second. I refuse the first because the departure of this misguided young woman has brought me to my senses and I refuse the second because he who keeps Perina away from me frees me not only from a strumpet and a thief but also from expense, shame and sin. Furthermore, if it were possible for one to believe oneself obliged to a ruffian guilty of every vice, I should confess that I owe a great deal to that creature, a poor imbecile nevertheless wicked and reckless in grain. I don't deny that the malevolence with which he may seem to have offended me deserves punishment. But I am content to leave my vengeance to the repeated returns of Perina's malady, which will torment him so fearfully that I feel almost sorry for him. Thank God, my friend, and rejoice at this event with a fervour equal to that which

---

[1] Some authorities insist that he was a gentleman who often passed the Casa in his gondola, or else that he was simply one of the young 'Don Juans' who visited Pietro.

would horrify you if chance had willed that I had been robbed of the light of understanding, the gift of virtue and the reward of my labours, instead of merely losing the vile, vain and pestilential delights of carnal rapture, since to be deprived of such pleasures is a triumph and to obtain them is a loss.'

Pietro's facile pen could sometimes be as eloquent in theological terms as in stage comedy, *reportage* or tavern invective. But he had to be cut to the quick like this to operate so effectively in the style of a Savonarola. The style of a modern gossip-writer, miraculously enough in that generally pompous age, came more easily to him. Ten days later he treated another correspondent, named Ferraguta, to a more secular type of literary exercise.

'Rejoice with me in my deliverance from the vilest servitude that ever fettered a human heart. If in the madness that forced me for five years to adore Perina I had never recognised the shoddiness of my idol I should blush for the poverty of my own self-knowledge, as she should blush for her own iniquity. It seems scarcely credible that one otherwise so attractive should never cease to repay the steadily growing indulgence I showed her with equal measures of hate. Yet as I had no water with which to quench so destructive a flame I waited for it to die down of its own accord. To have acted otherwise would have done violence to my own soul, as greedy boys twist the branches of a young tree in plucking down its fruit . . . fruit which is not yet even ripe. Those who truly love cannot cease to do so whenever they wish. Though love betrays us, we must endure its perfidies. The soul deprived of the presence and attention of what it loves is like a land devastated by the cruel violence of its enemies and only capable, as it confronts the fires that ravage it and the increasing ruin of its possessions, of weeping and wailing, hoping by its tears and prayers to be granted, if not mercy, at least compassion. . . .

'I don't propose to tell you how she came to my house with nothing to her name and how I provided her with all the pomp of silks, brocades, necklaces, pearls, comforts, honour and respect . . . you can read in Volume Two of my

Letters what I told Don Lope de Soria of my attentions to her while she was sick. In view of the ingratitude with which she has repaid so many benefactions, please consider whether woman, the root of all evil, is not made more in the likeness of the devil than man is made in the image of God. For that woman I speak of, in the midst of peace and prosperity, turned her thoughts to crime. Even as she vowed never to cease to honour me and I still believed that the words came from her heart, within that very hour, I say, she fled with a lover who practised openly every sort of vice. The more villainous the sin that she committed, the more pleasure she took in it. Sodomy, blasphemy, lying, cheating, adultery, sacrilege and incest encompassed the acts of her filthy existence as the signs of the zodiac encircle the motions of the heavenly bodies. Let her lover, whose triumph is due to the felonies he perpetrates, consider what the future holds for him at the age of twenty-six, if the wheel, the pincer, the knife, the gibbet and every other instrument of penal retribution permit such a scoundrel, loaded with public guilt as he is and afflicted into the bargain with the French Evil, to live on till he is forty.

'When I reflect on all this I am much gladdened, both because I am now free of that woman and because my recognition of the folly that made me her slave teaches me to care for women no longer than the act lasts which renders them subject to our will. Who thinks otherwise is fit only to change his human condition to that of an animal.'

Pietro rarely allowed himself so reckless and tearful an outburst of wounded vanity. His normal reaction on these occasions was a lofty, scarifying contempt. Yet in this hotch-potch of a letter, which ends in spiteful gabble, his literary instinct did not entirely let him down. The solemn, sententious beginning is followed by two admirable, genuinely moving similes, that of boys tearing at the branches of a young tree to get at the unripe fruit and that of a countryside devastated by invaders. Then the tone grows shrill, but only gradually. It had become second nature to this practised writer to build up his effects to a climax, even when he was personally excited by the subject, rather than blurt all his feelings out at once in a confused explosion. He preferred a constructive, serial process,

leading up to the shock at the end. It is true, however, that
the climax in this case appears vulgar and puerile, hardly
worthy of a mature public figure swindled by the sly little
harlot he had so fondly loved.

Perina's 'fire' – the word was used by Pietro to indicate both
her love of Marco and her hatred of himself – did 'go out' four
years later, when she returned to the Casa obviously the worse
for wear but onwontedly silent and haughty. She would not
say where she had been or how she had lived after being
deserted by her debauched young lover, though she did remark
that he had caught syphilis at some point in their travels.
According to Pietro he already had the disease at the time of
the elopement. But such statements were common items in
contemporary invective.

Pietro did not question her. He received the truant once
more into his noisy household almost as if nothing had
happened. Then the tuberculosis, aggravated perhaps not only
by recent hardships but also by venereal malady, seized her
lungs again. For the third time her devoted 'father' – their
relationship was now really paternal-filial – took her to his
villa on the Brenta. For three months she coughed blood, then
seemed to improve. He returned to Venice for a few days. She
died in his absence.[1]

Pietro exclaimed on hearing the news:
'I am glad that in her last hours she was at least able to
read the letter I sent her. Thus she could know what I really
felt in my heart for her. But I wish death had come more
swiftly. I have always loved her. I love her still. And I will
love her always, till the Last Day passes judgment on the
vanity of the senses.'

Two years later he had not ceased to mourn for her.

The third young woman he loved at this depth, but at an
earlier date, for she died suddenly in 1540, after he had lost
interest in her, differed considerably in character from both

[1] Such is the account given by the learned, painstaking and judicious
biographer T. C. Chubb (*Aretino Scourge of Princes*, New York, 1940). But
later Italian biographers insist that Perina 'died in Pietro Aretino's arms',
a sentence less specific than romantic and one which, moreover, seems to
contradict Pietro's own evidence.

Caterina Sandella and Perina Riccia. Angela Serena lived up to her name by a calm, ethereal presence. Yet significantly enough Pietro often refers to her as 'the Siren' rather than 'the Serene One'. She must have physically attracted him in some way; but he appears rather to have idealised her mentally.

Like Caterina she came of a noble family, Sienese in her case. Like Perina she could be gay. But she also wrote poetry and spoke in the melodious accents of her native city. Unlike both Caterina and Perina she was dark, with a great deal of splendid black hair – turned 'golden' by her eyes, wrote Pietro – and an alabaster complexion which glowed as though illuminated from within. Yet like the other two women she was already married when Pietro first met her. Once again the young husband had certain bad habits, largely homosexual, it seems, which let him in for a lecture – Pietro's usual technique on these occasions – from his older acquaintance.

'Too much money' – wrote the latter to Giovanni Antonio Serena – 'is the reason for those scandalous doings which cause tongues to wag about you. You are healthy and young and have agreeable manners. If you can only keep your vices in check you will lead a long and happy life. Get rid of your false friends and cleave to those who truly care for you. Associate with honourable persons, not with scoundrels. For the former will give you a good reputation and the latter will deprive you of whatever good reputation you may have. But I know I am talking to the wind!'

Intellectual intimacy with the long-suffering wife duly followed. The pair read each other their literary compositions. They discussed philosophy, love, virtue and religion in passionate abstractions like a couple of those early nineteenth-century Germans whom the amateur sages of sixteenth-century Italy so often resemble. He addressed her, for once, in not at all a bad sonnet, as different as possible, anyhow, from both his pasquinades and the *sonetti lussuriosi* he had once composed for Giulio Romano:

'My heavenly siren hath bright flashing eyes
that make her hair gleam even as the sun
and each blue orb to dart the gaze of one

166

who down to earth from angels' chorus flies.
Her cheeks the colour have of a blown rose
that burgeons on a hill all violet-strewn
and when she sweetly speaks, behold, the tune
of parted lips doth rubied pearls disclose.
Her luminous gay laugh and tender glance
do fill with such delight this earthly place
as only when in heaven you'd expect.
Her chaste breasts do forbid all dalliance,
yet she hath nature's wonder in her face
and all that's gracious in her intellect.'

But this idyll could not last. It would have culminated in a
bodily show-down, Pietro being the man he was, if Giovanni
Antonio Serena had not intervened. The Sienese nobility were
more straitlaced about their women than the Venetians.
Angela was summoned to a family conclave and told bluntly
to stop associating with a notoriously loose-living and plebeian
blackmailer. Thereafter she was 'not at home' to the visits of
her 'Platonic' adorer. She returned his letters unopened. She
cut him dead in a narrow street.

In a fury he wrote to Giovanni Antonio:

'Do you realise that there is no other great lady now living
who can boast that the man princes fear has sung of her so
that she will be remembered for ever? Are you aware that
popes, kings and emperors are happy when they are merely
not vituperated by my pen? The Duke of Ferrara has just
sent me a messenger with a pocketful of money merely to
induce me to visit him. A time will come when these very
words I send you, which I deign to sign with my own hand,
will constitute a claim to pride and rank by your descendants!'

Pietro had this letter copied fifty times and despatched it all
over Venice. But most of the recipients simply laughed at this
remarkable form of cover for what they assumed to be a com-
monplace adultery, like hundreds of others committed by the
loftily condescending aspirant to immortality who was known
at the same time to be at the beck and call of any good-looking
girl or boy impudent enough to smile an invitation to him.

For there were nearly as many catamites at the Casa Aretino

as there were pretty girls. About a dozen names survive, including that of the Medoro Nucci who gave away the secret of his master's birth to the Duke of Florence (see page 28). Two or three of these young men had literary tastes and really did act as secretaries to their exceptionally busy master, whose correspondence was enormous in bulk.

One of the grandiose nicknames Pietro invented for himself, 'Secretary of the World', had some justification. It is certain that, despite his own prodigious industry, he must have needed more than one private assistant and 'depository of secrets', which was the commonest meaning of the Italian word *segretario* in the sixteenth century and what Pietro intended to imply by his use of the term in relation to himself. There is no doubt, either, that he kept the noses of these youngsters pretty close to the grindstone when their persons were not otherwise required by him. But the rest of the lads were plain venal spongers of a common Mediterranean type, greedy, idle, treacherous, unscrupulous and definitely bisexual. They were the degenerate Renaissance successors of the 'wandering scholars' of the Middle Ages and the forerunners of the nocturnal haunters of Saint-Germain-des-Prés in modern times.

But Pietro Aretino always loved to be the centre of attention, any attention, from anybody. He treated these worthless scroungers alternately with lavish indulgence and bawling arrogance, both soon over. He married them off to either past or prospective mistresses. They undertook petty swindles on his behalf, in which he did not care to intervene in person. They would always swear on the body of Christ to any lie he wanted a third person to believe. Their extraordinary baseness actually stimulated his imagination when he wished, for the usual – financial – reason, to slander their betters. Most of them came from the gutter. But one or two were black sheep from respectable or even noble families, for instance, Polo Bartolini, the husband of Perina Riccia and a dealer in what was probably his father's business – since Polo himself seems to have been far indeed from the ideal sober merchant – of cotton and pepper. The lesser fry were perpetually robbing their grandly careless master. But occasionally they got well punished by somebody else.

'I shall take good care' – Pietro wrote to a small land-

owner – 'that the shirts you so kindly sent me do not suffer
the same fate as those of crimson and their accompanying
thirty *scudi* which you sent me from Mestre when you
stopped there on the way home from the war in Hungary.
One of my underlings not long ago decided to skip off to
his native Lucca. At three o'clock of a dark night he called
a gondola and placed in it a chest which contained the said
shirts together with other goods of mine worth in all two
hundred crowns. Then suddenly he remembered that he had
left behind a pair of velvet hose. He went back to get them.
When he returned, the gondolier had vanished, with his
gondola and everything in it. The story is now known to
every inhabitant of the obscurest canal in Venice!'

Those who worked as Pietro's secretaries in the modern sense
often imitated their director's own work, like apprentices in a
painter's studio. Lorenzo Veniero, perhaps the best educated
and best bred of them, though a conscienceless rogue, wrote
a couple of poems, 'The Wandering Whore' and 'The Thirty-
one' (see page 159) which were obscene enough to be generally
attributed to the master pornographer. He actually approved
them himself, though he repudiated authorship. He found
another really talented secretary, Ludovico Dolce, who never
pretended to be anything but self-educated, and encouraged
him to scribble away on his own account, as well as copying
the great man's manuscripts and negotiating with publishers.
Dolce, by the time he died at sixty, is said to have produced
no less than a hundred and twelve works, if translations and
adaptations are included.

These two were both useful and loyal to Pietro. But of the
others Ambrogio degli Eusebii from Milan, more fool than
villain, and Nicolo Franco from Benevento (also in Lombardy),
more villain than fool, (see page 35) did their benefactor a
lot of damage. An amusing letter to the first-named, who at one
time wished to enlist in the armed forces of Venice,
incidentally puts Pietro's views on warfare in a nutshell.

'It seems to me that you are mad even to think of enlisting
and absolutely crazy if you carry out your purpose. It is as
bad as if you wanted to be a courtier. Indeed, the court and
the camp are much alike. In the first you come upon want,

envy and premature old age, ending up in a poorhouse. In the second you acquire wounds, imprisonment and hunger. It is all very well to dream that you are a mercenary. For that makes a man one of the heroes of Troy in his own thoughts. But I disapprove of putting those dreams into effect. If all you want is to cut capers under the window of your trollop with your head decked out in feathers, you can do that just as well by stopping here at home. For a yell of "Forward, boys!" in front of a hen-roost you'll get no bread with your supper for a week. For a bundle of rags which will be all your share of the booty or for the captivity which will be your fate whenever God wills it, you'll gain as your reward the right to limp home on crutches and sell all your possessions so as to keep out of the hands of the sharks of moneylenders. You would do well to change your mind. And since you can compose a sonnet better than you can do arms drill I should advise you to go on having a good time at my expense. The big prizes in the lottery of war are very few. Pin that motto on your chest and then, if you like, go and buckle on your tin armour.'

Pietro had not forgotten his experiences on campaigns with Giovanni delle Bande Nere. During the period in 1537 of strained relations between Venice and France he advised another young military aspirant, one Battista Strozzi, how to proceed in battle. With the usual Aretinian imprudence these ironical counsels were offered in mixed company, at a time of general patriotic enthusiasm.

'Never take part in any actual fighting. But if you are on the winning side take care to come well to the front in the pursuit, keep your ears wide open to acclamation and march into the conquered territory with the stride of a heroic giant rather than an ordinary captain. But if your side is losing, come to a halt in double quick time and take to your heels. It will be better for your skin if people say afterwards, "This is where So-and-so ran away", than if they say, "This is where So-and-so fell". Glory is over-rated, you know. When Fame starts blowing her trumpets, in those stately and stirring measures of hers, we shan't hear them if we're dead.'

No one present considered this speech funny. Pietro was obliged to apologise and explain he was only joking. Strozzi himself was most annoyed, though it seems that he afterwards behaved in the field with ludicrous cowardice. There is a story, perhaps put about by Pietro himself, that while the recruit in question was hiding in a haystack and a horse came to nibble at it, the animal took to flight on hearing a roar from within of 'Mercy! I surrender!'

As for Nicolo, who could write and knew Latin, he tried first to cadge from the Duke of Mantua, who passed him on to Pietro in Venice. The penniless scribe arrived at the Casa, practically starving, in the autumn of 1536. The 'Scourge's' need for secretaries was then becoming urgent. His loss of two right-hand fingers in the assault on him by Achille della Volta in July 1925 and the incessant penmanship of the last decade or so was beginning to make writing a torture to him. Moreover, he had recently agreed with Marcolini, his publisher, to bring out an edition of 'The Letters of Pietro Aretino', the first compilation of this kind ever to be printed in Italy. As the letters themselves were also of a sort unprecedented in Italian literature, a vast sensation was expected. They were to be his best, a selection of three hundred out of no less than two thousand, some of which were in the hands of other people.

Nicolo Franco and Ambrogio degli Eusebii were entrusted with the donkey-work of this huge task. All through the long, hot summer of 1537 they toiled on. As a reward Pietro had some of their own mediocre sonnets published. Franco's were by far the best of this poor lot, so much so that Pietro wrote him a letter entitled 'Against Pedantry', which has come to be well known as the Divine One's theory of literary composition and therefore deserves a few paragraphs of quotation.

'Follow the path which life and reality has marked out for you if you wish your words to stand out from the page. Laugh at those who lift hackneyed phrases from other writers. Realise that there is a wide difference between accepting influence and blindly copying. Use the diction that your own ears have taught you. Readers are sick to death of "needs be" and "else thou shouldst". The sight of such expressions in a book raises the kind of snigger that would greet some swaggering fool prancing about on the

Piazza in full armour, with a steel helmet glittering on his head, adorned with waving egret feathers. He would be considered crazy or on his way to a fancy dress ball, though in the old days, of course, this was the correct rig-out for Duke Borso or Bartolomeo Colleoni.

'The best way to rival Petrarch or Boccaccio is to articulate your own ideas in a style as beautiful and skilful as they employed, not to plunder them of this or that idiom, which today sounds stilted, or to transfer whole lines of verse from their works to yours. It is only schoolmasters who suppose that the composition of poetry can be learnt by imitation. When they cackle away over their notes they change grace to rhetoric and the meaningless repetition of blocks of words they have got by rote. Now, O wandering tribe of scholars, know that poetry is simply the communication of a passionate mood of nature herself. It calls for naught but its own fine frenzy. If it lacks that it is like a tambourine without bells or a chimeless church tower.

'Our alchemists, although they employ every device that patience and avarice can suggest, have never yet made real gold, but only wretched travesties of it. Yet nature, without the least effort, produces the pure metal. There was once a wise painter who, when asked what models he copied, pointed in silence to a group of human beings. He meant that he studied only life.

'Consider the nerve and the sinew. Leave the skin to such flayers of it as stand about begging for the alms of fame, though they have no more talent for creative work than a pick-pocket. Be sculptors of what you feel, not word-painting miniaturists.'

The precepts are those of a Harold Ross.

Nicolo at once began to get too big for his boots. He believed he could outdo his master. The first step towards such a victory, he calculated, would be to discredit his mentor even further with the 'establishment' than was already the case. Whether Nicolo Franco arranged for Pietro to be charged with blasphemy by the Venetian magistrates is not perfectly clear, though likely enough. Definite accusations of sodomy, still a punishable offence, though widely practised, rather like exceeding the speed limit in motoring today, also began to be heard.

Whether or not Franco was implicated in these rumours, they were both certainly set going by a known homosexual, the Sienese aristocrat Giovanni Antonio Serena, whose wife, according to common gossip, had been seduced by Pietro. As the law stood at that time and place both blasphemy and sodomy could carry the death sentence, though it was rarely executed. Sodomites in particular might be hanged in a cage suspended from the Campanile in St Mark's Square and left there to die slowly under a shower of rubbish hurled at them by the citizens below.

Reckless though Pietro might be, he saw immediately that it would be no use facing out these charges in the courts. He had made too many powerful enemies in Venice to have the slightest chance of getting off, guilty as he was, like hundreds of other but less prominent Venetians, on both counts. He fled instantly to his villa on the Brenta, where he had once taken or according to some authorities actually met Perina.

Oddly enough, it was the Duke of Urbino, formerly his enemy because he was hostile to Giovanni delle Bande Nere, who came to the rescue of the exile. Completely exonerated, Pietro returned to Venice as arrogant as ever after only a few weeks in hiding. But in August of the same year, 1538, Nicolo almost certainly arranged for the publication, in Perugia, of an alleged 'Life of Aretino' by Francesco Berni, formerly the Secretary of Giovanmatteo Giberti and afterwards a well known comic poet. Berni, the author of the ferocious *sonetto codato* against Pietro of 1528 (quoted on page 132-4), had never ceased to hate him. But he had died in 1536 after rehashing old Boiardo's *Orlando Innamorato* nearly as expertly as Ariosto had continued it, and of course had nothing to do with the scurrilous compilation of legends and half-truths plausibly issued at Perugia under his name, as that of a known and brilliant antagonist of the Divine One.

The well advertised 'Life' significantly included the assertion that Nicolo Franco's 'Letters' were far better than the no less trumpeted collection of Pietro's own. Franco himself, it could hardly be doubted, had written this travesty of a biography of the man who had saved him from starvation but also dared to lecture him on literary composition and already enjoyed the poetic eminence Franco desired for himself. Pietro was not deceived by this trick. In a bellowing rage, he literally flung

Nicolo out of the Casa. The discomfited author tried to enlist one mutual friend after another to enable him to take his revenge.

> 'The Aretine cannot say I am ungrateful' – he wrote to the scholar Francesco Alunno, a correspondent of Pietro's ever since the latter's early days in Venice – 'for even though I admit he sometimes fed me, he cannot deny that I repaid this courtesy sevenfold by the work I did for him. Everyone knows that if it had not been for me he would not have had the skill to translate all those legends of the Holy Fathers which he embroiders and passes off as his own.'

The reference here is to three popular recapitulations of Biblical narratives, by means of which the Scourge had been trying to earn a reputation as truly 'Divine' and also to improve his financial standing. They were entitled 'The Seven Psalms of David', 'The Humanity of Christ' and 'The Story of Genesis'. Only the second-named had any real literary merit, being not unworthy of so notable a master of picturesque and dramatic detail. But both this and the 'Psalms' had been published before Franco reached Venice. No matter. It was known that Pietro was planning further edifying works of this kind and the implication for Alunno was that Franco had already translated the Latin sources of them for his inconsiderate host.

After Nicolo's ejection from the Casa he went on steadily assailing his former patron both in prose and in verse. But he made one bad mistake. He stated in so many words that his old associate Ambrogio degli Eusebii had been and even then was Pietro's catamite. He added, for good measure, that Ambrogio had prostituted his own wife, a charming kitchen-maid, to the 'monster's' lust. Both charges were probably true. But Ambrogio, for once, showed some courage. He went to Nicolo's new abode, called up to his window and demanded his presence in the street for a confidential interview. When the two rogues stood face to face Ambrogio, without another word, whipped out a knife and slashed his traducer across the face, scarring it to the bone. Then, though less severely, he cut the groaning and staggering poet about the body, paying particular attention to the ostentatious mantle, doublet and hose, all no doubt the gifts of the common benefactor of the combatants. Then Ambrogio sent his weeping adversary tumbling into the gutter and fled back to the Casa Aretino.

When Pietro heard the story he duly rebuked his employee, though more paternally than angrily, and then strode off to the nearest magistrate. He convinced that officer easily enough that Nicolo was well served for his treachery and the foul, false abuse he had spewed out against a kind master. On returning home, Pietro dashed off some jeering sonnets about nicely carved up gargoyles and sent Ambrogio to recite them under the invalid's window. The newly fledged swashbuckler obeyed these instructions so zestfully and repeatedly that his employer, who did not want a useful copyist stabbed by bravos when Nicolo recovered sufficiently to arrange such an assault, despatched the exuberant challenger to the French court to collect six hundred crowns recently promised by King Francis to his most eloquent correspondent.

But Ambrogio, prototype of many a blundering young ass in later European comedy, though he duly collected the six hundred crowns, lost them all at cards in the same house in Paris where he had received them – that occupied by Cardinal Gaddi of Ravenna – to a wily fellow-countryman named Strozzi, not the haystack hero but perhaps the later admiral of that name in the service of France.

It occurred to the appalled but not yet desperate courier that King Henry VIII of England, who had also often promised money to Pietro, might make good the loss. In London Ambrogio managed to make his way into the presence of the Lord Privy Seal, Sir Thomas Cromwell, the great Protestant reformer, then at the height of his power as instrument of Henry's dissolution of the English monasteries. But Cromwell told his Italian visitor, rightly or wrongly, that the sum in question, which he named as a mere two hundred crowns, had already been forwarded to Venice. He then condescendingly tipped Ambrogio eighty crowns and dismissed him. The anxious amateur diplomat got the same sort of reception in Flanders and Portugal. His master was known and admired in both countries, but not yet to the extent that their rulers would agree to subsidise him. From Lisbon it was easy for Ambrogio to cross the Atlantic to Brazil, whither, so he tactfully informed Pietro, he would now carry the renown of the Scourge of Princes.

Ambrogio, like the Texan who robbed the bank in the ballad, 'didn't really mean to be bad'. He was a weak, bombastic fool and more than a bit of a hypocrite. But he was not without courage and the will at least to be loyal to his master. Pietro, resigned to idiotic behaviour among those men and women whom he helped to get on in the world, after hearing of Ambrogio's misadventures in Brazil and Paraguay, never heard from him again. Whether the lad made his fortune in South America or succumbed to the alligators, barracuda, snakes and jaguars of that 'green hell', remains unknown. Pietro consoled Ambrogio's wife in the usual Aretinian style, only to see her run off, like other mistresses of his, with one of his young servants.

Meanwhile Nicolo Franco still meditated vengeance. He began by lampooning Lorenzo Veniero, one of the few secretaries at the Casa who permanently retained his employer's respect. Lorenzo, a youth of good family and some learning, lay in wait, with a few aristocratic friends, for the pseudo-Aretino and gave him a good hiding on his own doorstep. Nicolo also received a drubbing from the servants of another nobleman he had slandered in a further vain attempt to acquire the reputation of a 'Scourge'. A well known courtesan whom he had wooed followed suit. The Mantuan ambassador's mistress threatened to tear off his shirt-collar, a gift, actually, from Pietro himself, whom he was traducing at the time in his usual savage style. It is a wonder that Nicolo survived to be hanged for libelling the nephews of Pope Pius IV fourteen years after his old enemy's death.

At last Nicolo decided that Venice was getting too hot for him. The hated Pietro Aretino, despite all his vicissitudes, had by now become firmly entrenched in the city he loved so well. Franco took himself off to Padua, where he coolly told the scholar Sperone, with whom Pietro had not always seen eye to eye, though the two men still corresponded, that he, Nicolo Franco, was 'a friend of the great Aretine'.

Sperone lodged the embittered tramp of a poet for a while, then kicked him out. Few hosts could stand his malicious tongue, since it was unaccompanied by the truly Aretinian sense of humour. Franco had no better success as a schoolmaster in Milan. But at last he got a good job as the head of a Literary Academy at Casale, run by one Sigismondo Franzino, a dependant of the Duke of Mantua. Nicolo owed his introduction there to a story he told of having been driven out of Venice by the jealousy of an inferior but popular writer, a disgusting immoralist named Pietro Aretino.

Soon afterwards the Mantuan ambassador to Venice reported to the Duchy's regents (the Duke himself having died in 1540):

'Messer Titian told me that he went yesterday to the house of the Aretine, finding him in a state of fury. He was dashing off a pamphlet against your lordships and everyone else in the realm. Being reproved by Messer Titian for doing so, he retorted that his enemy Nicolo Franco was being sheltered in the house of Sigismondo Franzino and that Franco had dedicated to the latter a work slandering the speaker. He added, further, that this production was not unknown to your lordships and that he would be revenged upon you by writing and saying publicly all the evil that he can to your discredit. Messer Titian, who is your friend, considers that you should be made aware of this intention of the Aretine and that you should placate his wrath with a few reassuring words and moreover forbid Nicolo Franco to write against him.'

It was not the first time, nor the last, that the prudent artist gave good advice to everyone concerned in Pietro's periodical outbursts. For the friendship between the two men, one so far superior to the other in every kind of civilised behaviour and yet a far less remarkable personality, was deep and unbroken. Titian's interest in the Divine One is enough by itself to prove that the Scourge could not have been the monster he is still regularly represented as being.

The indefatigable Nicolo, a real 'viper', had written no less than two hundred and ninety-eight sonnets in the most foul and offensive terms, vituperating his former benefactor and employer. They were witty enough, in their vulgar way, to make a lot of important people laugh. Pietro felt he must take them seriously. To his now once more formidable enemy's charges of literary incompetence he replied by publishing two excellent comedies. The accusations that he consorted only with rascals and flatterers like himself were met by the second edition of his 'Letters', which included communications addressed to him personally by Bembo, Sperone, Michelangelo and Vittoria Colonna. He also characteristically found time, in the midst of the first fearful shock of Perina's elopement, to indicate more directly his contempt for his assailant, 'one of the leanest, most tattered pedagogues that ever gargled soup . . . a cur kicked from door to door and hated by everyone. . . . I have known frenzy, insolence, envy, spite, wickedness, destructive mania, cruelty, arrogance, fraud and ingratitude in men, but never any so extraordinary as his. . . .'

A letter of July 25, 1541 remarks in rather more dignified phraseology:

'I am bound to consider that the glory I obtain from these ignorant attacks on the part of a man with whom I was once intimate and who has now been abandoned by both fortune and hope exceeds the infamy with which he intended to cover me. Spite, envy and unwarranted presumption are ever snapping at the heels of the decent and the unassuming, who acquire more respect from the assaults of pamphleteers than they would acquire blame from the praise uttered by such creatures. . . . I am ready to admit that Franco's tongue is as glib as his understanding is obtuse. But must I therefore, I who have flayed the names of the great by mighty strokes of the knife of truth, lose my temper if my own modest name is nipped by the teeth of falsehood?'

Like an expert general, Pietro followed up this preliminary bombardment with a dexterous counter-attack. Nicolo had been reckless enough to criticise Charles V for subsiding Pietro. The latter promptly warned the regents of Mantua that as his disgruntled assailant now resided in the imperial dominions – Mantua being part of the Holy Roman Empire – the Emperor would believe the Mantuan State itself to have at least consented to this attack on its overlord. Pietro added to certain unofficial representatives of Mantua in Venice expressions of his grief and anger that so good a friend of the Gonzaga family as himself should be exposed to such dastardly calumnies emanating from their own territory. He went on to threaten direct action by both Charles and the Pope. But these menaces were ignored by Cardinal Ercole Gonzaga, chairman of the regents.

Pietro now turned his guns on the culprit's own person.
'I will now give you some bad news, you scoundrel' – he wrote to Franco – 'which is that I now find myself able to do more than ever. My health is so flourishing that you would die of fury if you merely laid eyes on me. Your writings against me arise more from your jealousy than from any elevation from which you imagine you can look down on me. Yet, because I once rescued you from starvation I can't be bothered hating you. If you want to be as famous as I am, write against vice, not against virtue, tell the truth instead of lying and stop shaming your talents by using them to attack a man who is as good as you are evil. Poor, silly little rapscallion that you are! (*"Poveretto, poverello, poveraccio, poverino"!*).'

Yet characteristically, when Nicolo fell ill in 1545, he wrote to the invalid:

'It would be right for me to rejoice at your misfortune, just as you lament my welfare. But I am so generous by nature that I feel very sorry for you. Take good care of yourself and hope for the best. The true doctor is God. Fortify your conscience and trust in Him. Then you will recover from your fever.'

Pietro certainly enjoyed his own magnanimity. It gave him that personal sentiment of superiority without which he could not live. But the impulse to it was genuine, as nearly all his dealings show. On the other hand, at this same time he told another correspondent:

'I am sick to my very soul to think that this fellow, whom I need not name, may be dying. I want him to live and suffer from the envy that gnaws him. If he dies, how can I look forward to my sweet revenge when he at last realises what a miserable villain he is?'

This was a typical half-serious, half-humorous Aretinian idea. Pietro must have known that there was precious little chance of Nicolo Franco repenting, even on a death-bed. But he could not resist representing himself to others as outdoing everyone else in implacable malignity.

It was not Franco, however, but his terrible opponent who died first. Nicolo's last words, in 1570, were as defiant as ever. 'This is too hard a punishment,' he said to the papal officers as the rope was tied round his neck on the Sant' Angelo bridge. Next moment the skinny, white-haired, white-bearded corpse, 'of venerable aspect', was dangling from the parapet. He had written so much and so readably about the man who had quite justly ejected him from the Casa Aretino that Pietro's poor press since then is largely based upon the Beneventine vagabond's vindictive abuse.

The Garden and the Desk

FORNICATION AND SODOMY, fraud and swagger, high politics, wordy warfare and material ambition were not the only fields in which Pietro Aretino, that 'literary brigand', as Titian called him, operated both as promoter and censor. Like nearly all Italians, especially Italians of the High Renaissance, he took plenty of time off from preaching and rascality to attend to man-made beauty.

Business men like Cosino de' Medici the Elder, stag and woman hunters like Francis I, ruthless political schemers like Ludovico Sforza, the 'Moor' of Milan, much admired and even paid for the paintings and sculptures of artists like Paolo Uccelli, Donatello, Cellini and Leonardo da Vinci. If these patrons had not loved art as well as ducats the ringing names of many fifteenth- and sixteenth-century Italians of supreme inventive genius would never have survived their own day.

Pietro Aretino, both patron and artist in his way, was no exception to this rule. But he added to his interest in art of all kinds a good deal of technical understanding of painting at least and an even greater capacity for making friends with men of creative talent, both major and minor. These two qualifications in him were much rarer than the general enthusiasm among his contemporaries for agreeable-looking objects. The practical craftsmen who made these found in Pietro much flamboyance, but a solid base of common sense beneath it. They saw that he had plenty of cunning; but it was seldom exercised at their expense. They recognised a dissimulation which anyone but a pompous prelate or conceited duke could see through at a glance; but they found that its perpetrator himself laughed at it. Above all, they could detect in their rumbustious acquaintance nothing at all of what could be called moral cowardice, a vice peculiarly distasteful to persons of an original cast of mind.

According to Pietro's own account of his investigations into pictures, Raphael was the first great painter who took any notice of him when he arrived in Rome. Perhaps Perugino, who had been Raphael's earliest master and whom Pietro must have met, if only casually, in Perugia, recommended the boy. Pietro was then merely a lackey in Chigi's palace, though a very talkative, knowledgeable and for that reason highly favoured servant of the magnanimous banker.

Pietro had also met, even before he reached Rome, Giorgio Vasari, a relatively mediocre practitioner in the studio but a jovial chatterbox and an industrious student of the lives of other painters. Sebastiano del Piombo was another almost life-long friend of Pietro's. It is highly significant that none of the many persons with whom the Scourge quarrelled permanently, after acquiring some degree of intimacy with them, were men of any real distinction, if one excepts the dubious case of Nicolo Franco.

As an indefatigable supporter of the visual arts Pietro, partly for the reason that he was not a man of rank, surpassed almost all the prelates and lay princes of his day. An example of his patience is furnished by his treatment of another Aretine, the goldsmith and sculptor Leone Leoni. Some critics thought him the equal of Cellini, who therefore became his deadly enemy. But Leoni's violent and incalculable temperament, closely resembling Cellini's own, gave his would-be protectors a lot of trouble.

The Aretine goldsmith complained to his powerful fellow-citizen that Cardinal Bembo had paid Cellini more for a wax model than Leoni himself had received for a fine portrait of the prelate in bronze. Pietro very reasonably pointed out Cellini's at that time superior reputation and personal friendship with the Cardinal, and counselled prudence and taciturnity. At a somewhat later date he gave the younger man, in the guise of an unctuous sermon, a leaf from his own well tried notes on the practical value of Christian forgiveness and charity. The fierce Florentine, Leoni's hated rival, happened just then, as the result of one of his many offences against law and order, to be languishing in a Roman gaol. Pietro recommended Leone Leoni, who was also in Rome at that time, to plead with the Pope for his fellow-goldsmith's release:

'Fra Tommaso, who brought me your letter, gave me the good news that you study no less to serve God than to delight your fellow men. You are right to do so, for all our knowledge and our capacity for labour come from Him. It is He Who moves your graver on the coin, inspires your genius in planning the design and mercifully accords you the honour you acquire with your chisel. . . . Through the grace of Jesus Christ the Pope gives ear to accounts of your talents. You have the treasure of a wife and children. He who persecuted you is in prison. You are in Rome, the glorious patroness of the arts, the mother of their fame and the source of wealth and fortune for their practitioners. Most important of all, you are young, in good health and admired. But, as I have already told you, such blessings must be attributed to the benevolence of God. If you take credit for them yourself you risk the enmity of fate. Hitherto you have prospered and you will continue to do so while you forgive those who injure you no matter how grave their offences may be. For the Son of the Most High is best gratified by proofs of the same spirit which led Him to forgive those who crucified Him and also to pray His Father to forgive them.

'I beg you therefore to petition the Pope to set your adversary free. The unfortunate man is an able craftsman and a hard worker. He was formerly beloved at the papal court. In addition, you owe more to him than to the Pope himself. For his Holiness would never have known the sum total of your abilities if the competition of so lofty a soul had not borne witness to them. It is certain that when he boasted that he would kill you he robbed himself of his own reputation and transferred it to you.'

The move advised would certainly have been a shrewd one. Cellini was raving to his gaoler at that very moment that he would kill the 'poisonous' Leoni as soon as he got out. But he could not very well carry out such a threat if he owed his freedom to the prospective victim.

Still later, in May 1540, Leoni himself tried to murder one of Cellini's friends, a German employed at the Mint in Rome. But the assailant was arrested before he could do more than slash his adversary's face. The bloodthirsty sculptor was at once imprisoned, racked and, when he stubbornly refused to confess that the German's accusations of counterfeiting coinage were true, sentenced to lose his right hand. This cruel punishment,

which would have meant lifelong beggary to the artist, was
however countermanded at the last moment. Leoni, by way of
alternative, was despatched to the galleys for as long as he
might survive the fearful harshness of that existence. To this,
deprivation of his right hand would perhaps have been prefer-
able. But coining was regarded as a most serious offence in the
sixteenth century, almost on a par with assassination.

Pietro used his influence with the imperial admiral, Andrea
Doria, to get the unhappy sculptor released from the oar. But
three years later the incorrigible Leoni was hiring bravos to
cut the throat of an assistant who had declined, no doubt with
reason, to return to his service. He was again arrested, in
Ferrara, and this time condemned to be hanged outright for
coining the Duke's money. Pietro again intervened. He saved
the convicted felon's life merely by persuading the art-loving
Ferrarese ruler, Ercole d'Este II, that Leoni was too skilled a
carver to be cleared off the earth before his time.

The Scourge's deep and genuine affection for all forms of
plastic creation led to the second great friendship of his life,
that with Titian. The two men instantly felt unquestioning and
unshakable admiration for each other. They seem to have
agreed about everything, from types of feminine beauty to the
misdeeds of princes, as well as in all problems of painting
technique. The sober and comparatively respectable Titian
even agreed, as already noted, to join Pietro's schemes for
blackmailing the irremediably delinquent rulers of Italy. At
the same time Pietro swallowed, without the slightest resent-
ment, lectures by the artist on his immorality which he would
not have put up with for a moment from any other man.
Titian, in his turn, meekly accepted Pietro's strictures on his
'greed' in turning out too many pictures too hastily and on
his 'pride' in not answering those famous Aretinian letters. In
one of these Pietro wrote to the painter, who was on a visit
to Augsburg:

'Although I have only received one letter from you since
you reached the imperial court, I will not yet believe that
the favours of his Majesty have so filled you with conceit
that you are scornful of old friends. Yet if that which I
cannot believe is true, I deplore your success instead of
congratulating you upon it. For good fortune becomes a

misfortune when it makes a man over-pleased with himself. Still, even if ambition has turned you into a snob, I advise you to act towards me with your accustomed modesty. I would certainly let the Emperor know what I thought of him if he treated me too mistrustfully. So clear yourself of all my suspicions of your motives by writing two or three lines to me. Meanwhile Sansovino and I send you our regards.'

Such a letter, full of real affection under the asperity, could not have been composed by a cynic. The two men, in fact, often addressed each other quite sincerely as 'brother'. Pietro once said: 'Titian is I and I am Titian. Titian is another myself.'

This statement was of course absurd presumption. The artist's professional gifts and the range and depth of his mind, to say nothing of his moral elevation, put him far above the level of journalism at which Pietro operated. One has only to look at the contrasting faces of the two 'brothers', both painted by Titian himself, to recognise the confident effrontery, the excessively coarse sensuality, of the younger man as in a different class altogether from the grave, thoughtful brows, the piercing yet melancholy eyes, of the incomparable master of pictorial vision. The former had little true sympathy, though he often pretended to have, with persons unlike himself. The other looked as deeply into his sitters' souls as into his own. At the bottom the distinction is that between studious contemplation and ruthless activity, between dreamer and fighter.

There were other differences. The austere Titian kept his large household under strict discipline. Pietro let his servants revel, rob and cheat him as much as they liked. They treated him as their equal or at best *primus inter pares*. The painter rebuked Pietro sharply for this folly – but the other answered coolly:

'The fact that my staff take advantage of me doesn't make me angry but happy. Just as Philip of Macedon, the father of Alexander the Great, prayed to the gods at the height of his victorious career for a little humiliation in his success, so I, who am feared rather than loved by the great ones of the earth, am glad that my grooms and kitchenmaids do not respect me. For that situation prevents me from getting a swelled head.'

This attitude was far from being that of a 'democrat' in the modern sense of the term, which has actually been applied to Pietro by some recent biographers. The strong strain of vulgarity in Pietro, a 'man of the people' himself, caused him to enjoy coarse company. But it would never have occurred to him that grooms and kitchenmaids could be in any sense his 'equals'. Like his dead friend Giovanni delle Bande Nere, who got on so much better with halberdiers and dragoons than with his own grand relatives and their rivals, Pietro appreciated a frank simplicity when he could find it, which was not often. But whereas the soldier had been frank and simple himself, Pietro was nothing of the kind, any more than a twentieth-century duke entertained by the earthy opinions of his gardener. A number of men of far greater genius than Pietro, for example Machiavelli and Peter the Great of Russia, have shown similar traits. Titian, however, the loftiest genius with whom Pietro was ever intimate, exhibited little trace of them. His own family being modestly distinguished, he held the conventional views of his time regarding those of humbler social position.

The artist, again, was happily married when Pietro first met him. After the death of his wife Cecilia in 1530 his sister Orsa came to keep house for him and he remained unaffected by serious love-affairs till the end of his long life. Pietro, on the other hand, kept a harem and fell deeply in love three times. The painter's temperament was equable, the writer's explosive. The bond between these otherwise so divergent personalities lay largely in their mutual relish of intelligent and amusing conversation in not too numerous a group – four for choice – gathered in agreeable surroundings.

Titian's garden could not have been more suitable as the scene of such meetings. It was situated in the Birri quarter near the island of Murano with its 'thousands of little gondolas, aboard which lovely ladies sang and played various musical instruments'. The grammarian Priscianese described one such occasion as follows:

'On the day of the Kalends of August I was invited . . . to the delightful garden of Messer Tiziano Vecelli, an excellent painter as everyone knows. Some of the most original wits of the city were present, for example Messer Pietro Aretino, that new miracle of nature, Messer Jacopo Tatti, known as Sansovino, Messer Jacopo Nardi' – a writer of comedies – 'and myself. . . . You could still feel the sun's heat but the place was well shaded. . . . Our dinner was no less well planned than plentiful . . . the viands most delicate and the wines most delicious. . . .'

Priscianese read out to the company a letter he had received describing a banquet, also held in a garden, where the host, a pedantic old prelate named Ridolfi, discussed literature. Titian's guests 'were a little annoyed at the incivility, not to say spite', shown in this address, when Ridolfi

'thrust the bitterness of grammatical argument into the pleasures of dining and merry conviviality. That handsome devil Aretino grew angrier than any of the others when he realised that the Tuscan tongue was being attacked. If we had not restrained him I think he would have been most cruelly abusive. For he called furiously for pen and paper while continuing to indulge in a flood of maledictions. But at last we calmed him down and the meal ended in gaiety.'

When Pietro was not present he took care that his letters should be. They were delivered to one or other of the guests or to Titian himself and read aloud. They were guaranteed to introduce an acid note into dialogues which in the nature of the case were liable to grow complacent, rhetorical or senti-mental. When he did show up and the talk consequently grew censorious, he was likely to call for writing materials, as Priscianese notes in the passage above, in case his own violent contributions should be lost for ever to the world.

As for feminine presences, they were welcome if they could sing and play the lute as well as kiss. 'If we are continually gay,' Pietro told his friend, 'old age, which is the spy of death, will not report that we are going grey.' Sansovino was generally there, with his ape-like head and short red beard. His nervous-ness and unaccountable changes of mood, as well as his appearance, contrasted strongly both with the somewhat aloof and self-contained behaviour of Titian and the Pietro's impulsive energy. One of the latter's gifts in mixed company was his miraculous ability to transform a rather vulgar if famous courtesan for the time being into a great lady.

Both Pietro and Sansovino, however, were as free in their public romps with courtesans as Titian was disciplined, though the latter was no puritan. 'I marvel at him,' quoth Pietro. 'For no matter with whom he is or where he finds himself, he always maintains restraint. He will kiss a young woman, hold her in his lap or fondle her. But that's as far as it goes. He sets a good example to us all.' Titian preferred his amorous dalliance, to which he devoted a considerable part of his leisure, to be in private.

Pietro's delight in children and the ease with which he got on with them had plenty of scope in Titian's household. The painter's eldest son Pomponio was an especial favourite with the huge and hugely bearded visitor, whose views on the treatment of 'youth' were as unconventional, for his time, as any modern theorist's. To one desperate parent he wrote:

'If there is such a thing as right, then certainly the wrongs done to you by your son would justify you in cutting him off without a shilling. Yet, if you stopped to think what you yourself did at his age, wouldn't you forgive him and also have a good laugh? You ought to pay him a hundred per cent interest on the money you have saved for him, spending the lot on clothing him extravagantly and paying his expenses with girls.'

When Pomponio, at the age of twelve, declined to submit to any further formal education while on holiday at the artist's villa, Titian asked the Scourge to reason with the young rebel. Pietro seized his pen at once.

'Your father' – he wrote to the boy – 'has just brought me the greetings you sent me. They pleased me almost as much as the two partridges that came with them. Incidentally, I gave the latter to myself, since Messer Titian told me to present them to some deserving gentleman. So you see how big-hearted I am. . . . Good health to you and my best wishes. But now I have some very bad news for you.

'It is time to get back to work. For, so far as I remember,

there are no schools in the country and in winter Venice is a very pleasant place. So do please come back here. Now that you are twelve, your Hebrew, Greek and Latin will drive all the learned scholars in the world to despair, just as your splendid father routs all the other painters in Italy when he puts brush to canvas.

'That's all! Now keep warm and enjoy your supper!'

This communication, with its shrewd emphasis at the beginning and end on food, which interests most boys of twelve more than anything else, and the midway appeal to the combative, ambitious instinct which is their next most conspicuous trait, proves how well this 'foul-tongued roisterer' understood the puerile mind. He was very like a boy himself in his automatic concentration on the satisfaction of his appetites and his craving for recognition by others.

Later on, when Pomponio, through Pietro's influence, had been given an abbey by Pope Paul III, the pampered young churchman behaved so scandalously when off duty that Pietro again intervened with a carefully composed homily.

'I realise the truth that old age is something that young people cannot believe is really possible, just as to old people youth is an extravagant fairy-tale. That is why youth laughs at old age when it should really weep and why old age weeps over youth when it should really laugh. I tell you this simply to prevent a young man like yourself from taking a moral lecture lightly merely because it comes from someone like me. Now, the other day your father came to my house in such deep grief that it pained me to see him. He said he wished you would change your mode of life. I must myself confess that to me your conduct resembles one of those vulgar farces which actors enjoy more than the audience. You should return to your studies and allow your fine mind to prove that it is the equal of any scholar's. It is all wrong that the wealth amassed by the brushes, the toil, the wisdom and the long journeys undertaken by so great a man as your father should be dissipated in riotous living. It would more become you to double the funds you have received.'

But not even this eminently tactful and morally unanswerable rebuke did any good. Pomponio did not mend his ways. At last Titian had him deprived of the canonry to which the Duke of Mantua, at Pietro's request, had appointed him. There is no more of interest to record of Pomponio. The Scourge no doubt thanked his lucky star that he had only daughters to look after.

Titian himself had not merely to thank his formidable friend for trying to help him in the hopeless task of whitewashing a black sheep of a son. The serious, modest and unbusinesslike painter was truly indebted to Pietro in his professional career. Bernhard Berenson wrote in *The Venetian Painters of the Renaissance*: 'Titian would scarcely have acquired such fame in his lifetime if that founder of modern journalism, Pietro Aretino, had not been at his side, eager to trumpet his praises and to advise him whom to court.' The Divine One's reputation as an art critic indeed stood high in Venice, a city of painters if ever there was one. He had the gift of laying down the law in these matters, and posterity has nearly always confirmed his judgment. Some of his casual notes on art are better worth remembering than most made in his time:

'Those who prefer Michelangelo are for the most part sculptors who think only of his draughtsmanship and force. They consider that the light and graceful manner of Raphael is too facile and hence not really artistic. They do not realise that ease is the best argument in favour of art and the hardest to acquire.'

'Leonardo was equal to the greatest. But his work suffered because his conceptions were so lofty that he was never satisfied with what he had done.'

'I grant that foreshortening is difficult. But it does not follow that the more often foreshortening is used the more credit the artist should be given. A painter should not demonstrate one capacity alone but all that he has.'

'The object of a picture is mainly to provide pleasure. So the practitioner who does not delight will stay unknown to fame. Yet I do not mean by delight that which pleases the vulgar eye or even that of a person who sees the painting in question for the first time. I mean by delight that thrilling sentiment which increases by familiarity.'

'Above all things the painter should avoid much revision

of his work. I believe that Apelles once said that although Protogenes was his equal and perhaps his superior in most tasks that had to do with painting, there was one respect in which Apelles himself could claim superiority. He always knew when to stop.'

'The three most important elements in making a picture are conception, design and colour.'

These remarks may be truisms today; they were not so in the sixteenth century.

Pietro realised that Titian was as great a painter as any that had ever lived. He said so, like the good journalist he was, in and out of season, telling Cardinal Salviati, for instance, that Titian's landscape drawing was superior in its naturalism to Dürer's and calling the attention of Count Maximilian Stampa to the former artist's skilful treatment of hair, skin, clothing and animals. He went on to buttonhole the Doge himself on Titian's behalf, to say nothing of visiting dukes, marquesses, counts, barons and prelates. One of the artist's most astonishing masterpieces, the portrait of Pope Paul III, now at Naples, owed both its inception and its instant renown to Pietro's tireless advocacy.

It was the same with the famous portrait of Charles V. Pietro shrewdly advised the painter not to charge too much for this production. The honour of the commission would be worth untold gold to him.

'Not Apelles nor Praxiteles nor any painter or sculptor of kings and princes could boast of having received gold or jewellery that even approach in value the reward your genius has obtained from his Majesty. That he deems you worthy of an invitation at a time of such great disorder is the finest tribute that could be accorded to an artist. For it proves that he considers you more important than any of the leagues or alliances he is obliged to contract against a world of enemies. He once said that he desired no portraits or statues to put him on a level with gods, but that he would be much better pleased to be carved and painted in the hearts of the good and wise. Yet now he has consented, merely as a compliment to your unique gifts, to your recording his appearance. Go therefore to him and, kneeling at his feet, revere him with all your being. And render your homage in my name also.'

It is true that Titian already had a high reputation, both as man and as painter, when Pietro first met him, the artist being then probably (for the date of his birth is still not certainly established) in his late forties. It is also true that Titian's high reputation was of advantage to Pietro's own much more ambiguous fame. Nevertheless, that energetic and colourful tongue and pen enormously enhanced Titian's standing, made him a fashion, almost an idol, the only unquestionable immortaliser of 'princes'.

The artist, for his part, had a good influence on his noisy, not over-fastidious friend, who began to show less rascality and more refinement in his general behaviour. Before Pietro encountered Titian he could not have written the extraordinarily perceptive landscape in words he set down for the greatest master of brushwork then living:

'Having eaten alone, my dear friend, which is contrary to my custom, or rather having eaten in the company of a vexatious quartan fever which did not even permit me to taste my food, I arose from table fed with the same despair in which I had sat down. Then, leaning my arm upon the window-sill and my chest, in fact almost my whole body, on my arm, I gazed upon the marvellous scene out of doors.

'An endless number of craft, some occupied by foreigners and others by our own citizens, entertained not only the onlookers but also the Grand Canal itself, which in its turn entertains all who are borne upon its waves. Near to me two gondolas, each manned by famous oarsmen, were racing, to the great excitement of the spectators. From the Rialto, from the fishmarkets, from the Santa Sofia wharf and from the Casa da Mosto, crowds of them watched the contest.

'After these groups had dispersed, joyously applauding what they had seen, I who stood there almost hating myself and scarcely knowing what to do with my thoughts turned to look upon the sky. Never since God created it had it seemed to me so beautiful in its subtle pattern of light and shade. Anyone who wished to record the quality of that atmosphere would have been consumed with envy at not being you. Read on and you will understand why.

'To begin with, the houses, though they were of stone, appeared phantasmal. The air in some directions looked transparent and alive, in others thick and dead. You must imagine, if you can, how I wondered at the clouds, which after all were nothing but condensed humidity. In the middle distance some seemed to touch the roofs, while others retreated far away. To the right they resembled a poised mass of greyish-black smoke.

'I was amazed at the variety of their hues. Those near at hand burned like fiery suns. Those in the distance glowed dully, like half-molten lead. The world's ingenious brush-strokes lent perspective to the atmosphere in recession behind the palaces, just as in one of your own landscapes. The bluish-green in some places and the greenish-blue in others seemed really to have been composed by nature with a capricious yet wonderfully skilled hand, lightening or subduing the tones in accordance, it appeared, with a personal choice.

'I who know your brushes to be the soul itself of nature exclaimed three or four times in succession: "Ah Titian, where are you?" I would take an oath by all that I hold sacred that if you had painted what I have just described men would have stood rooted to the spot with the same stunning admiration I felt as I beheld the scene and realised that its miracle would not last.'

The inspiration here is obviously genuine and the expression as elegant as Pietro ever achieved. He was now at the top of his form as a writer and it was during this last half of his life, the Venetian period, that the bulk of his voluminous literary works, good and bad, appeared. The most important of these productions were in 1532 two cantos of the epic *Marfisa*, in 1533 the comedy entitled 'The Master of the Horse', a light farce about a woman-hater, and in 1534 the first volume of the *Ragionamenti*, scurrilous dialogues of breath-taking vivacity and daring, probably the frankest pornography in Italian literature. In the very same year, characteristically enough, a rehash in popular language of the 'Seven Psalms of David, came out, followed in 1535 by another religious work called 'The Humanity of Christ'. In 1536 the second volume of the

Ragionamenti appeared, in 1537 the first volume of the 'Letters', equally vivid and arresting, and in 1538 a third pious tract, 'The Story of Genesis'. In 1540 a third comedy, 'The Hypocrite', was published. The first, 'Court Life', had been written in Rome before the author's flight from that city in October 1525. In 1542 a fourth comedy, 'La Talanta' (the name of a courtesan) and the second volume of the 'Letters' were issued. In 1545 came a curious and entertaining dialogue, 'The Talking Playing-Cards' – it will be remembered that Pietro would never allow gambling in his house – and in 1546 a fifth comedy, 'The Philosopher', the tragedy *L'Orazia* and the third volume of the 'Letters'.

Of these last works *L'Orazia*, a verse play in hendeca-syllables about the Horatii and Curiatii, whose quarrel is related by the ancient Roman historian Livy, has something of the lively and picturesque quality of the Letters. Here and there it may remind a British reader of Shakespeare's historical dramas, though there are no comic interludes. The whole tragedy is expressed in a grave, careful style quite new for Pietro, which he never repeated. Nor had he previously used it for his unfinished epic *Marfisa*, where the treatment is merely a disastrously clumsy imitation of Ariosto's magnificently romantic fantasy, so dignified even in its humour and so surely touching in its pathos.

L'Orazia, however, while not so grand as Corneille's refurbishing of ancient Roman themes, is a good deal more convincing in its realism and altogether more humane in sentiment. Without being Pietro's masterpiece, as he himself believed, it at least affords one more proof of his literary versatility and the vein of compassion that was never far below the surface, even in his most sardonic moods. It is likely that he hoped to attract the attention of Pope Paul III by this patriotic excursion into the glories of ancestral Rome, just as the religious tracts already mentioned were designed to counter the author's reputation among conventional churchmen as a mere impious pornographer.

Some idea of the way in which the stock characters of ancient Roman comedy are brought up to date in the above-mentioned plays may be gathered from the following passages. In 'The Hypocrite' a servant describes his young mistress, aged twenty-four, by noting:

'There is no font of holy water that she doesn't dirty with her fingers nor altar-step that she doesn't wear down with her knees nor saint's statue that she doesn't tire out with her prayers. She gets wind of every mass that's going, calls at every monastery and sweeps every convent into her net. She talks to everyone she meets in the street, asking soldiers for the latest news about the war and reminding urchins of all the spankings and kisses she has given them. She tells all the children that "Your mother and I are the greatest pals", teaches choirboys how to modulate their responses to the priest, peasants how to plant their cabbages, tailors how to cut their cloth, grocers how to pound their pepper, widows how to pray for the souls of their husbands and the plague how to eat away its victims down to the very bones of their ghosts.'

In *La Talanta* a snatch of dialogue between Branca the parasite and the boastful soldier Captain Tinsa runs: ' "Who wouldn't learn to be a good fighting-man in your company?" "All I need is the tarara of the trumpet!" "Ay, that's true." "Then we'll seize the darts Messer Cupid has plunged into our hearts for our delight and as soon as we have taken our revenge by sticking them in the spleen of anyone who wants them we'll be able to bind our prisoners and march them off in the fetters of love." '

In 'The Philosopher' the learned man's lackey delivers a monologue which could hardly have been bettered by Proust. 'I was just walking away wondering why on earth the philologist had bade me arm in such haste and rush off at such a rate, when I almost croaked of a confounded thirst that I got when I heard someone say to his companion that none of us drinkers really know how to drink, since something other is needed than just gulping the stuff down full of brotherly love. He said that wine should be poured out on musical principles. We should hold out the goblet at a certain distance from our chests and watch the liquor glittering, twinkling and fizzing, delighting in the pearls it produces, quite big at first then growing tinier and tinier till they disappear. He went on to say that we ought to drink from a perfectly full cup, taking care not to spill a drop, because by absorbing all that rich juice in two successive sips of the parted lips, wrinkling the nose and raising the eyebrows to signalise the solemnity of the occasion, till half of a large beaker has been drunk – a small one not enabling us to perform such miracles – our palate is refreshed, our gums revived by the liquid and our teeth cleansed, while the tongue as it explores the little lake of wine, which must not be swallowed at a draught, obtains the same satisfaction as the teeth, gums and palate. Finally, when the mind instructs the legs, the body the mouth, the mouth the thirst and the thirst the state of confusion arising from the desire to drink the whole glass up, the throat and gullet work together to guarantee wisdom. Whereby the belly, the lungs, the liver, the spleen and the bowels, thus activated, rise to float upon a sea of bliss. In this condition the senses of the spirits and the spirits of the senses render the face of the drinker rubicund, hot, cheerful, proud, bright, calm and vigorous. Such favours lend strength to the tongue, sparkle to the eyes, revival to the breath, enlargement to the veins, animation to the pulse, expansion to the skin and reinforcement to the nerves. Such was the discourse of that excellent man, in which he summed up the perfection of the grape, so light in its base, so gentle of body and sparkling in action and in which there is also a certain stimulating element which kisses, bites and kicks.'

When Pietro turns from such subtle sensuality to spiritual topics, his religious highlights cannot be altogether dismissed as devout rhetoric; there is real and unsentimental feeling in them. He always remained a good Catholic at heart, if by no means always in conduct. In 'The Humanity of Christ', when he comes to the arrival of the Virgin at the foot of the Cross he writes:

'Alas, behold the Virgin! Alas, that she should appear, alas, that at her appearance I am so afflicted by the grief that afflicts her that memory evades my subject, my subject my skill, my skill my pen, my pen my ink and my ink my paper!'

The account of the tempest at the Crucifixion has true eloquence:

'Meanwhile the darkness, which had lasted from the sixth

hour to the ninth, grew so black that it seemed day had hidden beneath the cloak of night. The clouds driving through the air and obscuring vision resembled a thousand banners of vast size arrayed against the eye of the sun. The sky itself groaned in unprecedented horror. The pallid lightning flashed. The very globe appeared about to dissolve in mist.'

The scene of the arrest of Christ is also a superb piece of word-painting, always Pietro's strong point in literary composition. Jesus 'resembled a stag about to be dragged down by hounds'. The actions of individuals in the milling crowds about Him are vividly described. The smoking torches, the flash of lanterns and of the steel of weapons that pressed on behind Judas are compared with those of a stricken field in battle or shepherds in flight before a raiding party or a wolf-pack.

The baptism of St. Thomas in Pietro's otherwise rather laboured life of that saint rouses the author for a moment to the invention of some picturesque detail. This biography took him as long as two years, during the most anxious period of his love-affair with Perina Riccia. He could not find enough material in the shape of documentary evidence to fill out the story and compared himself with 'a soldier whose officers think too highly of his worth and who is terrified at the prospect of the warlike feats expected of him, which he is compelled to execute, though he has no idea how to use his courage and his legs.' As usual Pietro solved this problem by letting his pen run away with him in imagined particulars. The beauty of the boy acolytes, with their 'laughing eyes and masses of unruly, curling hair and their cheeks like gardens of red and white roses and their diffident yet graceful attitudes', seemed more like that of angels or spirits than of living human beings. The golden vessels encrusted with jewels, the silver candlesticks, the 'glowing colours' of the infant's swaddling-clothes and the 'venerable matron' who held the child, surrounded by 'many noble gentlewomen, dignitaries of grave aspect and lords and ladies of the court', are described in just such admiring terms as a modern journalist would use in reporting a royal christening ceremony.

In 'The Story of Genesis' the author's profoundly sensuous

reaction to line, colour and mass in the ideal human figure, both masculine and feminine, again finds expression as he lingers over the individual elements composing the faultless brilliance of physique in both Adam and Eve, each of them as heroically proportioned, 'jocund' and 'tender' as any Greek divinity, though this comparison, which would be inappropriate in a Christian context, is not actually made.

Twentieth-century taste is in general averse from the contemplation of absolute perfection. But in the sixteenth century educated people were fascinated by it and the masses would settle for nothing less, their aesthetic sense being so largely identified with religious feeling. Pietro was well aware of this circumstance and exploited it with great skill, reinforced by his own perfectly genuine faith in Christian doctrine. He was deliberately aiming in these works at the widest possible public, which they duly reached. Consequently, though entirely adequate for their purpose, their literary value does not equal that of the best passages in his *Ragionamenti*, letters or even comedies. But a fair view of his personality should never fail to take account of them.

Prolific to a degree, Pietro produced at least three times the quantity of the material recorded above. But these minor efforts are of less interest to posterity. Though as a rule alert and pointed enough, they remain too closely tied to the conventions and idioms of their day to invite any but specialist readers. On the whole, however, Pietro was justified, between 1530 and 1546, in boasting: 'I live by the sweat of my ink, the lustre of which has never been extinguished by the blasts of malignity or the mists of envy.'

Yet like any other author, though probably less often, he could be despondent. In 1537, while editing the first volume of the Letters, he lamented:

'Old age is beginning to paralyse my wit. Love, which ought to wake me up, now puts me to sleep. I used to turn out forty stanzas in a morning. Now I can barely write one. It took me only seven days to compose the Psalms, ten each for Court Life and The Master of the Horse, forty-eight for the two dialogues and thirty for The Humanity of Christ. Yet I suffered for six months while I was writing the poems to the Siren' – i.e. Angela Serena – 'I swear to you by the truth which is my guide that beyond a few letters I have written nothing.'

All the same, talking of his comedies, he once declared to the Duke of Urbino: '*The Philospher* was completed in ten mornings and *Talanta* and *The Hypocrite* in twenty sleepless nights.' He was probably not exaggerating very much more than usual in these statements.

After his death certainly and to an extent in his lifetime he influenced manners and ideas abroad. The 'Discussions' (*Ragionamenti*) were read in a French translation before 1537. Less than a generation later these and other works reached Hungary, Poland, the Netherlands, Germany and England. In the latter country they accompanied those of Machiavelli in starting the vogue of 'Italianisation' so conspicuous in the plays of Shakespeare and other Elizabethan and Jacobean dramatists.

In Italy he acquired in his own day the same sort of fame as Byron did nearly three hundred years later. In Rome a correspondent allegedly wrote to the busy author in 1537:

'I never saw, even at the opening of the papal law courts, such a press of litigants striving to be the first to enter as there were men striving to be the first to buy your new book. Signs reading "The Letters of the Divine Pietro Aretino" were hung outside the shops. Instantly great crowds collected, with as much noise and jostling as when alms are distributed to the poor, in certain cities, on Holy Thursday.

'So many copies were sold that I can tell you plenty of prospective purchasers went away with empty hands. I myself would have been one of them, as I had not been among the first to rush up, if it hadn't been for a certain fool of a courtier. He and his companion each bought a copy. He started reading his then and there in spite of the shoving mob all round him. Then, in order to compare his copy with his friend's, he seized the latter and laid the former down on the counter. I immediately snatched it up and ran away with it. You should have heard him yell! He made more noise than all the rest of the throng put together. His cursing and swearing put such windy braggarts as Renzo, Jacobacci and Malatesta quite in the shade.

'Then he took to begging and pleading. He uttered more prayers than Fra Stopino has in all the years he has been trying to be made Bishop of Gaeta, or than that fellow Rimini has croaked in the hope of being nominated a cardinal. But his book was safe in my pocket and since then I have read it not once but ten times over.'

Either Pietro wrote this letter himself or revised it for publication, or else the alleged author of it, one Bernadino Theodolo, was a dexterous imitator of his friend's style.

Pietro's success, however, was not entirely 'scandalous'. Staid theologians and philologists consulted the 'divine' master of words. He was elected to literary academies in Siena, Padua and Florence. His reputation continued to grow in general esteem for hundreds of years. Corneille studied *L'Orazia* for his own tragedy *Horace*. Even in the early eighteenth century the English essayist and critic Joseph Addison, a decent citizen if ever there was one, declared that there could hardly be anyone living who had never heard of Pietro Aretino.

What everyone except Victorian hypocrites appreciated was his ability to speak the truth 'maliciously', without mincing his words like a don or a diplomat. From a literary point of view he certainly revived, more effectively than the magnificent Lorenzo de' Medici and that ruler's friend Politian, a language that had gone dead as Latin since the time of Petrarch and Boccaccio. But these two were inimitable, though imitated often enough, by the sixteenth century; the whole spirit of civilisation had changed. Scholars and gentlemen like Baldassare Castiglione and Niccolo Machiavelli, both contemporaries of the sketchily educated plebeian Pietro Aretino, did not possess his uncompromising revolutionary vigour.

Castiglione, however, championed a new approach to literature. In *Il Cortigiano* he makes Giuliano de' Medici say:

'I cannot and in reason ought not to contradict anyone who proclaims the superiority of the Tuscan tongue to all others. But it is true that Petrarch and Boccaccio use many words not now customary. I for my part would never employ such phrases either in speaking or in writing. Nor do I think that they themselves would still do so if they were alive today . . . it seems to me that he who does not avoid such antique expressions, except in the rarest instances, makes no less serious a mistake than he who in his desire to imitate times past continues to eat acorns after wheat has become available.'

Castiglione was attacking such pedants as Sperone Speroni, with whom Pietro carried on his usual type of correspondence, now flattering, now acrimonious. Speroni had complacently announced:

'Having in truth from my earliest years been desirous beyond all measure to speak and write my thoughts in our mother tongue, and that not so much with a view to being understood, which lies within the power of every unlettered person, as with the object of placing my name upon the roll of famous men, I neglected every other interest and gave my whole attention to the reading of Petrarch and of the *Hundred Novels*' – presumably an Italian translation of the French collection of short stories attributed to Antoine de la Salle (1388–1462) – 'I exercised myself for many months in these studies without a guide and with very little profit. Then, inspired by God, I betook myself to our revered master Trifone Gabrielli. With his kindly assistance I arrived at perfect comprehension of those authors whom through ignorance of what I ought to have noted I had often until then misunderstood.

'This excellent man and true father of ours first bade me observe the names of things, then gave me rules for the declension and conjugation of nouns and verbs in Tuscan, and finally explained to me articles, pronouns, participles, adverbs and other parts of speech, so that, collecting all I had learned, I composed a grammar for myself and by following this when I wrote I so controlled my style that soon the world held me for a man of erudition and still does so.

'Then when it seemed to me that I had taken rank as a grammarian, I set myself to making verses. My head being full of Petrarch and Boccaccio, for a few years I produced work that I considered wonderful. But after a while I concluded that my vein was beginning to run dry . . . not finding anything new to say I often re-wrote my old sonnets. Having recourse to a universal expedient now practised, I composed a rhyming dictionary or vocabulary of Italian phrases. Thus I classed alphabetically every word these two authors had used. Furthermore, I collected in another book their various ways of describing such things as day, night, anger, peace, hate, love, fear, hope and beauty. Consequently, not a single word or thought came to me that did not have its precedent in their sonnets or tales.'

In a later passage this prize pedant elaborated the theory of poetic diction which has since been periodically revered and execrated in the history of all literatures, a system of deliberately artificial ornament. Of such writers Pietro once exclaimed:

'It is better to drink out of one's own wooden platter than another man's golden goblet. One makes a braver show in one's own rags than in stolen velvet robes. I am content to be what I am and thank God I am not afflicted either with the bitterness of the servile or the rancour of the avaricious. I don't waste other people's time nor do I rejoice in the penury of others. I prefer, on the contrary, to share with my friends the shirt on my back and the mouthful at my lips. My maids are my daughters and my manservants my brothers. Peace is the furniture of my apartments and liberty my butler. I regularly enjoy simple fare and do not desire to be greater than I feel myself to be.'

On another occasion he wrote to one Giancopo Leopardi:

'I dreamed that I found myself in a market-place where starlings, magpies, crows and parrots were all making as much noise as a flock of geese. The birds were accompanied by certain toga-wearing, long-bearded and wild-eyed pedants whose only occupation was to teach their charges to chatter by the points of the moon. You would have laughed to hear a blue jay repeating "ne'er", "needs must", "lissom", "ofttimes", "hereby" and "hence". You would have burst your jaws to see Apollo, mad with fury, making a blockhead leap because he could not teach a nightingale to say "I' troth". He broke the frame of his lyre across the fellow's bum, while fame blew her trumpet so hard she split the handle.'

Pietro practised what he preached. Even his bad verses in the *Marfisa* have a singular vitality in their florid lushness, like gaudy tropical plants or the second-rate baroque and rococo art that succeeded the Renaissance style. In a sense Pietro himself forecast that change. He could not approach the light, subtle mockery of 'chivalry' by Ariosto in the *Orlando Furioso* or the tender relegation of the old-fashioned knight-errant to a lunatic asylum by Cervantes. But Pietro could throw big stones at the same sort of fatuity. That was what civilisation needed if it were ever to emerge from the clash of sword and lance into calm libraries and conferences. So much can be said for his less significant efforts, including his romantic and verbose religious tracts, which were at best fluent improvisation.

It is otherwise with the comedies, inferior only to Machiavelli's in their brightly pointed commentaries on the life of his age. The best of the Letters, again, some five hundred pages out of about four thousand, are as readable this year – the extracts already quoted may suggest their quality – as they were more than four centuries ago. Finally, the *Ragionamenti* are nearly as good as *Gargantua* and *Pantagruel*. They are not quite so indulgent and definitely less learned. Rabelais was by far the greater 'humanist' in every sense of the word. Pietro Aretino is more like Petronius, if one must look for a parallel. But he is unique in his versatility.

The Letters show him in a dozen utterly different moods, sharply perceptive, daring to the limit, calmly or playfully affectionate, sternly devoted, as in the description of the death of Giovanni delle Bande Nere, or again remorselessly savage or uproariously humorous. They cry out for selection by an anthologist. Fifty or sixty could serve as an incomparable self-portrait of a typical man of the High Renaissance. The comedies, all about fools and charlatans, lifted Italian plays of this kind out of the ruck of feeble imitations of Plautus and Terence which had held the stage till then. But the famous *Ragionamenti* are agreed by most critics to be the Divine Aretino's most effective text.

In the first dialogue of these 'Discussions' an old and a young courtesan, Nanna and Antonia, consider what they shall do with Nanna's little daughter Pippa. There are three alternatives. She could be made a nun, a matron or a whore. As for nuns, Nanna proceeds to give a frightful picture of their debaucheries, of course grossly libellous, with vivid accounts of every sexual perversion then rampant, the orgies being for the most part performed by several participants at once. This section largely explains the Divine One's lurid reputation in our own day as the most shameless pornographer between Petronius and de Sade.

For example, after the long and luscious description of a banquet in the nunnery where Nanna says she once lived as a novice, Antonia demands: 'Where did you go when you rose from table?' Nanna replies that they went into a large room on the ground floor, adorned with frescoes.

'*Antonia.* What were they about? Were they scenes of Lenten repentance?

Nanna. Repentance my foot! They were the sort of pictures pious bigots love to contemplate. The room had four walls. The first depicted the life of St Nafissa' – a favourite with Roman courtesans – 'showing the good-natured little girl at the age of twelve, chockful of charity, distributing her dowry to cops, pickpockets, priests, grooms and all sorts of other worthy persons. As soon as she has given everything away, she goes and sits down humbly on the Sistine Bridge' – a well known resort of prostitutes – 'having only her stool, her mat, her little dog and a cleft stick with a paper in it which she seemed to use as a fan.

Antonia. Why did she sit there?

Nanna. In order to clothe the naked. Fancy that, at her age! There she sat, with her face turned up and her mouth open, as if she were singing that ballad we all know, "What's my love doing, why doesn't he come?" Then she was painted standing up and facing a man who seemed ashamed to ask for what he wanted. She goes up to him so benevolently and kindly, and after taking him to the sepulchre where she was in the habit of consoling the afflicted, took off his doublet and undid his hose. There she found that little turtle-dove and gave it such pleasant entertainment that it grew quite arrogant and with the frenzy of a stallion that breaks away from its tether to rush at the mare went in between her legs. But she, not considering it decent to look it in the face and possibly, as our preacher told us, because she didn't wish to see it all so red and hot and excited, boldly turned her back on the thing.'

Antonia pretends to be very shocked at Nafissa's conduct and hopes her soul will suffer for it. But Nanna points out there is no question of any such thing, since she is a saint. Descriptions of other obscene frescoes follow, which may owe something to Pietro's acquaintance with the pornographic pictures produced by Giulio Romano in 1524.

'*Nanna*. The second wall illustrated the story of Masetto da Lampolecchio.' (This personage is the hero of the First Tale of the Third Day of Boccacio's Decameron. By pretending to be dumb he got himself engaged as gardener to a nunnery and so contrived to lie with all the nuns. 'And I swear to you by my soul that the two Sisters who took him to the hut looked positively alive while the rascal, feigning sleep, made his shirt swell like a sail while he stepped the mast of his carnality. *Antonia*. Ha, ha, ha!
Nanna. Quite so. And none of us there could restrain our laughter when we saw how the other two Sisters, on discovering the fun that their colleagues were having, instead of sneaking to the Abbess, joined the party and were amazed when Masetto, communicating only by signs, appeared to be resisting. The next scene showed the Mother Superior taking the matter in good part and inviting the gallant fellow to supper and bed with her, when he, to escape being skinned alive, suddenly found his tongue in the middle of the night. The rumour of this miracle spread over the whole countryside and the entire convent was canonised as a result.'

Antonia again laughs heartily and comments sarcastically on the subject of the third frescoe, a composite portrait of all the nuns of the Order, with their lovers and children, each figure being named.

'*Nanna*. The fourth wall depicted all the attitudes possible for men and women in the act of love. The nuns were obliged, before taking the field with their lovers, to try to adopt in real life the postures painted in the fresco. This rule was to prevent them from being clumsy in bed, like certain

women who simply lie there like logs and give their companions about as much pleasure as one has from bean soup
without oil or salt.

Antonia. Well, I suppose they had a fencing-mistress to help
them?

Nanna. Indeed they had. She showed those who needed showing how to stimulate lust in a man till he is ready to ride a
coffer, a stairway, a chair, a table or the floor itself. She had
to have as much patience as the trainer of a dog, a parrot, a
starling or a magpie. It would have been easier for the good
Sisters to learn the sleight of hand of a juggler than the art
of compelling that little bird to stand up when it doesn't
want to.'

The old courtesan then describes her seduction, as a novice,
by a young monk.

'I followed him as a blind man follows his dog. He led me to
a small room surrounded by many others. The walls were
of bricks so carelessly put together that you could see through
the chinks what was going on next door. When we got there
the sly young devil started telling me that my charms
exceeded those of any sorceress, calling me his soul, his blood,
his heart, his sweet life and all the rest of the endearments to
be found in the *Filocolo*' – Boccaccio's first work – 'and was
just getting ready to pull me down on to the bed in a con-
venient position when we heard a tapping sound that terrified
him and everyone else in the monastery as if they had been
rats in a barn when the door is suddenly opened and the
creatures gathered round a pile of nuts fall into such a panic
that they can't remember which hole they came out of. In
the same way our friends dashed wildly about, trying to hide
from the Episcopal Suffragan, the patron of the whole place.
For it was his tapping that frightened us all, like so many
frogs sitting up on their hind legs in a grassy ditch when
someone calls out or throws a stone, whereupon they all dive
into the water practically at the same time. He was walking
through the dormitory on his way to the Abbess's chamber.
She, in company with the Director-General, was preparing
a new version of the office of vespers as practised by her nuns.
The Cellaress told us that he had just lifted his hand to knock

at her door and I don't know what else when he suddenly refrained at the sight of a little nun kneeling at his feet who was as expert in chanting above or below the stave as Bovo d'Antona's Drusiana.'

This learned allusion is utterly incongruous in the mouth of the elderly bawd, who elsewhere regularly distorts and mispronounces, in order to raise a laugh from the reader, all sorts of titles and proper names, such as Suffragan and 'Vinezia' (for Venice). The author good-humouredly ensures by such improbable locutions that his readers will not suppose him to be describing actual scenes. His famous realism only appears in a detail here and there and in the closely observed similes of frogs and rats in the above passage.

As for the 'Bovo', which Nanna calls 'Buono', *Bovo d' Antona* is an anonymous Italian epic of the thirteenth century imitated from the French *Beuve D'Hanstone* and followed a few years later by the English metrical romance *Bevis of Hampton*, which however seems to incorporate elements from legends of the Danish invasions of England in the tenth century. In the *Bovo d'Antona* Drusiana, the daughter of the King of Armenia, is Bovo's wife. She sang so well that when she got lost on the seashore her wonderful voice led to her identification and rescue.

The First Day of the *Ragionamenti* continues with a meticulous account, in the language illustrated above, of an orgy which Nanna watches through a chink in a wall, the participants being the aged Suffragan, four nuns and three young monks. First the Suffragan is stripped and dressed up like a *condottiere*. Then the nuns and monks exchange clothing, except for one nun, who puts on the Suffragan's robes. When the latter's lust has been duly excited by the attentions of the Sisters he commits an act of sodomy upon one of them while himself undergoing the same indignity in an assault by one of the monks. At the same time the two others copulate with the other two nuns. The simultaneous orgasms of these seven persons, Nanna adds, are accompanied by her own, brought about by masturbation.

A number of variations of this scene ensue, in which artificial male organs are employed by the nuns, both on their own sex and on the other. Nanna also beholds, through another chink in another wall, the erotic transports of her venerable abbess and the latter's confessor, next the rape of a muleteer by several Sisters at once and a libidinous attack upon a porter by the mistress of the novices.

In all these cases Nanna has the good fortune to be accompanied by her original seducer, with results she again describes in the most vividly picturesque detail. These and many other obscenities, including flagellation and bestiality, are recounted with as much mocking humour as carnal relish and punctuated by shrieks of laughter from both speaker and listener. The total effect is both artificial in the utter absurdity and impossibility of the actions narrated, which no reader could possibly believe really happened, and also naturalistic to the highest degree, apart from occasional deliberate pedantries, in the reported conversation between Nanna and Antonia, whose personalities are as clearly rendered as the characters of any good novelist.

Next day the talk is resumed, the subject this time being married life. Nanna again takes the lead, for she has been a wife as well as a nun during her chequered existence. The text reads like a transcript of the evidence in case after case of divorce too appalling to be heard in public.

On the Third Day equally dreadful stories of the doings of professional harlots are told. But all the same Nanna decides to make Pippa a courtesan. For, says she, while the nun betrays religion and the wife the sanctity of marriage, the courtesan preys simply upon individuals who come to her of their own accord and consequently have only themselves to blame if they suffer for it. She is like the soldier who is paid for doing wrong and for that reason should not be held accountable for the miseries he inflicts. 'She is just a shopkeeper who sells you what you ask for.'

In Volume Two of the *Ragionamenti* the discussions are significantly called in the Foreword 'pleasant' (*'piacevoli'*) instead of 'whimsical' (*'capricciosi'*), which was their designation in Volume One. Pippa's education for her future career now begins. She is told, in so many 'easy lessons', how to make the most of the idiotic lusts of men, how to allure the timid, hold a restless lover and tame a brutal one, how to play off one rival aspirant against another and exploit their various weaknesses, such as vanity, jealousy, curiosity and so on, in order to keep herself in luxury. Guides to the lore of cosmetics and some elementary psychology are included. The arts of acting, as the

situation may require, every part from innocent schoolgirl to
cunning old rip, are inculcated.

On the Second Day Pippa hears of the different tricks which
her future lovers are likely to play on her. On the Third Day
both she and Nanna listen to a pair of repulsive old women
talking of the techniques of bawd and procuress. Other porno-
graphers had preceded Pietro on such topics. But their *dramatis
personae* had usually been figureheads and their language
tedious. Pietro's people and idioms carry complete conviction.
His strength was that he cared a lot for much else besides
pornography. Skipping does not pay in this case, and one can
read the *Ragionamenti* as one would enjoy good fiction, for the
characterisation and the story, not simply looking for the 'hot
spots'.

The sixteenth century was not shocked by the *Ragionamenti*.
The Spanish general Antonio de Leyva, no coarse debauchee,
though Pietro had once asserted that he was rotten with
syphilis, expressed a typical opinion when he declared: 'This
Pietro is more necessary to the human race than preachers. For
while the latter set simple folk on the road to righteousness, his
writings have reached the ears of the mighty.'

Pietro himself, however, disclaimed any such moral intentions in a letter to, of all people, the deeply devout poetess
Vittoria Colonna.

'I am extremely happy, most modest lady, that the religious
works I have composed are not displeasing to your taste and
your good judgment. I am aware that your doubt as to
whether you should praise or blame me for having used my
talents on any but sacred themes is prompted by your honest
spirit, which longs for every word and thought to turn to
God, the giver of all virtue and all wit. I confess, too, that I
am less useful to the world and less acceptable by Christ
when I spend my time on lying trifles instead of eternal
truths.

'But the cause of all this evil is the lewdness of others and
my own necessity. For if the princes of this world were as
truly pious as I am indigent, I would use my pen to write
nothing but *Misereres*. All men, most excellent lady, have not
the grace of divine inspiration. Most are ever aflame with
fleshly concupiscence. You yourself are lighted up every hour

with angelic fire. For you services and sermons are what masks and revels are to them. You would never spare a glance for Hercules on his funeral pyre. They would never hang in their apartments representations of St. Laurence on his gridiron or St. Bartholomew without his skin ... So you see that my trifles have at least this excuse, that they were written to earn a living, not out of malice ...'

The letter ends with a plea for Vittoria's good offices in screwing a debt of the balance of thirty crowns out of a certain Messer Sebastiano of Pesaro, which Pietro in his turn is being dunned for.

The nineteenth-century critic J. A. Symonds, who idolised Vittoria and detested Pietro Aretino, with whom Swinburne later compared him for his homosexual tendencies, considered this communication 'one long tissue of sneers, taunts and hypocritical sarcasm', giving 'the complete measure of Aretino's arrogance'. The charge is certainly not without foundation. But Symonds was prevented by his prejudices from noticing also the letter's complete candour as to the motivation of such money-grubbing 'trifles' as the *Ragionamenti*. Pietro did not mind people like Vittoria Colonna knowing what he was up to. His humorous depreciation of what is perhaps his greatest achievement from a purely literary point of view proves how little of a real 'pornographer' he actually was.

Last Round

BY 1534, WHEN the first volume of the 'Discussions' was published, the Divine Aretino had 'arrived'. He had no more financial need of patrons. But his inordinate ambition required more prestige than that of a best-selling novelist. He wanted the nod, however condescending, of kings. King Francis had already proved a disappointment. But there was always the Emperor, who had at least heard of him. Charles, however, had not so far shown any particular enthusiasm in replying to the letters he had received from his self-appointed counsellor.

Nevertheless, that prudent and harassed ruler had at last come to the conclusion that the fellow's tongue might be worth buying. The vast Holy Roman Empire was in serious difficulties with Protestant Germany and Holland, grimly anarchistic Spain, greedy France and the Sultan's hordes of bold, hard-fighting and tactically brilliant pirates. The Emperor himself, of cold and calculating character, and not really interested in art and entertainment, remained less than popular. The brutal sack of the centre of Christendom in 1527 had after all been carried out under his auspices and no Catholic Christian was ever likely to forget it. Charles V offered the Scourge of Princes two hundred crowns a year to say pleasant things about him and in particular to keep quiet about Beatrice of Savoy, the Emperor's sister-in-law, with whom he was known to be carrying on an affair.

Pietro accepted this gift with fulsome gratitude and duly began pouring out a steady stream of high-flown compliments. Charles was 'nearer to God than any man ever was', a regular 'torrent' in human history.

'Swollen with rain, snow and sun-melted ice, it floods the fields that apparently drink it, though in reality its proud waters make a bed of them. I salute the faith, the religion, the pious deeds, the mercy, the benevolence and the prudence of Caesar, the greatest ruler of all time. The new onslaught upon

211

you, believe me, will come to nothing, just as all previous
attacks against you have failed and every race, banner and
name that contends with yours is of no avail. For he who
fights Caesar fights God and he who fights God meets destruction ... All must agree that Your Majesty deserves shrines
and altars and a seat in heaven amongst the other gods. Yet
we writers feel that your wondrous deeds will not endure
unless record is made of them. We argue that pens and
tongues armed with steel that never fails to cut and fire that
never fails to burn will enlarge the realms conquered by your
fame as much as your captains increase the boundaries of
your empire.'

This pretentious rhetoric rings cheap and hollow today. But
it was what Charles wanted. Then as now a vaguely blustering
propaganda was found more effective by dictators in influencing
the minds of millions than a plausibly reasoned argument in
favour of their ideology and policies. Pietro, who could write
much better than he did in the above-quoted passage, knew
exactly what he was doing. His mentality was certainly not that
of a political or any other kind of philosopher. It was basically
that of a climber of the heights of wealth and power, and in
Renaissance Italy gross flattery had been proved again and
again the best armoury for such mountaineers.

The Empress Isabella of Portugal, a lady in fact as respectable as she was beautiful, also came in for the swelling organ-
notes of a highly decorative panegyric:

'Adorned, then, with the grace and beauty, you bring
serenity, with the simplicity that shines from your brow, into
minds that are clouded with affliction. The tranquillity
which calms the tempest in our hearts is radiant beneath
your eyelashes, where honesty and gravity dwell together.
Your modest glance consoles the spirits of all who look into
its sweet, affectionate depths. Its gracious gleam refreshes the
beholder like a vista of soothing green meadows. Our hopes
blossom in your cheeks. Your gaze alone is the virtuous man's
reward. Your nod sufficiently punishes the wicked. Your
slightest gesture is a lesson in good conduct and your countenance reveals the ideal aspect of a saint. Charity unfolds your
hands and mercy impels your feet. Constancy, humility and

concord are your ministers and companions. In your gait
and in your presence you disclose heaven. Faith and religion
bear witness to your good sense and innate dignity. With the
glory of the several moral excellences that embellish your
character your courtesy makes as many conquests as the
Emperor achieves in arms. Hence half the world is yours and
half his.'

Isabella must have shaken her imperial head over this
effusion, which nevertheless has precisely the kind of elegance
in eulogy that was fashionable in the sixteenth century, descending from classical models through the troubadours and Petrarch.

At this juncture Francis I played right into the hands of both
Charles and the man whom the French king had so often
treated with contempt after long ago promising to make his
fortune. Pietro had laid some of his most glittering prose,
showier even than the passage just quoted, at the monarch's
feet. But now Francis wanted Burgundy, Milan and whatever
else of the Emperor's dominions could be conquered with the
help of a powerful ally.

Suleiman the Magnificent, Commander of the Muslim Faithful and Barbarossa the pirate of Algiers wanted Vienna and
North Africa – where Charles had just recaptured Tunis –
respectively. In 1536 a treaty, said of course to be purely 'commercial', between Francis and Suleiman was made public.
Barbarossa's galleons promptly anchored off Toulon. It was
obvious enough that the French king, by this alliance, hoped
to bring the Holy Roman Emperor to his knees.

But this time Francis's reckless and insatiable aspirations had
taken him too far. Europe was scandalised at the sight of a
Christian monarch enlisting infidels against Christians. Charles
might be said to have at least connived at the sack of Rome;
but this was worse. Barbarossa's ships terrified the whole continent. For a Turkish invasion, let alone Turkish rule, meant the
infliction of atrocities that had not been heard of since the
hideous and still remembered nightmares of Hunnish and Avar
massacres in the fifth and sixth centuries. The universal panic
was the greatest political opportunity that ever came the way
of Pietro Aretino. He felt confident of being able to turn it to
his personal advantage.

He began his campaign quietly and subtly, not with a

romantic clarion call to Charles, but with two open letters to Francis. The first pointed out that Venice, whence His Majesty's present respectful correspondent wrote, had always been the ally of France against the East, but would now, if war broke out with Suleiman, be the first victim of Muslim cruelty and fanaticism. The writer also wondered how Francis's usual title of 'Most Christian King' would sound if its bearer wore a turban. He reminded the addressee of his ancestors Pepin and Charlemagne, the saviours of Europe for Christianity. He ended with a strong hint that revenge and ambition did not become so noble a monarch as the present occupant of the French throne.

'Ah, worst of all passions is the desire to rule! Ah, cruel is the longing for revenge! To think that such cravings should lodge in the mind of the most noble king who ever lived!'

The paragon on the throne of France did not reply to these exclamations. So the next letter was, metaphorically, a straight left to the jaw:

'I am aware that the world does not consider it decent to speak or write to a person of royal birth on a matter of such moment without invitation. Yet, since the Word of God forbids deceit and in Christ's republic there are no distinctions of rank, I have decided to add to my former communication, in which I doubted whether I could call you a "Most Christian" king. Now I regret bitterly, as your servant, that I can call you neither King of France nor Francis. For how can a man be called either king or "free", which is the epithet implicit in both "France" and "Francis", if he goes begging the aid of barbarians, foes of his race, and revolts against his own creed? My lord, for so I still address you, you have thrust the sword of the Ottoman into the heart of Christendom. By so doing you have fatally wounded the splendour of your hitherto unconquered glory. Moreover, while harming the Emperor hardly at all, you have strengthened all his reasons for recognising you as his enemy.

'Furthermore, is there any Christian prince who will not at least cease to sympathise with you now that you have chosen such an ally? Behold the wise King of England. Not long ago he was estranged from both Pope and Emperor. But no sooner did he hear that the Turkish fanatics were approaching the west than he turned his pious arms against you.

'Abandon, therefore, this unholy league. For only so can you justify your Christian faith and continue the glorious traditions of your country. In the days of Camillus your indomitable forefathers climbed the walls of Rome and invaded the Capitol itself . . . They entered Asia and left behind them the name of a province, Gallogrecia' – Galicia. – 'Under Charlemagne they subdued Spain, Germany and the Saracens. Yet now France is constrained to kneel to and plead for aid from the enemies of her people and her God, to beg for reinforcement from the banners of a greedy corsair, a vile, infamous pirate!

'Would that I could address you with that deference due both to your rank and to your past merits. But I cannot help being more conscious of an evil present than of a laudable past. For that reason I lament more your fault of today than I honour your correct behaviour of yesterday. Since you now act only from jealousy of Caesar you should either so control your impulses that his greatness does not trouble you or else so conduct yourself as to be equal or superior to him. Draw an honourable sword, as he has, on behalf of Christ. Cast out that venomous serpent from your breast. Do not permit the vaunting of Turkish arrogance in your cities, your palaces and the temples of your God. Sever your connection with that monster of pride, who is no friend of yours but a foe. Christian princes who fear the Turkish tyrant urge you to this step. Private persons who dread servitude to the barbarian do likewise. So also do women who tremble at the prospect of their honour and that of their daughters being stained by Turkish lust. So also does Christ, from Whom you received all the gifts that ennoble you.

'After taking such a measure you will pardon the insolence of your rash but faithful servant as readily as I hope you will pray God to pardon you. Indeed, if common opinion reaches your royal ears as it spreads elsewhere, you will not reproach me for writing as I have today. You will censure me for not having so written long ago.'

Pietro showed Francis clearly, by this language, that he

understood the King's main motive in this disastrous league with the Orient. The Frenchman had been impelled to it by mere hatred of the Emperor, who had always treated him with forbearance. Of course Pietro's whirlwind of remonstrance was sheer political rhetoric. Several popes and Charles himself had signed dangerous agreements with Turks before this period. And the very man who was now rebuking Francis would soon be addressing the 'infamous corsair' Barbarossa as 'illustrious monarch' and 'invincible warrior' in pursuance of his own private ends.

But this was the first time, since Hebrew prophets had thundered against the princes of Israel, that a private citizen had stood up to an anointed sovereign, believed by millions to rule by divine right. Pietro's own 'divinity', being purely literary, remained conventional in comparison. Yet here again he correctly foretold the future. From his time on fewer and fewer people experienced a specifically religious awe of monarchs, and during the ensuing centuries the latter would be assassinated, arrested, tried and sentenced to death for alleged misbehaviour. No one could even dream of such a thing in 1536.

The Emperor, pleased with Pietro's boldness, let it be known that he would double the pension of two hundred crowns if his new 'secretary' went on as he had begun. Then an old friend of Pietro's, one Hieronimo Comitolo of Perugia, serving in the French army, communicated the following information to Pietro.

'Yesterday, when I was riding with the Grand Master' – the Constable of France, Duke of Montmorency – 'on a visit of inspection to the fortifications, we met the Duke of Atri, who had known you in Venice. We spoke of you and the Duke said that the distinguished engraver Luigi Anichini had mentioned in his presence and that of the Grand Master that you had been granted a pension of two hundred crowns by the Emperor on condition that you recorded his deeds so that they would not be forgotten by posterity. A further condition was that you should cease to praise France as soon as you decently could. The Grand Master then declared that if you would write of the Emperor and the King of France in such terms as their actions truly deserved, recording them with the utmost accuracy, he would persuade King Francis to make you an allowance of four hundred crowns. He also stated that he would like to see some of your work.'

As it happened, the annuity of two hundred crowns granted by Charles was already overdue and Messer Pietro Aretino had no intention of throwing in his lot unconditionally with that of the Emperor. However, trouble had by then started with representatives of the French interests in Rome, who were plotting the overthrow of the base scribbler who had dared to censure the actions of the King of France.

An able man of letters named Alicante, who worked in Milan, had sometimes in the past supported Pietro's schemes of personal aggrandisement or vengeance and was to do so again in the future, notably in the case of the dead dramatist Francesco Berni whom Nicolo Franco mendaciously alleged, in 1538, to be the author of the obscenely abusive 'Life of Pietro Aretino' Franco himself had written. But the two associates had occasionally quarrelled. Alicante could up to a point imitate the Scourge's style; he now accepted bribes from the French authorities to issue a series of scurrilous attacks on Charles V and sign them with the name of the Divine Aretino.

Pietro emphatically denied authorship of these forgeries. He was relieved both to hear from imperial sources that no one but the French believed he had written such tripe and to receive his overdue pension. Yet at the same time he caused a rumour to circulate among Alicante's paymasters that he, Pietro Aretino, would be quite prepared to praise Francis again if it were made well worth his while. But this hedging did not amount to much. Gradually but steadily he took steps to imply that the Emperor, more generous than the evasive King, could command his services.

He was rewarded for this policy in 1543, by which time Francis had long been paying more attention to diplomacy than to belligerency in foreign affairs. In that year the new Duke of Urbino, Guidobaldo delle Rovere, son of the late Francesco Maria, acting on behalf of Venice, went to meet the Emperor, who was riding up from Italy to the Brenner Pass on his way to Germany. The Duke asked Pietro to accompany him. At Padua the citizens and university students poured into the streets to cheer the champion – Messer Pietro – of what neither he nor they yet called 'democracy'. He was welcomed also, though less tumultuously, at Vicenza and Verona. Then, near the little village of Peschiera, the Venetian party came face to face with the black double-headed eagles on the crimson banners of the Habsburgs.

A single horseman, riding ahead of the first lances, spurred forward to meet the small group of Venetians, who immediately dismounted to kneel in the dust with bent heads.

'Which of you is Pietro Aretino?'

The rider, a lean, eager-eyed, hook-nosed man in his early forties, with a sparse blond beard jutting from his long jaw, spoke without ceremony and wore plain black clothing. But no one could doubt that this was Charles V in person. Pietro looked up, meeting the other's piercing stare with dignified self-possession.

'I, Your Majesty.'

'Rise and ride with me.'

The Duke's party gasped. The bulky Pietro stood up at his leisure and remounted, while the Emperor waited for him. When the two men got into motion side by side, at a steady trot, it was the shoemaker's son who did most of the talking. Charles limited himself to an occasional compliment. But he was seen by his astonished staff to look a good deal more pleasant than he had lately. He kept his 'secretary' within call until the army reached Vicenza, where State affairs required the imperial attention.

Yet later on, at a banquet, he summoned Pietro to his side again.

'Come with me to Germany.'

'Majesty, I have sworn never to leave Venice.'

Next morning, before the troops moved out of Vicenza, Pietro was not to be found. He had already ridden off due east in the direction of his adopted city. It was a clever move, proving to the Emperor that the Scourge of Princes was no mere sycophant. As the latter had anticipated, the ruler of half the known world asked the Venetian ambassador what had become of him. Interrupting the embarrassed official's flustered apologies, Charles solemnly recommended Pietro Aretino to the especial care of the Doge, adding: 'Remember he is dear to our person.'

The rest of Pietro's story, however, is little more than anticlimax. It seems that he had, for a wonder, escaped serious syphilis. Nor did his truly amazing energy ever desert him. In mind at least he remained nearly as active as hitherto, though most men over sixty in his time – Titian was a notable exception – definitely relapsed into senility. Pietro was only more often grave than gay, looked even stouter and walked still more slowly than he had in his earlier fifties. But anyone can see from the portrait Titian painted of him in 1545, when the sitter was fifty-three, that there was not much the matter with him physically at that date. The subject himself remarked, rather menacingly, in a characteristically blunt and sturdy sonnet in celebration of this picture, 'Though I be painted I both speak and hear.' He unnecessarily added that he was neither poet nor prince but a truth-telling censor with a style of his own. Apart from the question of truth-telling, the portrait certainly bears out these statements.

Both Sansovino and his publisher Marcolini warned him against prodigality at this time (1545). He answered the sculptor:

'I am certainly not going to close against the crowds of my visitors the doors of that hostelry which has been open to them for the past eighteen years. For if I did so the act would be considered the result of insolvency rather than of a decision to reform.'

To one Captain Croce he wrote:

'I am perpetually being crucified, not so much by the beggars who come to my door, by applications from prisoners, by women in childbirth and others in similar troubles, as by monks accused of heresy, by priests pursued by calumny and by ill-treated domestic servants, to such an extent that I am driven to desperation by the general belief that I, powerless as I am, have the power to do anything.'

He told Don Lope de Soria, the Spanish ambassador at Venice, that:

'Everyone rushes to me as if I had inherited a king's treasury. If some poor woman bears a child my household is called upon to meet the expense. If anyone is clapped in gaol I have to provide him with everything he wants. Soldiers in rags and tatters, foreigners in need and all kinds of roving rogues take refuge under my wing. Anyone who falls ill sends to my "hospital" for drugs and even for my own doctor to cure him. Less than two months ago a young man who was wounded in the street not far from my house had himself carried into one of my apartments. When I heard the uproar that accompanied his entry and saw the fellow lying there half dead, I told the assembled multitude: "I'm quite well aware of being a good host, but I never knew before that I ran a hospital." '

To a correspondent named Mariano Borro Pietro wrote:

'It vexes me more to take up my pen as a duty than it would a miser to open his purse . . . If sometimes shame at my own laziness forces a pen into my hand I feel bound to use it in the interests of ordinary people, since they have all got it into their heads that no one, however high and mighty, would ever dare to contradict me. So I spend my whole time pleading with this man for that, with that man for this and with those men for these.'

People were always being unfairly locked up in those days. They could seldom be got out again unless some personage of social importance interested himself in the case, as he rarely would if not prodded by some other well known figure popular, like Pietro, with the masses. For despite the still rigid structure of society in sixteenth-century Italy, its natives had been for some hundreds of years much more republican in spirit than any others in continental Europe, including even the French, whose very name indicated the 'freedom' upon which the ancient Franks of Gaul so prided themselves. Consequently, the Italian magnates took more trouble than the great men of other countries to be cheered in the streets.

A great many begging letters from Pietro to influential characters on behalf of humbler citizens in trouble have survived. One may serve as an example for all. He told Cardinal Farnese:

'Mere sympathy is not enough in a case when, as a result of

false information, the omnipotence of your instructions holds captive within the four walls of a dreaded prison a wretched father, most miserably distressed, whose unending tears flow in petition to those who, to the prejudice of the law and in contempt of his innocence, have buried his body and soul alive.'

One remarkable attribute of Pietro in his prime was the way in which, though perpetually proposing bargains in hard cash for the use of his 'pen', he remained always at pains to demonstrate his utter incorruptibility in face of all the evidence to the contrary. He wrote, for instance, to one would-be but not over-generous paymaster:

'I return the ten ducats you sent me and would be glad if you on your side would give me back the praise I have accorded you. It doesn't seem decent to me to praise a man who depreciates my character in the way that you do when you suppose me capable of accepting alms more suitable to a beggar than a man of worth. Those who wish to buy glory should show themselves truly munificent when they give, not following personal inclination, but taking account of the status of him who sells them fame. We shabby scribblers are not interested in exalting a reputation earthbound by utter mediocrity.'

Again, on the question of Francis's vague offer to double the pension granted to Pietro by the Emperor, the recipient of pay from the imperial court informed the Duke of Montmorency, the Constable of France:

'So soon as the annuity of four hundred crowns enables me to meet my living expenses I shall speak with my usual candour of the merits of your king. For I am still the captain of troops that don't take payment for nothing and don't mutiny or surrender castles. They even, with their battalions of ink, and truth inscribed upon their standards, acquire more glory for the prince they serve than his armies can give him. My pen, moreover, pays out honour and dishonour where they are due. In a single morning I would make no bones about distributing praise and blame among those whom I do not necessarily adore or hate myself but who justly deserve to be adored or detested.'

He added calmly:

'I shall be that which duty demands that I shall be . . . Darius used to say that he would rather have Zopiro as his advocate than a thousand Babylons.'

He defended himself with equal aggressiveness to the Princess Molfetta, wife of Ferrante Gonzaga, Viceroy of Sicily. She had been indignant at Pietro's rudeness to certain ladies.

'My tongue and pen were certainly restrained by a recognition of the baseness of what I might have said. I did not go so far as to enforce such tributes as the princes pay me, though I could have rent the veils from the altars of Naples, Milan, Mantua, Ferrara and all Italy . . . I could have spoken of the feminine idiots and overweening blue-stockings, of the women who go in for trade, of prophetesses and female sages, of women who work miracles and steal and of each one of those other prodigies who infest the civilised world.'

As for less exalted and self-exalting ladies, Pietro could still satisfy the Angelas and Paolinas who were proud to share his bed without the usual cash payments. At about this period he wrote to Sansovino in buoyant mood:

'My dear Jacopo, the respect which I feel for you and Titian is the reason I did not let you know that I had Virginia to supper the other night. I kept this engagement entirely to myself, so that you and your good friend would not hear of it. To this secrecy I was impelled by my reverence for the – alas – somewhat advanced age of the pair of you. For it is only decent, honest and prudent that I should guard you two from all temptations to lasciviousness. The attitudes of love, perhaps, do not any longer allure you. But the beauty of Virginia is such that she would move continence itself to wish to enjoy her. So much is this the case that she can be compared with those dishes which not only entice the hungry to eat of them but also those who have just risen from table.'

The playful malice and personal complacency of this communication pinpoint the general tone of Pietro's casual conversation, which was nothing if not aggressive in tormenting even those he loved and in which he never hesitated to build himself up into a superman at their expense. He probably considered that it was good for people to taunt them with their misfortunes and shortcomings because it helped to develop in them a philosophic outlook on life.

Pietro certainly remained sexually as potent as ever into the late 1540s. Caterina Sandella, whom no one could suspect of betraying him with another lover, bore him a second daughter in 1547. He named the child Austria in compliment to the dynasty of his current patron the Emperor. 'I still have all my youthful powers,' he wrote soon afterwards to a friend, 'and not more than four or five months ago love and nature made me father of a beauteous daughter.'

In the previous year he had published his last comedy, 'The Philosopher', his verse tragedy *L'Orazia* and the third volume of his 'Letters'. Three more volumes of this collection of letters, making six in all, followed during the next five years. In 1551 he edited two stout tomes of written communications to himself 'by many lords, republics, worthy ladies, poets and other excellent persons', amounting to 875 closely printed pages. It was a great feat of production, especially as he may well have doctored a few of these missives to suit what he considered proper to his now long established fame.

He still had plenty to write about:

'With a goose quill and a few sheets of paper I can laugh at the universe. They say that I am the son of a prostitute. It may be so. But I have the heart of a king. I enjoy myself. I can call myself happy.'

The deaths of his sister Francesca and of Francis I inspired him to cast an almost sentimental light of memories and reverie over his normally hard-hitting style. But his quarrels with Michelangelo and thereafter with an English ambassador roused something of the old flashing fury of expression.

As for Michelangelo, who could be the terror of his friends, Pietro feared him less than he did the young Tintoretto, whom he had criticised publicly and who thereupon slyly invited him to his studio to have his portrait painted. As soon as the big visitor was seated the artist abruptly drew a pistol.

'What's that for?' cried Messer Pietro, who hated the very idea of bodily violence.

'To take your measure, my friend,' retorted the painter, with a certain ambiguity that increased the other's fright. Tintoretto retained his fierce frown while he proceeded to measure his sitter's giant frame with this improvised yardstick.

The Scourge of Princes quaked and even whimpered a little in his terror. For the artist at this time had the reputation, like Cellini, of a devilishly hot temper quite capable of leading him to commit murder for the merest trifle. But on this occasion Tintoretto, after a prolonged flourishing of the weapon, merely informed the trembling colossus that he was 'two and a half pistols tall', the pistol in question probably being a shortened version of the wheel-lock carbine then in use, which measured about three feet in length.

Pietro heard about this time that a greater sculptor than even Cellini had turned to painting, having been commissioned to cover the whole altar-wall of the Sistine Chapel with a prodigious representation of the Last Judgment. The figures were to be over life-size, huge as the dread and wonder imparted by the subject. This news stimulated in Pietro his usual irresistible impulse to be concerned with great events. He at once wrote what he considered to be an extremely tactful letter to the artist, whom he had never met and none of whose works he possessed.

After several paragraphs of flowery compliment Messer Pietro suggested to the addressee how he should set about the job:

'I see in the middle of a crowd Antichrist himself, with features such as you alone could imagine. I see fear written on the faces of the living, extinction on the sun, moon and stars. I see the spirit leaping up, as it were, from fire, earth, air and water. I see all nature horror-stricken, barren, shrivelled in decrepitude. I see time emaciated and shuddering, at his last gasp, seated on the withered stump of a tree. I see hope and despair guiding the cohorts of the good and the mob of the damned. I see the theatre of the clouds lit by rays emanating from the pure fires of heaven. There Christ is enthroned in awful majesty, surrounded by His

hosts. I see the splendour of His countenance and those flashing flames of light which fill the righteous with gladness and
evil-doers with terror. I see the ministers of the abyss glorify-
ing saints and martyrs, deriding Caesars and Alexanders,
since to have conquered oneself is a feat superior to conquer-
ing the world. I see fame with her crowns and palms trodden
underfoot, flung down beneath the wheels of her own chariot.
Finally I hear the Son of God pronouncing sentence. I see
His words descending in the forms of two arrows, one bearing
salvation and the other eternal punishment. As I watch their
flight, I hear fury cracking the machinery of the elements and
claps of thunder bursting and dissolving all. I see the illumi-
nations of paradise and the blazing furnaces of hell breaking
in upon the shadowy air of chaos.'

This highly baroque vision looks forward, with Pietro's usual
prophetic insight, to the extravagant allegories in the painting,
sculpture, architecture and literature of the succeeding century.
But the magniloquence is matched by the grossness of the
impertinence. Michelangelo, a poet himself and a mannerist at
that, could appreciate the foreshadowings of dreams by Rubens
and Bernini which always seem to hover in Pietro's prose when
he is deeply moved.

Perhaps the artist's instinctive recognition, in Pietro's ornate
phrases, of much that he himself might be working towards,
of much that might well come to characterise aesthetic expression in the years to come, caused him to reply with elaborate
courtesy, instead of either ignoring the presumptuous orator or
blasting him with a contemptuous thunderbolt. In any case
Michelangelo, in his answer to Pietro's effusion, deeply regretted
that, a large part of the fresco being already finished, he could
not avail himself of the conception of his 'peerless lord and
brother'. He reserved his irony for a last paragraph, referring
to what his correspondent had written about coming to Rome
to see the picture and thus breaking his oath never to leave
Venice: 'Do not break your resolve of never revisiting Rome
merely on account of the picture I am painting. That would
be too much.'

This covert thrust would have floored anyone but Pietro
Aretino. So would the jest by which the artist, when depicting
the flayed St Bartholomew holding, as convention demanded,

a piece of his own skin and a knife, gave the saint Pietro's face and the fragment of skin Michelangelo's own features, as though he were begging his insolent counsellor not to flay him alive, as he had flayed so many others. But the Scourge, quite unmoved by Michelangelo's final gibe, countered it by coming abruptly to the point he had been aiming at all along, as a corollary to his unasked advice. Could he have a cartoon, he wrote, or even a fragment of one, from the hand of the 'prince of sculptors'?

Michelangelo took no notice whatever of this communication or the many others that followed it, making the same request, for eight whole years. At last, in the spring of 1545, some copies by an inferior artist of some of the sculptor's own casual sketches reached the Casa Aretino. Nothing could have shown more clearly the scorn he felt for so assiduous a beggar. This time the insult stung the unlucky recipient in that tenderest of spots, his vast pride.

He resorted to his usual technique. After coldly informing the artist that he was not prepared to put up with mere imitations of his work, he dropped a broad hint to the effect that he might repeat, in his own inimitable and convincing manner, certain discreditable gossip he had heard about Messer Michelangelo's private and even professional life. Still no answer came. After waiting for some months the exasperated petitioner finally let fly.

'*Messere*,' – he began with ominous formality – 'I have now seen copies of your finished *Last Judgment*. I admit recognition of the distinguished charm of Raphael in its agreeable beauty of invention. However, as a baptised Christian, I blush at the license, so unworthy of a man of genius, with which you express ideas related to the highest aims and final ambitions to which our faith aspires.

'I find that the Michelangelo whose fame is so great, the Michelangelo whom all admire and the Michelangelo so renowned for prudence has chosen to display to the entire world an impiety, an irreligion, which is only equalled by the perfection of his painting. How has it been possible for an artist who, since he is divine, does not consort with human beings, to have done such work in the mightiest temple ever raised to God, over the highest altar erected to Christ, in the most sacred chapel upon earth, where the venerable priests of our faith, those great hinges upon which the Church turns, where the Vicar of Christ himself, join in solemn ceremonies and holy prayers, while they confess, contemplate and adore Christ's body, blood and flesh?

'It would be improper for me to compare my own procedure with yours. But I might well congratulate myself on my good taste when I wrote the *Ragionamenti*. It would be easy to prove the superiority of my discretion to your lack of it. My themes were lascivious and immodest, but my language remained comely and decorous. I spoke in blameless terms, inoffensive to chaste ears. But you, on the contrary, in presenting a subject of such grandeur, exhibited saints devoid of the common decencies observed in this world and angels without their heavenly insignia.'

This remarkable passage, in which the author of what seems to a modern reader the most obscene work in Italian literature declares that it is not obscene at all for the reason that it is well written, contains what was a truism in Pietro's own day and had been so for centuries in Christendom, not to mention previous civilisations. The Fathers of the Church themselves included in their manuscripts, intended for public perusal, statements and anecdotes which would have been the subjects of legal proceedings if they had been printed after the democratic revolutions of the eighteenth century had ensured general literacy.

Until then it was not the topic of eroticism itself but only the attitude to it of the person dealing with it that was open to censure. Moral reprobation of sexual depravity has always been a constant in Christian society. But it was held until comparatively recent times that the more moralists knew about immorality the better they would be able to suppress it. One could not defeat the devil, it was considered, without dining with him first. By this standard, therefore, Pietro was perfectly justified in calling attention to the elegant and striking fashion in which he referred, in the *Ragionamenti*, to things in themselves disgusting, but which, through the implications of his language, he absolutely condemned. Of course he enjoyed writing about orgies and hoped that others would enjoy reading what he wrote. But his tone of mocking contempt in doing so is so consistently maintained, even by the imaginary whores and bawds who are his mouthpieces, that no one could plausibly charge him with deliberately 'corrupting' young or silly people.

Pietro is unlikely, therefore, to have supposed that a general outbreak of lechery would result from the spectacle of Michelangelo's martyrs and virgins tumbling about in less than decent postures. He was concerned to discredit the artist among prosaic and literal-minded people who would be genuinely shocked by such unexpected revelations in a religious context. He went so far as to propose, in fact, that even the naked pudenda of the damned should be veiled in flames. The middle parts of the blest, on the other hand, he urged, ought to be made invisible by dazzling sunbeams. Such objections were to be later (1555–6) advanced by Pope Paul IV. The pontiff met, however, with a sharp retort from the artist, to the effect that His Holiness would be better employed in criticising the sins of his congregations than the management of pictures.

Pietro's long letter to Michelangelo would have been written very differently if the painter had let him have a few sketches. It reeks of unctuous hypocrisy and pseudopiety. The ideas expressed are deeply at odds with the writer's true mentality. He had a tendency at this date to use the language of the pulpit when snubbed by his cultural superiors; logic, common sense and aesthetic sensibility, so often conspicuous in his triumphant and confident moods, then flew out of his intellectual window, giving place to the cheapest brand of evangelical religiosity. But this was only a temporary cloak. As soon as he had blown off steam in such a way – the only way open to him, since he could not meet such giants on their own ground – he was instantly once more his old, generous self. Even the last paragraph of this egregious missive recommended Michelangelo to tear it up when he had read it.

No doubt he did. For that really was the end of the matter; Pietro never got a single scribble, plastic or literary, out of the colossus he had so tirelessly tried to bring down to his own level. Michelangelo was one of his few failures. No one, however, needed to feel ashamed of having been despised by an artist of such a calibre. There is no reason to suppose that after Pietro's first fury had subsided he thought much about his ignominious defeat. He was nothing if not resilient. Only death, never dishonour, could put him out of business.

King Henry VIII of England, in return for a typical complimentary effusion from Pietro, had promised him three hundred *scudi*. But this money never arrived. Henry died in 1547. A London friend of Pietro then rightly or wrongly informed him that the gift had long since been entrusted to Harwell, the English ambassador in Venice, to hand to him. Pietro immediately wrote one of his famous open letters to the Mantuan envoy, directly accusing Harwell of stealing the cash.

A few days later the burly author was swaggering down a narrow side-street in solitary state, his usual custom when on the way to or from an assignation, when he came face to face with seven Englishmen, Harwell at their head. The ambassador stood aside in scornful silence, while his servants flung themselves at his traducer. They beat him black and blue with the traditional cudgels of the island race, leaving him unconscious in the gutter.

Most Venetian citizens were scandalised by this affair. They were shocked by the cudgels. If Harwell had attacked Pietro personally with sword or dagger, or even knifed him in the back after dark, they would have thought little of it. But to set a mob of ruffians with sticks on to so distinguished and elderly a man of letters was considered characteristically English, sheer vulgar bullying and arrogance. The fact that Pietro neither lodged a complaint nor took the law into his own hands increased – as no doubt he had calculated – the general indignation. It spread beyond the city and caused even Italians of such standing as the Duke of Florence and Spaniards like Charles's ambassador in Venice to express the belief that Harwell really had stolen the money.

The English diplomat realised that he had been wrong to act in Italy as if he had been still at home. He called on Pietro and declared his regret at having misunderstood the implications of the letter to his Mantuan colleague. He also, which was more to the point, handed over the three hundred *scudi*, which he may or may not have appropriated, apologising for the 'delay' in settling this account.

Pietro's magnanimity had, as usual, literally paid off. He was as gracious as only he knew how to be to the Englishman. Harwell, whether or not a thief, must have been duly impressed by this display of nobility. The upshot was that which Pietro had in view from the start – his popularity rose to a new level.

But a bitter blow was now in store for him. In 1548 his

daughter Adria, at eleven, was advertised in the fashion of the day as ripe for marriage, or at any rate betrothal. She looked just like his mother, Tita Bonci, that celebrated beauty, proclaimed Pietro with tender pride to Vasari. A gentleman of twenty-nine named Diotalevi Rota, who lived in Urbino and possessed property worth five thousand crowns, applied for Adria's hand on condition that a dowry of one thousand in hard cash would come with her.

Pietro set about collecting the required sum. Cardinal Ravenna subscribed five hundred, the Spanish ambassador a hundred and the Duke of Florence three hundred. But the Duke insisted on paying Rota personally, not through such a spendthrift as the greatest friend of the Duke's deceased father, Giovanni delle Bande Nere, was known to be. 'From your natural liberality,' wrote the cool son of a hot parent, 'which is no vice, you might put the amount to some other use.'

Eventually, in June 1550, the whole dowry demanded was paid over to Rota, though not before Adria's excited father, in his anxiety to make up the total sum, had threatened to pawn a gold collar given him by the future Philip II of Spain. The marriage took place. The pair departed for Urbino. The Duke of that city, duly alerted by Pietro, himself came to meet them some eight miles from the gates and gave them a lavish reception. The union appeared in every respect splendidly successful. But it soon turned out that Rota and his family had no other interest in Adria but her dowry. They began to ill-treat the exquisite little bride of thirteen, perhaps with a view to extorting more cash from the outraged father. They repeatedly locked her up in her boudoir, kept her short of food and took away a lot of her clothing and jewellery. She seems also to have been beaten and taunted with her illegitimacy.

At last she managed to escape, fled to Venice and complained to her parents. Yet after a few days at the Casa she returned to her callous husband and of course suffered the same ill-usage as before. Pietro thereupon wrote to the Duke of Urbino, who arranged her transfer to his own household. But it was too late. The unfortunate girl seems really to have loved the worthless Rota. Her disillusion at his conduct broke her heart. Soon she was dead.

But at this very time of domestic mourning the public prospects of the far-famed Pietro Aretino were once more

improving. In 1550 Pope Paul III had been succeeded by
Julius III, who had been born in Arezzo. His fellow Aretine
remembered that the 'chameleon' Clement VII had once, very
vaguely, intimated that high office in the Church might well be
available later on to so able a diplomat and phrase-maker as
Pietro Aretino – if he chose to behave himself. Pietro, however, in Clement's view, had not done so. The offer, if it
had ever been seriously meant, came to nothing in Clement's
lifetime, which ended in 1534.

His successor, Paul III, had also been approached by Pietro's
friends regarding the matter of a possible cardinalate. The
pontiff's grandson, Ottavio Farnese, is related to have urged
Pietro's claims in the following terms:

'Every day of your life, Holy Father, you make men who are
poor and of low degree cardinals, for no other reason than
that they have served our family faithfully at all times. You
have acted wisely and laudably in so doing. But if such
persons have seemed to you fit for such high promotion, what
would you not gain by bestowing a similar advancement on
Pietro Aretino? He may be poor and baseborn. But he is on
good terms with every prince in the world. If he should
receive this dignity from you he would render you immortal.'

But the Pope had refused to act on Ottavio's suggestion and
suffered the usual penalty of lampooning by the disgruntled
candidate. Would Julius III, as an Aretine himself, and apparently an easy-going old fellow, be more amenable to flattery?
Off went a complimentary sonnet, of mediocre but tolerable
quality, to the Vatican. Pietro also dedicated Volume Five of
his Letters to Julius's brother and followed this up with an
interminable monument of dull sycophancy in rhyme.

The first result was his appointment as honorary chief magistrate of Arezzo. The second was a thousand crowns. The third,
a knighthood of St Peter, carried a salary of eighty crowns a
year. The fourth, perhaps the most important of all, conveyed
to him the information that he was coming to be very highly
regarded in Rome, where Julius himself had expressed esteem
for his capacities.

A certain Vicenzio di Poggio, in Rome on his way to Pales-
tine, wrote:

'Everyone not only speaks well of you but does so with all the affection and sincerity imaginable. I think that all poets should envy you, for not only do the great lords give you deserved praise and wish you every happiness, but in the streets and houses of the citizens bets are offered and taken on the honours that await you. It is publicly said that his Holiness and his friends love and esteem you beyond measure, comparing you with the hydra which grows seven new heads in the place of every one cut off . . . your old enemies now act and speak as if they were your fathers, sons or brothers, according to their respective ages . . . at an assembly of the Knights of St. Peter I was surrounded by the members, who all asked for news of the lord Aretino, crying, "How is he and when will he be coming to Rome?" I was delighted to be able to answer their clamorous enquiries with the tidings that you are well, coming soon and prospering in your affairs.'

Then the Duke of Urbino, who was due at the Vatican to take office as Captain-General of the Church, invited Pietro to help him to beguile the tedium of the journey to Rome, as he had invited him ten years before to ride with him to meet Charles. Just as he had introduced Pietro to the Emperor in 1543, so now he offered to perform the same function in the case of Julius III. After considerable hesitation, due to fear of a possible trap, and after composing a characteristic begging letter to the Duke, Pietro broke his vow never to leave Venice. The letter read:

'The worthy Messer Jacomo Terzo has just paid me a hundred crowns in the name of Your humane, kindly and courteous Excellency. In acknowledgement of this further generous and helpful act the knee of my poverty bends lower than the ground. I thank you with affection and will repay you with praise. I am most sincerely obliged to you.

'But since this goodly sum has been, as they say in Rome, but a bowl of soup for twenty friars, I beg Your Magnificence to send me an additional fifty. For I do not want to appear at the Papal Court in my own worthless character, for which any old rags would be good enough, but clothed as befits a follower of yourself, the great Duke of Urbino, whose merits equal those of any prince or king. If you do not allow me this further sum I shall have to spend in your honour the dowry of my youngest daughter, which stands banked to my credit.

'Half of what I have already received from you has been expended upon a robe of wool and velvet, no less seemly than handsome, and I need four others to wear at our receptions and on the road. Nor have I even now mentioned such articles as hose, cloaks, caps, shoes, slippers, riding-boots, hats, hand-bags and trunks. Then there are the necessary liveries for my servants and lodging-money for those who will attend me to Urbino, as well as wages for the caretaking staff I must leave in my house at Venice.

'I would also ask you to remember that the treasury of St Mark and the strength of Hercules would not suffice to persuade me to leave Venice for a single day and that by cajoling me into coming to Rome you alone have accomplished what the Emperor, the Pope and the Duke of Florence could not.'

He added, just in case Duke Guidobaldo might change his mind in the face of this catalogue of requirements:

'Nevertheless, my dear patron and benefactor, I am making this journey simply because you command me to do so ... I would like to ask for a boat to meet me and an escort, but if that is too much to expect I will come in any case.'

Pietro met the Duke eventually at the latter's own city of Urbino, where Adria and her scoundrel of a husband were then still living. There is no record, however, of what was said or done, either at Rota's house or in the ducal palace on that occasion. But it was not one when private affairs could be settled. The public prospect overshadowed everything else. No doubt florid compliments were exchanged, in the High Renaissance manner, and that was all.

By the end of May 1553 Pietro was riding with the Duke across the Campagna, taking the opposite direction to that of his precipitate flight nearly thirty years previously, with the scars made by the dagger of Achille della Volta on his chest and his right hand barely healed. He had often thundered in his letters and plays against the courts to which he was now, at the age of sixty-two, about to return.

'As for courts, – 'he had scribbled furiously to one correspondent – 'I personally would rather be a gondolier in Venice than a chamberlain in one of those places. For consider the plight of the courtier. He spends his life on his feet. Cold makes a martyr of him and heat devours him. Where can he find a fire to get warm at or water to refresh himself? If he falls ill, can he find even a stable or a charity ward to lie in? Rain, snow and mud assail him when he rides out with or on behalf of his patron. Where is he to obtain a change of clothing? What is his reward for all this suffering? It's heart-rending to see children who have been appointed court servants grow into bearded men before their time and the hair of young men turning white after a lifetime of waiting at table, in the entrance-hall and at the doors of privies. I knew a good and learned man who in his old age was hunted to the gallows because he refused the office of a pander, exclaiming, "Such work is not for me!"

'Don't mention courts to me! It's better to live on bread and capers than the odour of delicate viands served on silver platters. Ay, there's no pain to match that of a weary courtier who has nowhere to sit down, nothing to eat when he's hungry and must keep awake when he's sleepy. And there's no pleasure like mine when I take a seat as soon as I feel tired, eat whenever I feel like it and go to bed when I choose. For all my hours are my own! How abject must be the souls of those who find ample compensation for all their servitude and fidelity when they are allowed to go staggering to the comfort of a straw mattress! In my own case my very indigence makes me happy, for I have no need to doff my hat to any papal favourite.'

He had peremptorily commanded another friend to block all efforts to bring him back to Rome:

'Please put a stop to any movement that may be afoot for that purpose. I wouldn't live in Rome with St Peter himself, let alone with his successor. I'd sooner spend ten years in gaol than ten in a palace.'

He had ridiculed with bitter scorn a certain Messer Pietro Piccardo, the very spit and image of an old-fashioned courtier.

'I could spend whole days listening to his stories of how Pope Julius II, when a cardinal, won sixty thousand ducats from my lord Franceschetto, Innocent's brother, and used the money to build his palace in the Campo di Fiori. Or again, how Cesare Borgia unwittingly poisoned both himself and his father from flasks he had doctored for their Eminences. Piccardo remembers the blow which Julius struck Alexander on the bridge. He has been present at all the schisms, jubilees and councils. He has watched all the erotic revels. He saw Jacobazzo go crazy. He knows how syphilis originated and all the other court jokes. There ought to be a marble or bronze effigy of him over the door of every servants' hall, with a Bible at his feet containing the names of all the popes and cardinals he was so familiar with.'

Yet reluctant as Pietro may have been to join in the court life he knew so well and had satirised so often he realised that it was now or never for a cardinalate – the road, perhaps, to the papacy itself. Times had changed. Berni and Giberti, his former enemies, and Giulio Romano, his friend, were dead. But there were many more recent acquaintances, mostly cordial enough, to welcome him. Julius, after due ritual, received him with 'fraternal tenderness', even rising from the papal throne to raise his fellow Aretine from his knees and kiss him on the forehead.

Yet all through that oppressive summer nothing was said about 'high office in the Church'. By the middle of August Pietro realised that the Pope had not the slightest intention of elevating him to the Sacred College of Cardinals. Old scandals were being revived by envious rivals. Possibly he himself had not always behaved with entire discretion since his arrival in Rome. In any case the low-lying city was unbearable in the heat. Like many other prominent personalities Pietro left for the north.

He returned first to Urbino, then to Venice, which he reached in early September. There he characteristically hinted that he had been offered a cardinalate but had declined the honour. He did not, however, attack Julius in his usual manner for neglecting to reward his merit as it deserved. After all, he was still officially in receipt of his pension from the Vatican as a Knight of St. Peter, though those eighty crowns a year were as long in coming to him as any other salary he had ever been granted.

A more unexpected vexation awaited him. His landlord, Bolani, would not renew his lease of the Casa Aretino. The evicted tenant of course pretended, with typical arrogance, that he was leaving of his own accord. He wrote acidly to Bolani:

'Distinguished and honoured Lord, I herewith restore to you the keys of that house in which I have dwelt for twenty-two years and to which I have given the same care as I would if it had been my own. My reason for this step is solely that it is falling to pieces in all directions, so that I can no more repair its decrepitude than I can shore up my own old age.

'I have no wish to refer to the lack of respect you have shown me, though the Emperor himself interceded on my behalf, requesting his four Venetian ambassadors to secure for me the goodwill of the Signory. But if you had in fact treated me as someone dear to His Majesty, he would have acknowledged himself eternally in your debt. I will only say that if you care to inspect the chamber in which I had hoped to live out my days happily, the figures painted on the ceiling, the grace of the terrace and the decorations over the bed and mantelpiece will all combine to prove to you that I repay even discourtesy with its opposite.

'The daughters which have been born to me, the treasures known to all the world and the works which are on view to all have been procreated, amassed and composed in this house. I therefore have the best of causes to love and reverence for evermore not only the building itself but also Your Excellency. Accordingly, when I depart to-morrow, may it please God with good fortune, to occupy the splendid and commodious apartments which I have taken in the Riva del Carbon at twice the rent of my present quarters, it will be with the desire to remain the same humble servant and friend to you that I have always been. For no perverse injury inflicted upon me can make me change my nature.'

Pietro's old technique when cornered by an adversary on

perfectly justifiable grounds was here at work. The opponent was to be made to feel thoroughly ashamed of himself, quite apart from the merits of the case, simply for inconveniencing so virtuous and eminent a champion of civilisation as Pietro Aretino. In this instance, however, the magnificent bravado had little to stand on. The apartments on the Riva del Carbon, though decent, were not a patch on the Casa. And this is the first we hear of its having fallen into disrepair. As for Bolani's alleged 'lack of respect' for his blustering tenant, there is much reason to suppose that the latter had always been behindhand with the rent and some doubt whether he had ever paid it at all during his twenty odd years of occupation.

Pietro's next row concerned Cosimo de' Medici the Younger, now Duke of Tuscany, who had shown very little of his glorious father's partiality for Pietro. Cosimo saw no reason why he should pay this elderly survivor from bygone days a pension. Pietro raged through Venice, cursing both the Duke and his ambassador, one Pero. That astute diplomat tried to avoid meeting him. But one day they bumped into each other at the house of the Spanish envoy. Pietro did not hesitate to insult the Duke to Pero's face. The latter lost his temper, laid his hand on his sword and retaliated with a torrent of abuse nearly as bitter as the other's. Pietro played his usual trump card of public revelations about the ambassador which would lead inevitably to his disgrace and recall. The infuriated Florentine wrote to his chancellor:

'This ruffian deserves as many beatings a day as the Duke gives him ducats a year. He never shuts his loud mouth. I am credibly informed that the Emperor's ambassador is aware of his wicked life and has taken it upon himself to awaken His Majesty's conscience in regard to the pension he has paid him these many years.'

Pero did not change his attitude, though Pietro changed his. 'I have no pleasure in being praised by Aretino,' the embittered diplomat observed when he heard of a complimentary letter about him written to the Duke of Urbino by Pietro. 'To be praised by that sort of man seems to me more evil than good.' The famous 'Letters of Pietro Aretino' now alternated, in fact, between laudatory hymns to those from whom he

successfully begged and to himself for his similar charity to
others. One to an unnamed woman begins:

'I have read the note you sent me. It was composed more by
the pen of misery than by your own. Therefore I despatch to
you a ducat by the servant who brought it. I wish I could do
more. But my endless endeavours to help my neighbours have
rendered it impossible. During the last two months I have
given away more than two hundred gold crowns. Yesterday
I subscribed to a man's funeral expenses. He was so poor that
even a Turk would have pitied him. In addition, one
gondolier after another comes to me to ask for my purse as
godfather to his children. Now it is near Christmas and I am
hoping to get through that season without going bankrupt. I
may do so if street musicians, beggars, friends and my over-
staffed household do not force me to pawn my very flesh and
blood. Even at this moment, while I ask your pardon because
I can give you little or nothing, here is a note from a poor
scholar demanding a cloak to prevent him freezing to death.
I myself live but from hand to mouth. So you must just
forgive me, my dear lady, if I don't do any more for you at
the moment.'

By 1556 many of Pietro's old friends and patrons were gone.
King Henry of England and King Francis of France had both
died in 1547. The Emperor had abdicated and was in 1557 to
go into complete retirement from the world, at the lonely
monastery of Yuste in Estremadura. Yet at sixty-four the ageing
'chief brigand of literature', though physically failing after
so many years of reckless sexual debauchery and exhaust-
ing quarrels, still had a lot of aggressive mental vitality in
him.

Yet another would-be Divine One, the same Francesco Doni
who had seen him romping with his little daughter Adria, herself now dead, roused the veteran publicist to as fierce a paper
cavalry charge as ever. Doni had tried to worm himself into the
favour of both the Duke of Urbino and Marcolini, Pietro's own
publisher, by slandering the most effective slanderer of the
century. The latter warned the rogue that he was going to strip
him of every shred of credit he might suppose himself to enjoy
with the Duke and Marcolini. Doni retorted, quite spiritedly,

with a verbose production entitled in the grandiloquent style
of sixteenth-century polemics:

'The Earthquake of Doni the Florentine, with the Ruin of a
Great Bestial Colossus, the Antichrist of our Age, A Work
Written for the Honour of God and for the Defence and
Welfare not only of Prelates but of all Good Christians,
Divided into Seven Books, the Earthquake, the Ruin, the
Lightning, the Thunder, the Thunderbolt, the Life and
Death, the Burial and Obsequies.'

This prolix and pretentious effort took the form, imitative
of his rival, of a series of 'Letters', some to Pietro himself, super-
scribed with such phrases as:

'To that disgraceful scoundrel, source and spring of every
rascally deed, Pietro Aretino, stinking organ of devilish lies
and true antichrist of this era.'
  'To that long-faced coward, Pietro Aretino, clumsy fool of
our age and disgrace to mankind.'
  'To his Divine Hogsheadedness, formerly Messer Pier of
Arezzo, a Divine Wine-jug.'
  'To Aretino, the tiltyard dummy of all worthless rascals,
gilded without but wooden within.'
  'To the hoggishness of that wild boar Aretino, venerable
gulper of roast pig-meat.'

Other 'Letters' were addressed in more conventional terms
to the Dukes of Urbino and Tuscany, to the Doge of Venice
and even to the Emperor himself. The contents were mostly
absurd rant, unfounded libel and mere spite, not worth answering. But the author ended with a specific prophecy that the life
of this 'deadly sickness to all his friends' would end in that very
year of 1556.
  The book came out in March. But its victim remained as
lively and popular as ever, though now his hair was snow-white
and his great beard heavily silvered. The spring passed, then the
summer and the first few weeks of autumn.
  On the night of October 21 Pietro was feasting at a tavern
near his house among a gay group of friends of all ranks, from
nobles to humble tradesmen. Suddenly the big Aretine gave

vent to one of his mighty roars of laughter at some obscenity
he or one of the party had uttered. He threw up his vast,
bearded chin to the rafters. His chair tilted backwards; his
ponderous frame overbalanced it; it crashed to the floor and
he with it. He did not rise. His face was unnaturally flushed,
his breathing laboured. Apoplexy! His friends carried the
great, groaning body, with considerable difficulty, the short
distance to his quarters in the Riva del Carbon.

A doctor and a priest were sent for. Pietro remained delirious
in bed for some hours. Towards morning he sank into a coma.
At dawn the doctor pronounced life to be extinct. It is not
certain that he confessed to the priest, though an affidavit
exists to that effect, even testifying, with rather less probability
than sententiousness, that the dying man 'wept bitterly withal.'

When Doni's bold prophecy came true it seemed to many
Italians that sheer vindictiveness had killed the man who, for
all his ferocious calumnies, had never been truly vindictive.
Everyone who counted in Europe felt some degree of regret at
the news of the passing of so conspicuous a figure.

But the debunkers were soon on the quenched luminary's
track. Said Pero, the Florentine ambassador to Venice: 'No
decent man was sorry to lose him.' Less exalted persons swore
he had been telling stories in the tavern about his two sisters'
debaucheries, when he laughed too loudly and so cracked his
skull. They put scurrilous 'last words' into his mouth, a verse,
for instance, mocking the oil of extreme unction. 'I'm all greased
up now, so keep the rats away,' he was said to have grunted.

An epitaph which may, however, have been current at a
much earlier date was rushed into print:

'Here lies the Tuscan poet Aretino.
He slandered all but God, Whom he left out
because, he pleaded, Well, I never knew him.'

Some authorities ascribe this jeer to the year 1525 and quote
Pietro's reply to it, written in the belief that it was the work of a
certain Bishop Giovio:

'Here lies our top reporter Giovio.
He slandered all but asses, for, said he,
How could I slander my own fellow-creature?'

An epitaph closer to the truth was carved on the wall of the church of San Luca in Arezzo:

> 'Base-born Pietro Aretino rose
> to such heights in the scourging of foul vice
> that those who held the world in fee paid price
> to him in fear of even fiercer blows.'

According to some authorities, one of the prices, the magnificent gold chain with vermilion tongues given to Pietro by King Francis I, was sold to defray the funeral expenses. Others affirm that it was broken up and distributed to the poor during the obsequies, which one can be sure were well attended.

The life of Pietro Aretino illustrates clearly the not so subtle difference between a rogue and a scoundrel. The Scourge was unquestionably the first but never the second. There was a certain innocence, often characteristic of self-educated men, about his sinfulness. It was utterly unlike that of the guilt-ridden or indeed of the sensual average of humanity. He did not misbehave like ordinary people but in a way peculiar to himself, in that he remained invariably ready to make practical amends for his offences, while not admitting the right of others to judge him.

He fought society, but did not want to change it. He learned no true wisdom from experience but only how to sharpen wits already more effective than most. Yet it is difficult to avoid the impression that he loved his enemies much more than many Christians far exceeding him in pious observances. His own natural resilience and gaiety caused him to wish others to show similar qualities. Rather than meet the glum glares of those he had got into trouble, he hunted tirelessly for means to acquire their esteem and gratitude. He often succeeded in this quest.

Self-centred to a high degree, he yet felt a deep solidarity with the rest of mankind, especially the unfortunate. His prodigious complacency was repeatedly accompanied by a wry, not altogether 'mock' modesty. The irony goes as deep as the pride when he muses:

> 'You'll get the rue for your subtle whores' dialogues, nettles
> for your biting sonnets about priests, lots of banknotes for

your gay comedies, thorns for your religious tracts, cypress for the immortality you have given others by your writings, olive-branches for your reconciliations with princes, laurels for your poems of war and love and oak-leaves for the incorrigible extravagance with which you shamed avarice. Well, I accept all these decorations and they make me laugh. For anyone seeing me with such a collection of foliage on my head would recommend me for canonisation as out of my wits.'

A bundle of contradictions, violently antipathetic to the sterner sort of logical intellectual, Michelangelo for example, Pietro Aretino easily won the sympathy of those equally cultivated but of lighter, more sceptical and optimistic temperament, such as Ariosto. But if everyone disliked him at one time or another, for one reason or another, everyone also at different times for different reasons yielded helplessly to the charm and vigour of his personality. There have been very few prominent men indeed, in any age or country, of whom the same paradox could be so confidently upheld.

His posthumous misfortune was that one of his most conspicuous traits, frankness in admitting his erotic manias and peculiarities, repelled, more than any other conceivable shortcoming could have done, the British literary censors of the nineteenth century, who were for that very reason fascinated by so outspoken a 'villain'. Remy de Gourmont called Aretino 'the scapegoat of moralists delighted to find a personage weighty enough to stand their invectives without collapsing'. The reader who is neither pedant nor bigot cannot feel that he has been wasting his time on a mere pornographer-blackmailer. On the contrary, such a reader may reasonably conclude that Pietro the Divine Aretino has better claims to immortality, both as writer and as human being, than a good many figures readily accorded it. The Scourge of Princes has never yet received from historians the respect that a close acquaintance with the evidence seems to warrant.

Appendix

POPES CONTEMPORARY WITH
PIETRO ARETINO (1492–1556)

ALEXANDER VI (Rodrigo Borgia, 1492–1503). Spaniard. Father
of Cesare (b.1476) and Lucrezia (b.1480) by Vanozza dei
Cattanei, wife, successively, of three husbands. This most
corrupt of popes lavished power and wealth on his many
bastards, was a cynically vicious murderer, swindler and
tyrant, but also a shrewd diplomat and connoisseur of the
arts.

JULIUS II (Giuliano della Rovere, 1503–13). From Liguria,
part of former Republic of Genoa. Strong character, expert
diplomat, reformer and art patron. Founded Vatican
museum.

LEO X (Giovanni de' Medici, 1513–21). First patron of Aretino,
who always liked him. Second son of Lorenzo the Magnificent. Excommunicated Luther in 1521. Made Rome politically supreme and the centre of European culture. Generous
and outwardly pious but essentially self-indulgent and
utterly unscrupulous in public affairs.

ADRIAN VI (Adrian Dedel, 1521–23). From Utrecht. Tutor to
Charles V. Meant well but a hopeless bigot. Hated by Aretino.

CLEMENT VII (Giulio de' Medici, 1523–34). Bastard of Giuliano, younger brother of Lorenzo the Magnificent. Cultured
and economical but narrow-minded and politically unreliable. Later subservient to Charles V. Refused Henry VIII
a divorce. Many dealings with Aretino, who never trusted
him.

PAUL III (Alessandro Farnese, 1534–49). From Parma in
Emilia. Cultured, easy-going, worldly type of good business
man, but irresolute on questions of reform. More interested
in advancement of family than in job. His sister Giulia had

been the favourite mistress of Alexander VI. Aretino could make little headway with Paul III.

JULIUS III (Giovanni Maria del Monte, 1550–55). A lazy pontiff with little public spirit. Neglected Aretino after receiving him effusively.

MARCELLUS II (Marcello Cervini, April 9 – April 30, 1555). An obstinately conventional character.

PAUL IV (Giovanni Pietro Caraffa, 1555–59). Neapolitan. Had been in England as nuncio. Bad-tempered and pompous. Had famous row with Michelangelo over nudities in the *Last Judgment*. Finally forced England (under Elizabeth) out of papal ambit. Generally unpopular for stupidity in politics and personal bigotry.

GENEALOGIES

The Habsburg Family

Rudolph I (d. 1291)

Albert I (d. 1308)
Rudolph II (d. 1290)

Rudolph III (d. 1307)
Frederick III (d. 1330)
Leopold I (d. 1326)
Albert II (d. 1356)
Leopold III (d. 1386)

William (d. 1406)
Leopold IV (d. 1411)
Frederick IV (d. 1439)
Ernest the Lion (d. 1424)
Frederick V (d. 1493)

Maximilian I (1459–1519)

Philip I, Duke of Burgundy
and King of Spain (1478–1506)

Charles V (1500–58),
m. Isabella of Portugal
Ferdinand I (1503–64)

Philip II (1527–98)
Don John of Austria
(illegitimate)

Don Carlos (d. 1568)
Philip III (1578–1621)

The Medici Family

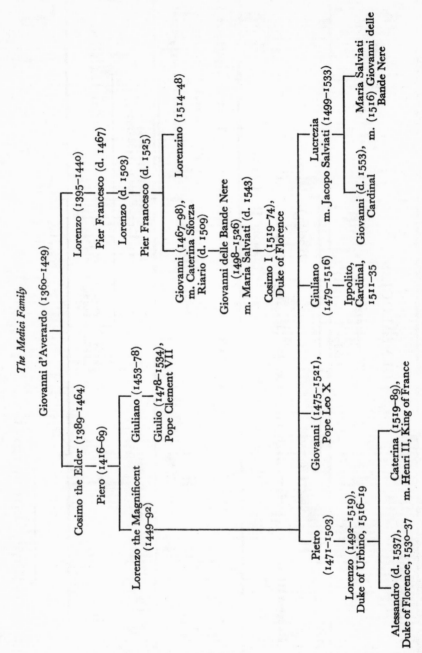

The Gonzaga Family

Lodovico I (d. 1382), m. Alda D'Este
|
Francesco I (1366–1407). m. (i) Agnese Visconti; (ii) Margherita Malatesta
|
Gianfrancesco (1395–1444), First Marquess of Mantua, m. Paola Malatesta
|
Lodovico II (1414–78), Second Marquess
|
Federigo I (1442–84), Third Marquess
|
├─ Francesco II (1466–1519), Fourth Marquess, m. Isabella D'Este
│   │
│   ├─ Federigo II (1500–40), Fifth Marquess and First Duke of Mantua
│   │   │
│   │   ├─ Francesco III (1533–50), Second Duke
│   │   └─ Federigo (1541–65), Cardinal
│   │
│   ├─ Ercole (1505–63), Cardinal
│   │
│   └─ Eleonora (1494–1570), m. Francesco Maria della Rovere, Duke of Urbino
│
└─ Elisabetta (d. 1526), m. Guidobaldo da Montefeltro, Duke of Urbino

Chiara (d. 1505), m. Gilbert de Montpensier
|
Charles (1482–1527), Duke of Bourbon, Constable of France

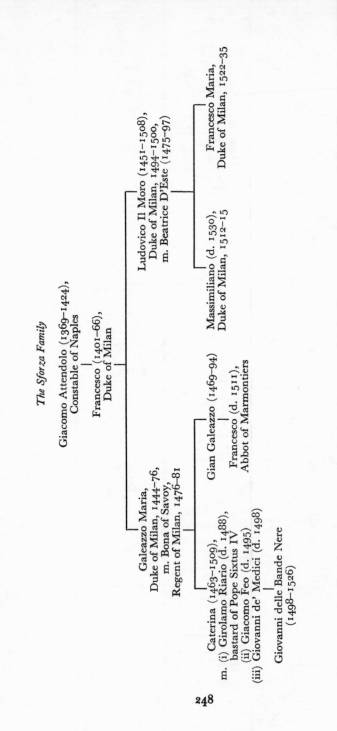

The Sforza Family

Giacomo Attendolo (1369–1424), Constable of Naples

Francesco (1401–66), Duke of Milan

Galeazzo Maria, Duke of Milan, 1444–76, m. Bona of Savoy, Regent of Milan, 1476–81

Ludovico Il Moro (1451–1508), Duke of Milan, 1494–1500, m. Beatrice D'Este (1475–97)

Gian Galeazzo (1469–94)

Francesco (d. 1511), Abbot of Marmontiers

Caterina (1463–1509),
m. (i) Girolamo Riario (d. 1488), bastard of Pope Sixtus IV
(ii) Giacomo Feo (d. 1495)
(iii) Giovanni de' Medici (d. 1498)

Giovanni delle Bande Nere (1498–1526)

Massimiliano (d. 1530), Duke of Milan, 1512–15

Francesco Maria, Duke of Milan, 1522–35

Bibliography

Apart from general works and articles in periodicals, I have consulted the following publications:

Aretino, Pietro. *Opera Nuoa.* Venice, 1512.
— — *Lettere.* Paris, 1609.
Berni, F. (et al.) *Opere Burlesche.* London, 1734.
Dujardin, B. *La vie de Pierre Arétin.* Paris. 1750.
Mazzuchelli, G. M. *Vita di Pietro Aretino.* Brescia, 1763.
Guicciardini, F. *Istoria d'Italia.* Pisa, 1819–20.
Berni, F. *Vita di Pietro Aretino.* London, 1821.
Barthold, F. W. *Georg von Frundsberg.* Hamburg, 1853.
Peignot, E. G. *De Pierre Arétin.* Paris, 1836.
Caselmann, H. W. *Das Leben des Georg von Frundsberg.* Ansbach, 1863.
Berni, F. *Opere.* Milan, 1864.
Doni, A. F. (ed. Daelli, G.). *Il Terremoto.* Lucca, 1864.
Cappelli, A. *Pietro Aretino.* Modena, 1865.
Villanti, G. *L'Aretino in Roma.* Palermo, 1869.
Chasles, V. E. P. *L'Arétin. Sa vie et ses écrits.* Neuchâtel, 1873 (limited ed.)
Landoni, T. (ed.) *Lettere scritte a Pietro Aretino.* Bologna, 1873.
Crowe, J. A. and Cavalcaselle, G. B. *Titian: his life and times.* London, 1877.
Samosch, S. *Pietro Aretino und italienische Charakterköpfe.* Berlin, 1881.
Sinigaglia, G. *Saggio di un studio su Pietro Aretino.* Rome, 1882.
Franco, N. *Delle rime di M. Nicolo Franco contro Pietro Aretino.* London, 1887 (privately printed).
Luzio, A. *Pietro Aretino.* Turin, 1888.
Virchow, R. L. C. and Holtzendorff, F. von. *Sammlung gemeinverständlicher wissenschaftlicher Vorträge.* Berlin, 1890.
Rossi, V. *Pasquinate di Pietro Aretino.* Palermo-Turin, 1891.
Pasolini dall'Onda, P. D. *Caterina Sforza.* Rome, 1893.
Gauthiez, P. *L'Arétin.* Paris, 1895.

Grasso, D. *L'Aretino e le sue Commedie*. Palermo, 1900.

Doni, A. F. (ed. Alia, C.) *Il Terremoto*. Lucca, 1901.

—— *La vita dello infame Aretino*. Citta di Castello, 1901.

Bertani, C. *Pietro Aretino e le sue opere*. Sondrio, 1901.

Gauthiez, P. *Jean des Bandes Noires*. Paris, 1901.

Mari, G. *Storia e leggenda di Pietro Aretino*. Rome, 1903.

Jerrold, M. F. *Vittoria Colonna*. London, 1906.

Luzio, A. *Un prognostico satirico di Pietro Aretino*. Bergamo, 1906.

Van Dyke, P. *Renascence Portraits*. New York, 1906.

Vaughan, H. M. *The Medici Popes Leo X and Clement VII*. London, 1908.

Apollinaire, G. *L'Oeuvre du Divin Arétin*. Paris, 1909.

Levi, Eugenia. *Dell' unica e rarissima edizione degli Strambotti alla Villanesca di M. Pietro Aretino*. Florence, 1909.

Cellini, B. (ed. Butti, A.) *La vita di Benvenuto Cellini*. Milan, 1910.

Hare, C. *The Romance of a Medici Warrior*. London, 1910.

Dolce, L. *L'Aretino. Dialogo della Pittura*. Florence, 1910.

Aretino, Pietro (ed. Nicolini, F.) *Corrispondenza. Scrittori d'Italia*, vol. 53, etc., Bari, 1910, etc.

Fochessati, G. *Gonzaga di Mantova e l'ultima duca*. Mantova, 1912.

Allodoli, G. *Introduzione alle Prose Sacre di Pietro Aretino* Lanciano, 1914.

Franco, N. *Rime contro Pietro Aretino*. Casale Monferrato, 1541.

Parodi, T. (ed. Croce, B.) *Poesia e letteratura*. Bari, 1916.

Symonds, J. A. *The Renaissance in Italy*. London, 1920–27.

Hutton, E. *Pietro Aretino*. London, 1922.

Putnam, S. *The Works of Aretino*. Chicago, 1926.

Bontempelli, M. (ed.). *Le piu belle pagine di Pietro Aretino*. Milan, 1927.

Aretino, Pietro (ed. de Sanctis, F.). *Lettere*. Milan, 1928.

Armstrong, E. *The Emperor Charles V*. London, 1929.

Allodoli, E. *Giovanni dalle Bande Nere*. Florence, 1929.

Berenson, B. *The Venetian Painters of the Renaissance*. New York, 1930.

Foschini. A. *L'Aretino*. Milan, 1931.

Roeder, R. *The Man of the Renaissance. Four Lawgivers: Savonarola, Machiavelli, Castiglione, Aretino*. New York, 1933.

Rodocanachi, E. *Histoire de Rome*. Paris, 1933.

Hackett, F. *Francis the First*. London, 1934.

Antoniade, C. *Trois figures de la Renaissance*. Paris, 1937.

Dublin, P. G. *La vie de l'Arétin*. Paris, 1937.

Chubb, T. C. *Aretino, Scourge of Princes*. New York, 1940.

Riggs, A. S. *Titian*. London, 1946.

Castiglione, B. (ed. Cian, V.) *Il Libro del Cortigiano*. Florence, 1947.

Petrocchi, G. *Pietro Aretino*. Milan, 1948.

Terrasse, C. *François Premier*. Paris, 1949.

Vita, A. del. *L'Aretino 'uomo libero per grazia di Dio'*. Arezzo, 1954.

Mattingly, G. *Renaissance Diplomacy*. London, 1955.

Aretino, Pietro (ed. Foschini, A.) *I Ragionamenti*. Milan, 1960.

Bailly, A. *François Premier*. Paris, 1961.

Plumb, J. H. (ed.). *The Penguin Book of the Renaissance*. London, 1964.

Index